PENGUIN B

BLACK KETTLE AND FULL MOON

Geoffrey Blainey is one of Australia's most significant and popular historians. His thirty-two published books include *The Tyranny of Distance*, *The Causes of War*, *A Short History of the World*, *A Shorter History of Australia*, and a history of Aboriginal Australia, *Triumph of the Nomads*. Professor Blainey taught at the University of Melbourne for many years and chaired the Australia Council from 1977 to 1981. He was delegate to the 1998 Constitutional Convention and has served on many Commonwealth boards and councils, which include the Australian War Memorial, the Australian Heritage Commission, the Literature Board and the National Council for the Centenary of Federation. He is one of the few Australians whose biography appears in *Encyclopedia Britannica*.

GEOFFREY BLAINEY

BLACK KETTLE AND FULL MOON

Daily Life in a Vanished Australia

PENGUIN BOOKS

PENGUIN BOOKS

Published by the Penguin Group
Penguin Group (Australia)
250 Camberwell Road, Camberwell, Victoria 3124, Australia
(a division of Pearson Australia Group Pty Ltd)
Penguin Group (USA) Inc.
375 Hudson Street, New York, New York 10014, USA
Penguin Group (Canada)
10 Alcorn Avenue, Toronto, Ontario, Canada M4V 3B2
(a division of Pearson Penguin Canada Inc.)
Penguin Books Ltd
80 Strand, London WC2R 0RL, England
Penguin Ireland
25 St Stephen's Green, Dublin 2, Ireland
(a division of Penguin Books Ltd)
Penguin Books India Pvt Ltd
11 Community Centre, Panchsheel Park, New Delhi – 110 017, India
Penguin Group (NZ)
Cnr Airborne and Rosedale Roads, Albany, Auckland, New Zealand
(a division of Pearson New Zealand Ltd)
Penguin Books (South Africa) (Pty) Ltd
24 Sturdee Avenue, Rosebank, Johannesburg 2196, South Africa

Penguin Books Ltd, Registered Offices: 80 Strand, London, WC2R 0RL, England

First published by Penguin Books Australia Ltd, 2003
This paperback edition published by Penguin Group (Australia),
a division of Pearson Australia Group Pty Ltd, 2004

1 3 5 7 9 10 8 6 4 2

Design by Karen Trump © Penguin Group (Australia)
Front cover image by permission of the National Library of Australia
Author photograph by Irene Lorbegs,
courtesy National Council for the Centenary of Federation
Typeset in 11.5/17.7pt Fairfield by Midland Typesetters, Maryborough, Victoria
Printed and bound in Australia by McPherson's Printing Group, Maryborough, Victoria

National Library of Australia
Cataloguing-in-Publication data:

Blainey, Geoffrey, 1930– .
Black kettle and full moon: daily life in a vanished Australia.

Bibliography.
Includes index.
ISBN 0 14 300266 X.

1. Australia – History. 2. Australia – Social life and customs – 19th century.
3. Australia Social life and customs – 20th century. I. Title.

994

CONTENTS

PREFACE

This is a history of how most Australians lived – from day to day – during a crucial and fascinating period of their history. It is a story of everyday things, of the little habits and happenings and sometimes the large.

The book looks at tasks and pleasures that everyone once knew about but are now largely forgotten. What did people eat? How did they cook over a fire? Who drank alcohol and when did the cigarette become popular? When did the typical family begin to own a clock? What bread did they eat and how did they pay for it? When did the Southern Cross capture the imagination?

How did people cope with the summer, the season of the year feared the most? Some coped by importing shiploads of ice all the way from Boston. And how did they make use of the moonlight? Some of the dramatic events in Australian history could take place only when the moon was full. What kind of tea did they drink? To my surprise they drank almost nothing but Chinese tea in the 1850s though later they changed speedily to Indian and Ceylonese tea.

The book is in two parts. The first looks at the sky and climate, moonlight, candles and gas and kerosene lamps, clocks, ships and cameras, the printed newspaper and bank-note, the coo-ee and the bullock bell, and the conveying of messages by word and by wire. The second part looks at cooking, food and drink, smoking, and shopping. It looks at the dinner table and the black kettle singing on the hot kitchen stove. Daily life refuses to be tidy and orderly, and some of the themes in the book overlap or intersect.

Covering about seventy years, the book extends from the eve of the first gold rush to the First World War. For most of this period, rural life and mining towns were flourishing but the cities were advancing rapidly. Melbourne was larger than Sydney in most years, and Ballarat, Bendigo and Newcastle were usually larger than Perth. The book begins when Australia held fewer than 400 000 white people and an uncounted but falling number of Aborigines; and it ends when the total population reached five million people. It begins when males far exceeded females, and ends when they were about equal in number. It begins with billy tea and candles, and ends with ice cream and the telephone. While it is now accepted rightly that a unique transforming of eating, drinking and habits has taken place in the last fifty years, another unique transforming had already taken place, in the period spanned by this book.

This is mostly the story of average Australians – the nine of every ten who were neither rich nor very poor. It says little about the rich. It says little about the transported convicts whose numbers were dwindling by 1850, and little about the Aborigines: both groups, of course, sat near the bottom of the income ladder. The traditional ways of life of the Aborigines – a nomadic life, probably pursued by half of them in 1850 but few in 1914 – are described in an earlier book of mine, *Triumph of the Nomads*.

I have written little about clothes and houses, except kitchens and verandahs. Churches do not receive the attention they deserve, nor do sport and toys. My intention had been to make this book more comprehensive. But the more I read and listened, the more I realised that even to write realistically about meat – at a time when Australians were said to be the world's most voracious eaters of meat – was to call for a wide amount of detail. A whole book could be written about each of the two dozen separate topics that are covered in these pages.

Geoffrey Blainey

PART ONE

Ocean and Moon

1

MOON, SUN AND STARS

The moon above Australia was believed to show a lustre unknown in the British Isles. A Scottish visitor in the 1860s thought that 'the Australian moon' was one of the noble sights of the world, for it seemed 'like a globe of fire, lighting all around'. Another voyager, approaching Western Australia, marvelled at the path of moonlight stretching across the ocean and thought that the rising moon seemed larger than in England. Certainly the moon was more visible, for the skies were clearer and the fogs and mists and rain clouds appeared less often. On the spacious Australian plains the moon seemed to dominate the sky in a way not quite attainable in the more crowded landscape and streetscape of England. In the pioneering era, too, numerous Australians, whether shepherds or gold diggers, were out of doors at night, even sleeping outside, and so they noticed the moon's presence or absence.

The moon had an influence on many daily activities. Some people killed livestock only when the moon was on the wane. Some farmers were inclined to follow the old English proverb: 'sow peas and beans in the wane of the moon'. At the turn of the century some farmers in Tasmania followed the rule that seeds should be planted only when the moon was waning. They were also careful to begin no project on a Friday, another day for the superstitious.

When Will the Moon Wane?

Attempts to forecast the weather were often based on the moon. Old sayings arrived from the British Isles and, tested in Australian conditions, were repeated aloud even though the evidence in their favour was sparse. Perhaps the sayings were precious reminders of home as well as guides to the weather. Farmers, about to harvest the wheat, were likely to recall the old saying:

> If the moon shows a silver shield,
> Be not afraid to reap your field.

When expressed in simple rhymes, the predictions were easily remembered:

> The full moon brings fair weather
> Pale moon does rain, Red moon does blow;
> White moon does neither rain nor snow.

The moon was believed to wield power over health and sickness. People were warned that if they fell asleep while lying directly in the moon's rays they would be 'moonstruck'. Those who lived in the tropics and fell asleep while the moon was shining on their face were said to be likely to catch that temporary blindness known as 'moon-blink'. The most feared power of the moon was madness. A lunatic was one who was affected by the moon, *luna* being the Latin word for moon. These warnings, part of English folklore, were not so easily obeyed by those Australians who carried their swag and slept night after night in the open air.

Most newsagents and bookshops sold annual almanacs which set out, to the nearest minute, the predicted movements of the moon for that year. Every diary carried an almanac in its front pages, and many country newspapers issued annually a printed almanac which told, for every day of the year, when the sun and the moon would rise and set. The almanac set out the phases of the moon, stating when the moon would enter its first or last quarter, when the moon would be full, and the hour and exact minute when a new moon would appear. At the foot of each page were often hints or instructions for farmers and home gardeners.

In rural areas, people planning a journey, or fixing the date for a ball, carefully consulted the almanac to see when the moon would be brightest. When Rolf Boldrewood in his novel *A Colonial Reformer* comes to describing the bachelors' ball, which was the glamorous event in the town's social calendar, he notes that the night selected for it should have 'the clearest moonlight procurable'. Using his finest prose he called the moonlit sky 'the wondrous dark-blue dome'.

Mary Gilmore, in her recollections of childhood, recalled the importance of the full moon: 'When will there be a moon?' asked her uncles as they prepared the bullock or horse teams for a long overnight journey. 'Bring me the Almanack!' replied her grandfather. Mary explained that in the later era of made roads, railways and streetlamps, the moon 'lost her high throne in the heavens'. But in earlier days most people consulted the almanac to see if the moon would be favourable for their journey on half-made bush roads during the hours of darkness. When country people were to visit neighbouring homesteads for an evening, they hoped for a full moon. Sometimes they stayed and danced and sang until daylight because it was dangerous to ride home in pitch darkness.

The moon shining above the Presbyterian Church at Bathurst. On the night of a full moon, more people attended church services, dances and public meetings in the countryside and inland towns.

When Melbourne was becoming the largest city in Australia, its streets were still rough and dimly lit. Accordingly the leading Presbyterian preacher, planning a series of evening lectures in 1855, selected the 'moonlight nights', so that his congregation could ride or walk home in relative safety after hearing his lectures. In pioneering towns, organisers of concerts and balls would commonly include in their advertisements the simple word 'Moonlight'. This was not the name of a pop group: it was rather an affirmation that the night had been selected with care. Today it is doubtful whether one in every five city residents, if suddenly questioned at night-time, would know whether the moon was old or new, or whether it was visible or not in the night sky.

The Moons of Ned Kelly

Ultimately we will learn more about some of the celebrated events in Australian history if we turn to the old almanacs and their tables of the moon. Ned Kelly probably used an almanac or carried in his head a knowledge of the phases of the moon. He knew that after some exploits he might have to make long rides on horseback in order to evade the police. So he was likely to select the full moon for his daring robberies. A glance at old almanacs reveals that he made his two celebrated raids on banks – at the small town of Euroa in December 1878, and Jerilderie the following February – when the moon was full. The raids were carried out when the moon was in such a position as to be favourable to their enterprise.

7

The raid on Jerilderie was astonishingly daring. The four members of the Kelly gang were already the target of a highly organised hunt, and they had to cross the plains with alertness. Their point of departure, somewhere in the Victorian ranges, perhaps near Beechworth or Wangaratta, is not known with certainty; but they probably had to travel close to 200 kilometres, allowing for the detours made in order to avoid towns and townships, in order to cross the Murray River and reach the New South Wales plains town of Jerilderie. And then they had to ride back a similar distance again. Wisely they selected a short run of nights when the fullish moon rose soon after sunset, and illuminated the sky for the remainder of the night. They travelled on horseback, two separate pairs of men. When they reached the outskirts of Jerilderie on a Saturday afternoon, they cut the telegraph line connecting the town to the outside world. Robbing the bank with ease, they rode away late on the Sunday. Before they reached their hideaway in the Victorian ranges the news of their raid reached the cities, and the search for them was intensified. They were finally surrounded and trapped in a bush hotel in the winter of 1880. Significantly, they had set out for the hotel at the start of a cluster of moonlit nights, which suggests that they had it in mind – if necessary – to escape on horseback with the aid of the moon.

The large-scale thieving of cattle usually required a moonlit night. A popular Australian word for stealing cattle was 'moonlighting'. The word is now used mainly to describe city people who work at a second job at night. After moving from the country to the city, the word largely retains its illicit connotation.

A military event planned for the hours of darkness required a knowledge of the phases of the moon. When in December 1854 the armed miners confronted the policemen and soldiers at Ballarat, both sides must have been conscious of the role that night and day, and moonlight and darkness, could play in their struggle. The eve of the battle at the Eureka Stockade coincided with the full moon. Was this a coincidence, or was the moon crucial to the planning of that battle? Did the miners guarding their stockade believe that, as most of the hours of that night were lit by the moon, they were safe from a surprise attack? Whatever the reasons, the rebels' leader allowed most of his men, on that crucial night, to leave the stockade and visit their families and friends. His stockade was thus poorly manned.

The government forces were assembled in their camp at about 2.30 a.m. on that morning. Half an hour later, they set out quietly to attack the stockade, which was less than 3 kilometres away. The first part of their advance was aided by the moonlight. The mounted police, cavalry, soldiers and policemen on foot moved through the broken terrain in 'excellent order, and with perfect silence'. For a time they halted: they had almost one hour to spare; the sun would not rise until after 4.30 a.m. The setting of the moon gave them protection as they moved closer to the stockade. With the onset of darkness they approached the stock-ade without being detected. They fired their first shots in the dawn, before the sun had risen above the hills to the east. Attacking the poorly defended stockade, they won a decisive victory. In the quick battle about thirty miners and five soldiers were killed. The rebellion was over.

Explorers in peril tried to use the moonlight. Sometimes the moon was their special ally. In 1861 in tropical north-west Queensland, Robert O'Hara Burke and William Wills, walking south after successfully crossing the continent, were approaching disaster. The days were so hot and steamy that they planned to travel, when practicable, during the night and to sleep in the heat of the day. Perhaps they could reach help before their pack camels and horses fell exhausted and their supply of food ran out. They could travel at night, however, only when a bright moon was in the sky.

On Saturday 23 February, Wills observed that the humidity was so high, he had a 'helpless feeling of lassitude'. As he noted, 'we started in the evening to try a trip by moonlight'. Wills does not record in his journal the time of the moon's rising, but he was an astronomer and undoubtedly, with a few mental calculations, could tell days in advance when the moon would rise and set. In fact the moon rose at about five o'clock that afternoon and set at about three the next morning. The explorers did not travel far in the moonlight that evening, partly because the horses suffered from the wet heat.

Wills's journal is so sparse that he does not always record their travels for the day, but on 26 February we learn that they travelled until midnight. The next day they spent resting, and at 2 a.m. on the following morning they resumed their journey. A glance at the records and calculations of the US naval observatory at Washington reveals that at their particular latitude and longitude during those days in 1861, the moon was rising after sunset and shining for most of the night. Probably for a week or so the explorers tried to travel on the more favourable nights. It meant that they successively postponed their start each evening, because the moon rose later and later.

We know that they were travelling at night at the start of March because, 'while crossing a creek by moonlight', they rode over a very large snake. From time to time the half-silent journal mentions night journeys, but there was probably even more moonlight-travelling than was recorded. Burke, with some just-ification, is now regarded as a poor and even incompetent explorer, but he and Wills have never been given credit for their skill and persistence in harvesting the moonlight.

As they moved further south the days ceased to burn so intensely, and several of the nights almost became chilling. Moreover there came those inevitable days when the moon, in the course of its cycle, shone more in the hours of daylight than in darkness. So the advantage of travelling in the moonlight receded.

Four months previously, Burke had left a relief party in the centre of Australia, at Cooper's Creek. The instructions given to this small party, led by William Brahe, were to wait and wait – until Burke returned from the north. And wait they did, in their small fortified 'stockade', built to protect them from possible Aboriginal attacks. The stockade, fenced by branches and saplings, protected a tent containing guns, ammunition and ample supplies of food. Month after month the four men waited in heat that they agreed was almost unbearable: one day the temperature inside the tent reached 117 degrees Fahrenheit.

The waiting men had now virtually fulfilled their instructions. What had happened to Burke and Wills they did not know. They resolved to abandon the stockade and travel south towards civilisation. Just in case the explorers should eventually reach the site of the stockade, they dug a hole and buried a small lot of flour and other provisions.

In fact the surviving explorers – Burke, Wills and their camel man, King – were fast approaching the depot. Their legs were feeble, their morale was low, and their daily progress was slower than they had anticipated. They now jettisoned surplus supplies: they had to, because only two of their camels remained. Earlier, on 15 April, steady rain had slowed them down. Then their ill colleague, Charles Gray, died. In burying Gray they lost another day; and that delay deprived them of much of the gain made through their previous night travels.

On the morning of 21 April 1861, the guardians of the stockade prepared to set out for the south. They left at about 10 a.m. They did not know, as they rode away, that Burke and his depleted team were fast approaching the stockade from the opposite direction. Indeed, they were only nine hours away.

On that last day Burke on his camel, and his two colleagues sharing their camel, travelled maybe a total of 50 kilometres – one of the longest treks of their whole journey. They knew that the stockade was within reach. They imagined the welcome, the hearty meal and the companionship awaiting them. The sun set at about 5.40 p.m. but the moon was already in the sky. In the twilight and then the eery moonlight the three explorers pressed on. Around 7.30 p.m. Burke imagined, from his high position on his camel, that he could glimpse the stockade. No lamp was burning, no fire was glowing, but he imagined that in the near distance he could see the tents. He called out loudly, giving one coo-ee and then another. He even called the names of the men who, he felt sure, were patiently waiting for his return. No coo-ee came in reply. Burke and Wills were to die in that region, after attempting more travels in the moonlight.

Nine years later, the 22-year-old explorer John Forrest, making the first west–east journey between Perth and Adelaide, was worried that his horses had drunk no water for two days. He decided to travel before daybreak, conscious that 'there is a good moon' and believing that settled country and a supply of drinking water could not be far away. Arising at 1 a.m. to search for his horses, he spent so long in finding them that it was almost dawn before his party set out. The next morning he again wasted the early hours searching for his horses instead of travelling in the light of the moon.

Aborigines had long known the value of moonlight for their ceremonies. When John Glover, S. T. Gill and other British artists witnessed a corroboree and painted the scene, they usually left behind a record of the night sky. The moon or moonlight is visible in their paintings: it is usually a full moon.

The Moon as a Headlight

Along the coast, in deep water, ships normally continued their voyage whether it was day or night. The narrow sea lane between the Great Barrier Reef and the Queensland coast was dangerous, and here some ships anchored for the night. But if the moon was bright the captain was usually persuaded to proceed.

One of the worst tragedies in the history of the Barrier Reef occurred when a bright moon persuaded a captain to keep his ship moving long after the sun had set. On 28 February 1890 the mail steamer *Quetta*, on a voyage from Brisbane to ports in South-East Asia, was steaming in the moonlight near Thursday Island. It was about 9.30 in the evening and the social life of the ship was probably at its merriest. A pilot familiar with the waters was on the bridge. The sea was flat, and in the soft light all seemed safe. Suddenly the ship hit an uncharted rock. One side of her iron hull was ripped open, and she sank within three minutes. Most of the Asian passengers were on deck and were saved. Most of the Europeans were below deck and drowned.

On a moonlit night in warm weather there was special pleasure in boarding an excursion steamer on Sydney Harbour.

On a winter's night in our time, several million cars and trucks shine their headlights on the road, but the only powerful headlights in 1860 were fixed to the few locomotives. The lonely lighthouses, with their oil lamps, transmitted a bright light across the ocean, but nearly all other outdoor lamps were weak. Country roads were unlit, and traffic virtually halted when night fell.

But did the coaches of Cobb and Co travel at night? Before the era of television, the popular image of those night coaches came largely from Henry Lawson's poem, 'The Lights of Cobb and Co'. His first verse takes us to a wayside hotel in the middle of the night. The hotel is astir because soon the long-distance coach will arrive, the tired horses will be replaced, and the passengers will eat their quick meal until there arises the call, 'All aboard!' Lawson shows us the separate sources of light in that little hotel:

> Fire lighted; on the table a meal for sleepy men;
> A lantern in the stable; a jingle now and then;
> The mail-coach looming darkly by light of moon and star;
> The growl of sleepy voices; a candle in the bar

In Lawson's verses the three oil lamps, hung on the moving coach, shine their light on all that lines the road – the old diggings, pools of water, a covered wagon, clumps of scrub, and the sandstone cuttings in the steep hills. But the poem's horses and coach, racing through the night, do not belong to the gold rush years. They belong to a later era of smoother roads, an era when the roadside is fenced and the sheep and cattle cannot easily stray. They belong to an era when as many as five kerosene

15

lamps, each with shining reflectors, have supplanted the simple candle lamps on the coach.

The lights of Cobb and Co, brilliant in the imagination, could be dim in reality. Moonlight was infinitely more powerful than the simple headlights carried by a horsedrawn vehicle.

Southern Cross – a Kite or a Cluster?

Those who travelled to Australia in the nineteenth century were nearly as conscious of the sky as the sea. The average sea voyage in most decades took not less than three months, and much of that voyage would be spent beneath skies clearer than Europe's. The passengers eagerly scanned the changing night sky when they went on deck, especially in the tropics. On balmy nights near the equator they watched the familiar stars of the northern world slip from sight, and new stars glide into their place. Many passengers viewed with sadness or nostalgia the vanishing northern stars, for they were the last trace of home. Louisa Anne Meredith, emigrating to Sydney in 1839, thought in retrospect that she suffered more through the loss of the North Star than from any other parting:

> Night after night I watched it, sinking lower – lower; and the well-known 'Great Bear' that I had so gazed at even from a child, that it seemed like the face of an old friend, was fast going too; it was like parting from my own loved home-faces over again. I thought of so many times and places associated in my mind with those bright stars; of those who had

16

gazed on them beside me, some of whom had for ever passed from earth, – and of the rest, who might say that we should ever meet again? Those stars seemed a last link uniting us, but it was soon broken – they sunk beneath the horizon, and the new constellations of the southern hemisphere seemed to my partial eyes far less splendid.

Ludwig Leichhardt, making his first and only voyage to Australia – he was to vanish mysteriously in the far interior – marvelled at the little things. In all his early life, his own shadow, when the sun shone, had pointed to the north, but after crossing the equator his shadow pointed in the opposite direction. At night he watched the constellations rise majestically in the east and stride slowly 'in sublime silence' over the sea, and lower themselves in the west. This nightly procession of stars slowly changed, and some of the bright personages in the procession were seen no more, to be replaced, as the ship steered south, by brighter, unfamiliar stars. 'If only', he wrote when he reached Sydney in 1842, 'I could find words to tell you how deeply I was stirred.'

Migrants in sailing ships, long before they reached the equator, sought out the signpost of the Southern Cross on clear nights, but many seeing it in its full glory were slightly disappointed by its irregularity. 'It isn't a cross', wrote Samuel Butler, who was a sheep farmer in New Zealand in the early 1860s. 'It is a kite, a kite upside down, an irregular kite upside down, with only three respectable stars and one very poor and very much out of place.' This brilliant kite is highest in the Australian sky in autumn, and in April and May it hovers almost directly above Canberra. But in the late spring it lies so low in the southern sky that the bottom part of the cross is invisible in the tropics of Australia. If the main city had been Darwin rather than Sydney, the Southern Cross would never have become a popular national symbol: it was too low in the sky.

Out on the never-ending plains the explorers and shepherds – if they were curious – looked at the night sky. Many marvelled at what they saw, night after night. In the dry regions, clouds at night were unusual. The dome of the sky was rarely veiled by cloud, fog, mist or dust. Leichhardt, exploring in tropical Queensland in June 1845, was delighted when, moving closer to the equator, he could see not only a myriad of the southern hemisphere's stars but some of the northern hemisphere's too. At 17 degrees from the equator he saw stars that were invisible in Sydney:

> Sleeping in the open air at night, with a bright sky studded with its stars above us, we were naturally led to observe more closely the hourly changes of the heavens; and my companions became curious to know the names of those brilliant constellations, with which nightly observation had now, perhaps for the first time, made them familiar.

One morning at four o'clock he awakened his men and pointed out the Great Bear, alias the Big Dipper, a star that must have been familiar in their childhoods, for nearly all had been born in the northern hemisphere. The sudden reappearance of such familiar stars 'touches us like magic', he wrote. Whether he spoke for everyone is far from certain. Some of his men must have cursed when, jolted out of a deep sleep, they were made to stand in the cold darkness and gaze upwards.

For several generations the night sky had a significance that now has faded. People marvelled at the stars which – as the poet Binyon was to write – moved in marches across the heavenly plains. A much larger proportion of Australians then lived beyond the Great Dividing Range, where the night skies are usually clearer. Even those who lived in the cities walked into the open air at least once each evening, to gather firewood or visit their outhouse: in those days, in most suburbs, the lavatory was an outhouse.

On virtually every night of the year, passenger ships were steaming along the coast. Unless the night was windy or wet, people left the saloons to take the night air on the decks and to gaze at the procession of stars. Likewise, on the stock routes the flocks and herds were halted near nightfall, and the drovers – in watches consisting of two to four hours – took their turn to keep awake. They watched the black sky dusted with stars. 'Banjo' Paterson's hero, Clancy of the Overflow, was one horseman who saw, all around him, 'the sunlit plains extended, And at night the wondrous glory of the everlasting stars'. Hundreds of thousands of Australians, in that starlit era, knew his poem by heart.

Early settlers began to think that the Southern Cross should symbolise the continent. Thus the stars of the Southern Cross appeared on the big flag of the Anti-Transportation

League in Victoria and Tasmania in 1851; they dominated the large flag – about 3.5 metres wide – which flew at Eureka in 1854; and they appeared on the new flag of the Australian Federation League in the 1890s. When a competition was held in 1901 among the citizens of Australia – and, curiously, New Zealand – to design a Commonwealth flag, more than half of the 33 000 entries carried the Southern Cross. The Union Jack was nearly as ubiquitous. Indeed the five prize winners submitted almost identical designs.

Eventually the Southern Cross, as a powerful symbol, became as important on the flag as in the night sky. The cross we now see in the sky perhaps lacks the visibility it possessed in the late nineteenth century. Increasingly the nation has concentrated itself in a few big cities where at night the blaze of electricity – so strong that it can often be seen as a pale puff of light from 100 kilometres away – has dimmed the stars.

The Burning Sun: 'This Country is Curious'

The moon and stars caught the imagination of many Australians. The sun burned deeper into their minds.

Most newcomers who experienced their first summer in Australia complained of the heat. In Adelaide and Sydney the hot wind from the interior – variously known as the sirocco and the brickfielder – was especially dreaded. The British Isles knew no such wind. In the far interior the temperatures were higher, and a shade tree was often a rarity. The explorers of the interior faced heat and dry terrain such as they had not imagined. Some wondered whether their descriptions would be believed by those who, on the far side of the world, read their published journals.

Melbourne is now often viewed as a cold city but in the 1850s it was seen by most of its new residents as a furnace in summer. The hot winds blowing dust from the dry interior or from roughly made suburban streets were an additional nightmare. Even in the tall rooms of the fine Parliament House in 1858, reporters on a hot night felt a 'sensation of headache and faintness', partly from the heat of summer and partly from the heat emitted by the new gas lamps. Prefabricated iron buildings sent out from England were valued, especially as Melbourne was short of builders, but an all-iron building on a hot day became an oven. An iron lockup or jail, erected in Bendigo in the late 1850s, was so hot that a canvas tent was placed over it. Even so the prisoners inside pleaded for relief on hot days.

In the Hunter Valley an Irish migrant, Michael Normile, depicted the warm climate in his letters home. 'This Country is Curious, dear Father', he wrote. It was hot at the very time when it was cold in distant Derry. The wheat fields were so dry that they were in danger of catching fire, while grass was burned down 'to the very clay'. When he went out walking, the metalled road was so hot that it burned the soles of his feet. On 1 April 1855 he summed up the long summer: 'I Seen this last Summer 4 months without a drop of rain and all that time hot scorching weather.' The heat was so oppressive that many newcomers found themselves panting. 'I would give a mouthfull of money for a mouthfull of fresh air', he wrote. All in all he was not a complainer and felt pleased with his new life near the winding, soothing Hunter River. The town of Brisbane was much hotter; and Biddy Burke, writing home to Ireland, complained that 'I did feel the heat so much both night & day we could not sleep'.

Tasmania and the South Island of New Zealand were thought then to possess the most favourable climates. Even the mild summer of Hobart, however, had its perils. The Reverend John Martineau, a visitor from Melbourne, liked the climate of Tasmania but issued a warning in 1869. While invalids, the tubercular and the rheumatic would revel in the climate, he claimed that 'the strong and the active seem to lose something of their vigour'. He thought that children in England gained from 'the nipping of the keen frost' and the cold winds but the vigour of Tasmanian-born children would slowly be impaired because frosts were rarer. As for Queensland and South Australia, he did not think that they were intended by nature as a home for 'the English race'.

Whereas the heat of summer was feared, winter – all over the land – was a sensation to those who arrived from western Europe. Ada Cambridge, who first came ashore in 1870, exulted in the winter. Her ship berthed at Port Melbourne in the cool darkness. When she awoke she felt a radiance in the air: the morning was 'full of sunshine and freshness'. The clarity of the daylight delighted her. Warned that the climate of Australia was like the inside of a glasshouse, she agreed that there was almost a tropical feel in the air, even in what was one of the cooler regions of Australia. When she ate a whole pineapple – in England almost a forbidden fruit because of its expense – she felt that she was near the Garden of Eden. Her first smell of a bunch of Australian violets, carried aboard her ship, made her nostalgic for her English homeland and yet grateful that she was now in the land of all the perfumes and fruits. Tens of thousands of immigrants shared her delight, especially if they arrived in late autumn, winter, or early spring. It was the summer that was overpowering.

Climate lives partly inside the mind. What is roasting weather to some can be pleasing to others. Moreover successive generations, adjusting to a novel climate, alter their daily ways and their permanent attitudes: the Australian-born were more likely to tolerate the hot climate. Even in the middle of the nineteenth century many new settlers preferred not the dry breath of the brickfielder blowing over Adelaide but the moist

Brighton Beach near Melbourne in the 1880s. Most visitors wore long sleeves and carried umbrellas to protect themselves from the hot sun, whereas beach-goers now lie in the sun.

heat on the southern Queensland coast. There the hot day was relieved by the sea breeze.

In trying to cope with summer, Australians responded in distinctive ways. The importing of ice from the far side of the equator was one scheme, and it belongs to a later chapter. In the suburbs and country towns, houses with verandahs became common. On the farmlands where water could be scarce, the green South American 'peppercorn' tree was planted near the homestead, and within a few years it provided precious shade.

For the people of the cities, spacious public parks and botanical gardens dotted with shade trees were cultivated. For the governors of the chief mainland colonies, a summer residence was built in the nearby hills or on a cooler stretch of the coast. The cool southern highlands of New South Wales, Mount Macedon in Victoria and the port of Robe in South Australia were chosen as retreats for the governors and their families. Tasmania's governor needed no such summer retreat: the whole island was a retreat. In the 1880s during the summer it became fashionable for the wives of richer men to escape the mainland heat by holidaying for a few weeks in Hobart or voyaging in a ship to Milford Sound. A century later, climatic preferences having turned a somersault, their great-granddaughters fly to Surfers Paradise and lie in the hot sun.

Largely for climatic reasons, a shorter working week became the goal of several of the early trade unions. Stonemasons and other outside workers pointed to the dangers of working too long under the summer sun and successfully claimed the eight-hour day.

Well-dressed women attending a concert were careful to take their pretty silk fans and wave them to and fro, to cool their flushed faces. When Nellie Melba sang for the first time in Perth, one music critic noticed that, quietly competing with her voice were the swish and rustle of hundreds of hand-held fans in the hot and crowded theatre. Inland, where the heat was most intense and the afternoon sea breeze unknown, travellers had a strong desire to swim in rock pools and the deeper reaches of half-dry rivers. Drownings were all too common. In the big cities on public holidays people in their thousands sailed in the pleasure steamers and felt the sea breeze, or sat beneath shade trees in the parks. Some nationalists now resent the old elms, oaks and other English trees lining streets and parks, but the trees were chosen not only for nostalgia but because they offered an expanse of shade that eucalypts and most native trees could not provide.

In the cities the hot days fostered diseases and odours. The garbage in backyards stank; the waste at the back of the butchers' and fishmongers' shops stank; the fat that was the main ingredient used at soap and candle factories stank; and those who walked along the city lanes could smell sewage here and there.

To stifle the more offensive odours, charcoal was some-times used. As James Johnston wrote in 1855, in praise of charcoal: 'Mixed with fermenting night-soil, or with the contents of our common sewers, it sweetens them almost immediately, and it produces a like effect upon almost every variety of decaying animal and vegetable matter.' Many women dabbed

25

themselves with perfume, or carried a perfumed handkerchief, not just to project a pleasant scent but to protect them from the unpleasant.

The vogue for eucalyptus oil arose partly from its merit as a deodorant in hot weather. It became the habit well before the 1880s to sprinkle a towel or cloth with eucalyptus oil and hang it in a sick room. In Hobart in 1876, Gould's Blue Finch Brand of Eucalyptus, when rubbed on the limbs of the patient or sprinkled in the air, was said to prevent the spread of typhoid and scarlet fever from the sick room. Those who did not mind the raw taste of this oil were tempted to experiment when that astonishing invention, eucalyptus ice cream, appeared in Australian shops. Of course eucalyptus was such a cure-all that it was hailed in winter, too, as the healer of footballers' bruises and children's colds.

It was feared that the warm climate would, generation after generation, slowly debilitate and enfeeble young white Australians. That fear helps to explain why Australians, with their tiny population, were so elated when their team defeated England at cricket – the very game that was symbolic of English outdoor virtues. (Victory in cricket tests, however, was really a victory only of eleven men, not a whole nation.) Again and again the fears resurged. John W. Fortescue, a young British critic, wrote in 1893 an influential article on 'The Influence of Climate on Race'. Queensland, in his opinion, was too tropical to be the home of a vigorous people. He argued that in summer even Sydney people showed the 'limp, parboiled appearance' sometimes visible in 'degenerate whites' in the West Indies.

The most forbidding climate, in the eyes of Britsh migrants, was in Queensland. There, in response, a distinctive architecture arose. By the 1890s the common house in a vast area of Queensland and inland New South Wales stood on high wooden legs, so that the under-house formed a retreat in hot weather. A high pyramid-shaped roof of iron and gabled ventilators allowed the air above the ceilings to circulate. A wide verandah provided further protection from the sun. In turn the verandahs were sometimes shaded by an outer sloping roof, known as the Charters Towers verandah. That town, standing on a plateau south-west of Townsville, was once the largest in tropical Australia.

To cope with the summer, Queenslanders preferred high ceilings. If a congregation could afford the additional expense, they built churches with roofs that were sometimes Scandinavian in their steepness. In many of the new towns in north Queensland, people wore wide hats or white pith helmets and carried a Chinese-made umbrella to fend off the sun. Chinese storekeepers imported these blue umbrellas in their tens of thousands. Larger than a woman's umbrella, they were carried by men and women alike. When babies slept outside, a blue umbrella was placed over their head. The direct rays of the summer sun were usually avoided throughout the land. Sunstroke often appeared as the certified cause of death, even in the cooler colonies. Whether the real cause of death was dehydration, asthma, or multiple causes, sunstroke was the frequent diagnosis.

It was emphatically believed that white men and women could not safely work in the open air of the tropics, beneath the rays of the hot sun. Accordingly Pacific islanders were imported to work in the sugarcane fields, and Cantonese came of their own accord. Even the white women who worked indoors were seen to run a risk. As late as 1914 a leading Melbourne physician, Sir James Barrett, feared for the health of all those Queensland women who faced not only the humid heat of summer but the heat radiating from the wood-burning stove in the kitchen. His learned article claimed to detect a 'contrast between the robust appearance of the average man in Queensland, and the debilitated appearance of too many of the women'. Would the health and vigour of the next generations of Queensland children be impaired? He pondered the question.

Even in the far south of Australia, people were surprised by the strength and tanning powers of the sun. A young man working in the bush not far from Melbourne, while waiting for a dray to bring him supplies, sat down to inform his mother of how his appearance had changed since they last met in England. F. J. Meyrick confided that he had put on so much weight that his clothes were skin-tight. 'I am 5 feet, 11 inches in height, burnt black with the sun, as strong as a bullock, with a great beard upon my face', he added. To be burned black, a rare experience in England, was common here even in 1840.

In that era the colour of the face was often a sign of the work that people performed. Today, in contrast, the financial consultant who goes to the beach in the summer or the snow in winter will be suntanned, and will have the same facial complexion as someone who labours outside at unskilled work. Today most people enjoy a higher ratio of leisure to work, and so their facial skin often shows the signs of leisure activities spent in the open air. In contrast, in the nineteenth century daily work dominated life, and this was reflected in the faces of those who laboured out of doors.

The Scottish actors, the Kennedys, touring Tasmania in the 1870s, observed the faces around them as they travelled by train. They noticed many 'clean-shaven men, with florid, full faces, portly paunches, and all the appearance of the typical John Bull'. On a Sunday they walked to the Scottish church in a township near Deloraine and found about a hundred people crammed inside, sitting on forms without backs. The Kennedys judged them, because their skins showed 'a high healthy colour', to be people who worked in the open air. Occasionally a clergyman fresh from the British Isles would, from the height of the pulpit, look down on his Australian congregation and remark to himself how brown, how un-European, the faces appeared. More women than men tried to preserve a white skin.

The peaches and cream complexion, favoured by young women in the British Isles, was valued highly in some female circles in Australia. The canvases of the open-air painters of the Heidelberg School show fashionable young women of the late 1880s, most shielding their fair skin from the sun. Thus Charles Conder, painting in an unkempt orchard on a day of cloud and sunlight, depicts women fending off the spring sun with hats, long, full-sleeved dresses and parasols. Tom Roberts, in *A Summer Morning Tiff*, depicts a woman standing in a dry paddock and wearing a white hat and ground-rustling white gown with long sleeves. Only her hands and lower wrists are

These families travelling in a day-excursion steamship are 'rugged up', not against the winter wind but the summer sun. Helena Rubinstein, a temporary migrant to Victoria, devised her face cream for women such as these.

exposed to the sun. One of the most famous brand-names in the world was created in the belief that the hot Australian sun so wrinkled and freckled the faces of women that it called for a protective cream. Helena Rubinstein migrated as a teenager from Cracow in Poland to the Victorian town of Coleraine where in the 1890s she concocted a face cream. She later vowed – she moved successively to Melbourne, London and New York – that the cream had already proved its worth in a land 'as ruinous to the complexion' as distant Australia.

A revolutionary stance of the Heidelberg School of painters was to praise the summer more than the winter. They gloried in hot winds and blue skies. While they did not paint the real outback – they did not visit it in the 1880s – they guided

Australian eyes towards an appreciation of a dry landscape that previously was alien.

It was a slow process, creating a national respect for a fierce blue sky and dry landscape and a hot, unrelenting summer. 'Banjo' Paterson's poem 'Waltzing Matilda', while seemingly set in the outback, displayed an untypical corner of that landscape. It depicted shade and water – the shade of the coolibah and the water of the billabong. It described a thoroughbred horse and a jolly jumbuck: a jolly sheep is obviously not a skinny one. The poem of 1895 could almost have been set in the well-watered country of the lower Hunter or the upper Murray. If instead it had described stony desert and the bones of dead sheep and a swagman whose billy was empty, it would not have appealed to that generation of Australians.

How to Celebrate a Brown Christmas

Christmas came at the wrong time. This puzzled nearly every new immigrant. Some could not hide their disappointment that snow would never fall on Christmas Day.

The local novels intended for circulation in the British Isles usually contained a chapter on the Australian experience of Christmas Day and how odd it was. Henry Kingsley, living in Victoria in the late 1850s, wrote a popular novel, *The Recollections of Geoffry Hamlyn*. His twentieth chapter is titled 'A Warm Christmas Day'. The setting is the house of Major Buckley, a squatter in Victoria's Western District. On Christmas

Eve his wife complains of the heat and calls out, 'My dear husband, please refresh me with reading the thermometer!' He dutifully looks at the thermometer and replies with a chuckle that it is 109 in the shade. 'Ah, dear!' Mrs Buckley sighs. The thought comes to her that if only 'the dear old rheumatic creatures' living out their days in the almshouse in their old English village could be here, how their creaking bones would be warmed.

Anthony Trollope, the novelist, reached Melbourne just before the Christmas of 1871. He was astonished at the heat. On 21 December it was 100 degrees Fahrenheit in the shade: the next day was 106. It was almost too much for him. He recorded that as 'the hot winds were blowing as they blow only in Melbourne', he moved from a house in the city to a friend's house in a suburb. He could not escape the heat. What was worse, the aqueduct that conveyed water from the reservoir to Melbourne was unable to satisfy the thirst engendered by a heatwave, and not enough water arrived even to fill a bath.

Far from their homeland so many people felt nostalgic for their chilly, childhood Christmases. With remarkable resilience they began to create their own version of the day. It became the custom for women to decorate the verandah posts of their houses with green bushes. They did not yet think of growing baby pine trees in readiness for the occasion. Instead on Christmas Eve a few men with axes and a horse and dray would go into the bush and come back with native bushes piled high, or the children would enter the nearby bush and return with their own freshly cut branches. And so the verandah posts were concealed 'behind a wall of greenery'.

Henry Lawson recalled how in Gulgong some of the rich diggers, having no children of their own, lavished money on boys and girls on Christmas Eve. He wrote of diggers who spent the big sum of one guinea to buy 'a toy for a child that reminded them of some other child at home', or escorted children into the general store and 'slapped a five-pound note down on the counter and told the little ones to call for whatever they wanted'. And he wrote of the generous Chinese storekeepers Sun Tong Lee & Co, who handed out 'strange, delicious sweets that melted in our mouths'.

Christmas dinner was the meal of the year, and made more exciting – for families that could afford the money – by the growing practice of hiding the small silver threepenny coins in the hot plum pudding. In many households the money was too precious, and mother, when the meal was over, collected the coins from the children, washed them and put them away to buy the next day's bread. At a few dinner tables tiny nuggets were hidden in the plum pudding. In Bendigo and other big gold towns those dentists in need of work must have looked forward to Christmas, for it would have brought them patients with broken teeth.

The German custom of erecting a Christmas tree, loaded with decorations and maybe presents, was slow to appear. But towards the end of the nineteenth century, in the weatherboard halls of a few townships, a tree would annually be set up, usually on Christmas Eve. Near Scottsdale, in Tasmania, according to John Skemp's *Memories of Myrtle Bank*, the chosen Christmas tree was a native species and often 'a shapely mountain pepper'. Chopped down and then erected on the stage of the local hall, it was trimmed with coloured paper and candles, and laden with a simple present for each child. As the tree was green and sappy, the candles could safely be fixed to the branches. And so the farming families arrived in their horsedrawn vehicles before sunset; and after the darkness set in, the adults and children in the packed hall watched the lighting of the candles. Each child was given a number, and numbered presents were cut from the tree. When a number was called, a child would rush forward to receive the wrapped trinket. For many bush children it was the momentous event of the year.

In big cities the theatres staged Christmas pantomimes, with lavish dresses and children's themes, while in the town halls large choirs sang Handel's *Messiah*. But the full-blooded Australian Christmas, as we now know it, was barely in its infancy. It was not yet a time for present-giving on a large scale. Large numbers of children in 1880 received no Christmas present. There were no giant retailers who week after week advertised their Christmas specials, and often the small shops that did advertise referred to their wares as 'Christmas and New Year Gifts'. It was not yet a season of extended holidays, except for children, and in the interval between Boxing Day and New Year's Day most breadwinners were hard at work. Miners, factory and rural workers, wharf labourers, domestic servants, washer-women and train shunters would have resented an extended holiday, because they were not paid on those days when they were away from their work.

As a religious festival, Christmas was honoured in spirit more than it is today. For devout Anglicans and Catholics it was a revered day. The other major religions, however, were slightly wary of Christmas. Most Presbyterians, being people of Scottish descent, put their heart into New Year's Day, and some of the now-famous sporting carnivals, such as the highland games at Maryborough, were in full swing even in the 1860s. The Methodists, who probably erected more church buildings in Australia than any other sect, were uneasy about celebrating on Christmas Day. If it fell on a weekday most of their churches were closed: if it fell on a Sunday their churches were open, and often packed. The Methodists were more likely to attend church on the last hour of the last day of the year, when they held a special service, than on Christmas Day.

During their long period of unease about a hot Christmas, Australians rarely noticed that they had more access than their British relatives to a vital part of the traditional Christmas story: 'the stars in the bright sky'. Eventually they ceased to lament that their Christmas came in hot weather.

The Trickle of Muddy Water

Australia is said to be the driest continent but some of the early settlers did not think it was exceptionally dry. They knew India, which also has its dry regions. Indeed, for decades most of the climatic regions of the eastern half of Australia tended to be viewed optimistically rather than realistically by their new inhabitants. The information passed on from Aborigines did not necessarily curb the optimism. While the Aborigines knew the climates, they had no measurements of temperature and rainfall that they could pass on. They knew that severe droughts came, but the droughts were less dislocating to them because they owned no domesticated livestock and used water sparingly. The optimism of the new settlers was also aided by the procession of abnormally moist seasons in much of eastern Australia from the mid-1840s to about 1890. It was a bitter blow when the following period of sixty years proved to be drier.

The penalties imposed by a very dry continent were at first barely noticed. All the early towns were built near the mouths of freshwater rivers. Sydney sat alongside the tiny Tank Stream, Newcastle was on the Hunter River, Hobart had its rivulets, Adelaide was on the freshwater Torrens, and Perth and Brisbane were built on river banks, close to where the tidal salt water flowing upstream met the fresh water coming from the ranges. Melbourne, too, was founded at such a spot, a rocky ledge which usually prevented the salt water of the navigable lower Yarra from fouling the fresh water just upstream. These infant towns were rarely short of water for essential needs.

In 1850, most houses in the capital cities did not yet possess the luxury of running water. In central Sydney, only about 1000 of the 8000 houses possessed running water. Instead their fresh water was carried in containers from a pipe in the street, or by a water cart which drew water from the nearby river. Garden plants were not watered, except with a bucket. Household lawns were few. Horsedrawn vehicles were not washed down with a hose. The factories that called for a steady flow of water drew it from the nearby river. Tanneries, boiling-down and wool-scouring works, and other factories that required a high flow of water extracted it from the river and then poured most of it back again as effluent, somewhat polluted, a few metres downstream.

In the farming districts and in the outback, water was sometimes scarce. On many farms a small, shallow earthen dam was excavated, with the aid of a horsedrawn scoop. In many pastoral districts the supply of water for sheep and cattle was dramatically increased by the widespread discovery of artesian water following the success of the first well, drilled in 1879. When severe drought persisted, the deaths of livestock came more from a lack of feed than a lack of water. Irrigation water was still a rarity in 1900.

It is not easy to find a careful analysis of the purity of the drinking water in a rural district. There survives an observant estimate of the water drunk by Pacific islanders living on ten large sugar plantations in Queensland in the early 1880s. On six of the ten properties, the water was classed as clean, having been collected from iron roofs and stored in iron or hardwood tanks. But on Eaton Vale, where 117 men lived in grass huts, the 'indifferent' water was collected from a chain of waterholes. On three other plantations the water was 'bad' or 'very bad'. Some of the free settlers drank 'bad' water too. In farming regions those houses clad with an iron roof invariably collected a clean supply of drinking water; but if their tank ran dry, the discoloured and sometimes polluted water of the dams had to be drunk.

In dry regions the local Aborigines knew where to find water at nearly every time of the year. That they had been able to survive for so long in this dry land puzzled the newcomers.

The reasons for their survival in the deserts slowly emerged. In the dry country certain trees yielded water. The mallee, especially the red species, yielded water after its long roots were excavated and broken open. A particular she-oak produced water. In the trunk of the spotted gum, small hollows often carried water. In the mulga country of Western Australia, a tree not unlike the mulga was known as the water tree.

New settlers sometimes learned from Aborigines and sometimes they learned by trial and error. William Morton offered guidance to anybody travelling in the dry terrain beyond the Darling River: 'If he sees emus, magpies, parrots or pigeons, he may be certain that there is some water not far away.' On the other hand, the presence of dingoes and crows were not necessarily a sign of water. When Morton saw pigeons and other smallish birds flying in a set direction just before sunset, he guessed that their goal was a pool of water.

After a short shower had fallen on dry land, travellers sometimes used a sponge to collect water from the neat shallow holes created in the soft earth by the impact of horses' hooves. The same sponges could be used to collect the morning dew. With patience a small sponge, used again and again, might eventually fill a quart pot. To gain water for a thirsty horse, an old blanket could be dragged gently and slowly over the wet tops of bushes until the blanket was saturated with water, and then it was so squeezed and wrung that a bucket or dish was needed to hold the water. There were other ways of collecting water. Ingenuity in finding water, first an Aboriginal skill, became a widespread talent in the bush.

When water was found it might be the colour of brown milky tea or black with mud. John Forrest, the Western Australian explorer, finding a tiny pool of water in a narrow rock hole, ladled out liquid which he described as 'about two quarts of something between mud and water'. Pulling out his pocket handkerchief he used it to strain mud from water. His colleagues thought the water was drinkable but their standards, after spending time in the dry country, were low. Of course, horses needed far more water, and to find enough could be difficult. Forrest organised his exploring around the principle of sending scouts ahead to find water, and only then could the whole party move forward.

In many districts travellers had to carry water, often on packhorses, or their life would be endangered. Initially, large leather or skin bags were used to hold water, with canvas being adopted later. A canvas bag was much lighter, and its water remained cooler. For those travelling on foot and carrying their own supplies and equipment, the canvas bag was a boon. The explorers Burke and Wills recorded on 17 December 1860 that the water scooped from a sandy waterhole was 97.4 degrees Fahrenheit but that when they poured the same warm water into their bags it quickly cooled down – 'to our astonishment' – to 78 degrees. After drinking a pannikin of the water they decided that it was 'too low a temperature to be pleasant'. One generation later, in Western Australia, a canvas water bag was carried by most prospectors.

Few people died of thirst in a typical decade. Even today it is widely said, in everyday conversation, that Burke and Wills died of thirst near Cooper's Creek. The idea is folklore: in fact the creek held plenty of water.

The nation's economic life depended on keeping sheep and cattle alive during the very dry years. Water had to be found for mobs of cattle on the move to market and for slow-moving flocks of sheep so large that they were beyond accurate counting. In droughts, livestock were moved long distances in order to reach a region where there was hope of grass and water. Sometimes a mob of thirsty cattle, sniffing water in the distance, would rush towards it, endangering the lives of drovers. Edward Sorenson, a drover, observed how the faint scent of a tiny volume of rainwater, lying in small potholes in the distance, aroused the cattle in his charge:

> They smell water at a long distance. You may be moving along quietly, your charges steady but sullen, when suddenly a puff of wind comes from the direction of the potholes. You notice an electric-like movement pass through the mob; every head is raised, and a thousand throats announce the proximity of a drink. Thenceforth they are noisy and restless.

As the cities became larger they constructed dams in nearby hills. By 1880 most inhabitants of the larger cities could, in their own house, turn on a tap which released fresh water that had flowed by pipe from a nearby reservoir. Water, however, was not used in washing away the sewage. The lavatory was outside, and the smelly metallic can was collected – usually once a week – by the nightsoil man and placed on the back of his wagon or cart. Market gardens absorbed much of this refuse: it was spread over the ground as fertiliser. In those days, squares of newspaper were used as toilet paper, and after they'd dried in the sun they were blown about by the wind.

Unsewered cities, as they grew larger, endangered health. In the 1870s and 1880s the death rate of children under the age of one was much higher in Sydney's suburbs than in rural New South Wales. For a family to move from the country to the city was to increase their chance of prosperity and also their chance of losing an infant. Periodically, typhoid was a killer, especially of young adults. The incentive to build a sewerage system for the larger cities would have been stronger but for the fact that Australians were inclined to boast of their healthy way of life.

Adelaide took the first steps towards higher standards of hygiene. It built the first Australian sewerage farm, and animals grazed on its grasses. By 1910 the typical house in an Australian city was connected to a network of underground pipes that carried sewage out to sea or to a treatment farm beyond the outer suburbs. But maybe half of the people in Australia, especially those living in small towns, the countryside and the newest suburbs, still used an outhouse. It was often a shed or shelter built over a hole in the ground. Eventually the hole was filled in with earth, and the shelter was moved to a new site where a fresh hole was dug.

Even when the cities gained a reliable supply of water, many of the household taps were turned on sparingly. A kitchen sink did not readily replace the tub and water bucket. An enthusiasm for regularly washing bodies and washing clothes was late in coming, but by the early 1900s it was noticeable. Evelyn Clowes, arriving in about 1902, was surprised to see at the dock the 'extraordinary cleanliness' of the wharf labourers. She reached the conclusion, spelled out in her book *On the Wallaby*, that the Australian workingman was the cleanest in the world.

Outback towns obtained their own water as best they could. Some dammed a creek. The typical house had its own iron tank that collected rainwater from the roof. In the backyard was sometimes a man-made well, and the water hauled up in the bucket was cool, if the well was deep.

Large mining towns that sprang up in the outback faced, as they grew, an acute scarcity of water. Early Broken Hill was known for the thousands of human faces coated with red dust. The early residents of Kalgoorlie mainly used salt water that had been condensed and made drinkable at high cost. A bold solution was finally found for what was soon the tenth-largest city in Australia. In 1903, for the first time, a chain of steam engines pumped water along a steel pipeline running all the way from a reservoir near Perth to the goldfields. It was a foretaste of the Snowy Mountains Scheme of half a century later.

Across the land, the water that was boiled in billies, saucepans or kettles for the making of tea came in a surprising range of colours, but was rarely neutral. From bush houses with a roof of bark, the water collected in a tank or barrel had a distinctive colour. Water flowing from a new shingle roof was 'wine-red' for several years and water flowing from a roof of stringy-bark had the colour of tea for an even longer time. Coffee-coloured water and creamy-coloured water were found inland. Black water, stained by tannin, was common in western Tasmania. The taste of the water was as varied as the colour. In the Northern Territory two experienced travellers reported that one pannikin of water tasted of goats and another tasted of rats. One reason for the intense popularity of tea was that it improved the taste and appearance of water.

When rain fell on the bark roof of this bush house, it was collected in barrels standing on the ground. Sometimes the water was coloured red by the bark.

2

THE DIMMING OF CANDLELIGHT

The candle was once the light of Australia. In most houses and huts it burned and spluttered after dark. In retrospect its light, though usually dim, gave off a romantic glow. Hugh McCrae, the poet, surrounded by his books in the evening, and looking back on his youth spent in the nineteenth century, rejoiced in 'the yellow pleasure of candle-light'. The more expensive candles provided a pleasant light – enough to read a book with ease. On the other hand the cheaper tallow candles used in most huts and humbler houses gave off an offensive odour. They also smoked excessively. When protected by a glass covering, they smeared the glass, thus calling for the use of the cleaning rag each morning.

Children had to be taught the danger of placing a lighted candle even for a minute on a ledge or cupboard close to a window. On a summer night the window might be open and a sudden change in the wind could rustle the curtains, and suddenly they would be alight. Many children were burned to death by a fire that caught on the window drapes. When the wide, bell-shaped dress, the crinoline, was in fashion mid-century, it could too easily brush against a candle or an open fire. Another hazard was to read in bed with a naked candle held in the hand. Some family doctors, unduly fearful, warned their patients on no account to read in bed because the practice would permanently impair their eyesight.

Rewards and Perils of the Yellow Light

Almanacs and yearbooks warned their readers: 'When you discover your clothes to be on fire try to retain your presence of mind. *On no account rush about wildly*. If you are alone seize any loose rag or woollen article and wrap it tightly about you: this will extinguish the flames at once.' If no such articles were at hand, the advice was to roll on the floor. If a woman's clothes caught fire, a man – so it was said – had a positive duty to step in, forcibly throw her onto the floor and, taking off his own coat, wrap it around her.

In many districts, mosquito nets usually enclosed a bed at night. Even in Sydney a carefully woven net, made of lightweight yarn, was desirable if mosquitoes were to be kept away in summer. The Reverend John West, who moved from Launceston to become the editor of the *Sydney Morning Herald* in 1854, was sometimes called upon at his Paddington house at night by a shorthand writer who needed his views on a late item for the last edition. West would light a candle and, sitting up in bed, dictate a few sentences to the scribe. He soon realised the danger of a candle burning near the inflammable mosquito net. On his orders an enclosure of metal gauze, lightly perforated, was built around his bed.

It was by candlelight that pages of books were read aloud to the family at night – novels, books of travel, history, and the Bible. One girl affectionately recorded in the 1860s a scene that was repeated in thousands of homes: 'Father would read aloud night after night to Mother while she sat with her sewing. Two home-made candles in tall brass candlesticks gave a mild light. Kerosene lamps had not yet come so far into the country.' It should be added that her house was in the Daylesford district, less than 100 kilometres from Melbourne, but the cost of carting tins of kerosene in wagons and drays was presumably dear. 'A pair of snuffers on a brass tray at Father's right hand were used frequently to keep the candles from getting dull. He was always nervous and fidgety, and the snuffing made a relieving interlude, and a chance to rebuke someone for making a noise.' Today the word snuff often means to extinguish a light. But in the heyday of the candle, snuffing usually signified the process whereby, with the help of the twin metal handles of the snuffer, the half-burned end of the wick was cut or pinched so that the candle could burn with a new brightness.

Tens of thousands of rural households made their own candles by pouring fat into a metal mould. Like so many of the simple manufacturing tasks, it was open to error. If the fat was heated incorrectly, the candle did not burn effectively. In many rural districts the main light was a homemade slush lamp. A large tin, perhaps a jam tin, was half-filled with clay, and then topped up with dripping left over from roasting meat or from the specially cooked fat of an animal. Into the fat was inserted a long, homemade wick, consisting of wood wrapped in cloth. The wick was lit, and the lamp spluttered and then began to burn. 'The smell of the smoke was something to remember, but it gave a good light', recalled Jane Goldsmith of South Gippsland.

In winter many people in the bush used few lights at night. They had to use candles in the first hour or two of darkness, but they went to bed early, partly to escape the cold. There was also a fear, in some frontier districts, that a light might attract bushrangers or other robbers. The writer Mary Gilmore, recalling the western plains around 1870, regretted that by going early to bed, the settlers suffered one fleeting deprivation: 'people were usually asleep when the moon was in its glory, or the stars a blaze of splendour. But I have known my father to wake my mother out of sleep to look at the moon, and lift me out of bed to show it to me'.

In the open air a naked flame needed protection from a puff of wind. Several kinds of glass vessels were used to cup the flame. For a time a common lantern was made from an empty beer or cordial bottle. The bottom of the bottle was neatly removed and a candle was fixed in its throat, thus protecting the flame from the wind. In parts of Victoria by the 1870s this was known as a Ballarat lantern, but elsewhere it had other names. A sophisticated version of the Ballarat lantern was equipped with a wire handle.

On mining fields, when the men on the afternoon shift finished their work, this homemade lantern guided those who had to walk home along unlit roads. In hilly fields such as Mt Lyell, wives living in the valley, and still awake after midnight, recalled how reassuring it was to see the procession of tiny lights coming down the hill.

In the goldmines, for decades, the candle supplied the only light. The stearine candle, made from purified fatty acids, was preferred because it emitted no smoke. Some miners stuck the end of the candle into a blob of clay and fixed the clay to their hat. A long sharpened piece of iron, fixed to the mine's timber or rock wall, was a neat holder for candles. It was popularly known as a spider. By 1900 the busier passageways of large goldmines were lit by electricity, while in the remote corners the carbide lamp was beginning to challenge the candle. In the coalmines a naked flame was dangerous, and the safety lamp was used.

If a political rally was held on a moonless night, the wooden torch was useful. It was used less to illuminate the crowd than to light up the speaker's face and the gestures of his hands. The torch was essentially a long, rounded piece of resinous timber, sometimes with a rag tied to the top end, and the rag soaked in tallow. When in 1857 the young politician Henry Parkes addressed a huge crowd in Wynyard Square in Sydney, even those listeners at the edge of the crowd could see him, standing on the tray of a wagon, his face illuminated by a burning torch. The street procession, marching with the aid of torchlight, became almost a mark of the trade unions. In pioneering districts, a funeral procession, running behind time, was illuminated by torches. 'The night was dark', it was said of a burial in a Gippsland forest in April 1888, 'and torches made of bark were lighted to show the way.'

In June 1880 the outlaw Ned Kelly and his gang planned to derail and destroy a police train approaching Glenrowan, on what is now the main Melbourne–Sydney railway line. When their plan was found out, a warning had to be delivered to the driver of the oncoming train. A schoolteacher decided to warn him. As it was long past midnight he had to devise a way of attracting the driver's attention. According to one report he took one of the glass-covered lamps used on a horsedrawn buggy, lit a candle and placed it inside the lamp. To make the light more vivid he placed a red scarf around the lamp. Standing by the lonely railway line in the darkness he waved his lamp and succeeded in halting the train. Another account reported that the teacher had only matches, which he lit against the background of a red cloth.

In its heyday the candle was used at the rate of tens of millions a year. Dozens of Australian factories manufactured candles and soap, for both commodities used tallow – usually rendered from the fat of sheep – as their main ingredient. As candles were fragile and could accidentally be broken, they were packed tightly in strong wooden boxes. In the grocer's shop the empty candle box was not wasted. At any one time, tens of thousands of these boxes were used as seats in simple Australian homes. Arranged one on top of the other, they served as cupboards. Outside, drivers would sit on a candle box as they drove a cart or dray.

Towards the end of the twentieth century the lighted

candle again became popular, though only for special occasions. A curiosity, it waved the wand of nostalgia. Candles lighted tables at banquets, and were lit for Christmas dinner. The liking for candles – even though electricity was available – was also a sign of the decline of evangelical Protestantism, which earlier had viewed the ornamental candle as a symbol of papacy. The candle was popular again partly because the brick house has replaced the bark, slab or rough-timber house with holes and cracks that let in the wind.

More than one century earlier, the candle was less romantic. It was so fragile, so easily blown out, when the winds were whistling through the thin gaps in the slabs of timber that constituted the walls. Thus the drover's wife, the heroine of one of Australia's best-known stories, possessed only a dwindling candle to light up the kitchen on the frightening night when a snake was hiding behind a wall. Henry Lawson captured the scene with a few words:

> The thunder-storm comes on, and the wind, rushing through the cracks in the slab wall, threatens to blow out her candle. She places it on a sheltered part of the dresser and fixes up a newspaper to protect it. At every flash of lightning, the cracks between the slabs gleam like polished silver.

The rain pelts down. The night creeps by. She watches continually for a sign of the snake but the light from the candle is now fainter and flickering. Lawson depicts her plight: 'Her candle is nearly done; she forgot that she was out of candles.

Some more wood must be got to keep the fire up, and so she shuts the dog inside and hurries round to the woodheap.' The inadequate light adds tension to the scene. Eventually the snake is caught, by the dog.

Hurricane lamps and their strong light arrived after the heyday of the candle. They came with the increasing prosperity, for the kerosene in these lamps was expensive. The smell of kerosene also seemed slightly less offensive than fat and some of the other fuels used in candles and lamps. At night, with a hurricane lamp to light up the rough road, people could safely set out to attend a dance at a neighbouring farm. Those who could not go to the dance – or for religious reasons did not believe in dancing – saw the procession of lamps bobbing along a lonely track where week after week not a lamp was to be seen.

The kerosene lamp was popular by the 1870s. Made from oil increasingly available from the United States, kerosene and its virtues were so heavily advertised that Australian children knew the names and the insignia of Snowflake, Evening Star, Light of the Age and other American brands. Kerosene tins were imported in wooden packing cases, which were later used for making primitive furniture. The tin itself, once the kerosene was emptied, was washed out, equipped with a wire handle, and used for carrying water, milk and oats. By 1900 the kerosene lamp must have been the most widely used source of light in those numerous houses that had no access to gas or electricity.

A night operator at a telegraph station. At night, the light was often bright when it was gas or kerosene, but feeble when it came from a candle.

The Gaslight – Soft and Pleasing

While the candle still prevailed, the central streets of the largest cities were lit by gas. Sydney was the first to be gas-lit. On the opening day – 24 May 1841, the birthday of Queen Victoria – twenty-three streetlamps were lit. The Sydney *Herald* exulted in the 'soft and pleasing' light shed on those standing beneath the lamp, while the gas flame itself was 'was almost too dazzling to look upon'. Melbourne's first gasworks was opened by the governor Sir Charles Hotham just before Christmas 1855. At the ceremony he caught what was called 'a violent cold', and he died on the eve of the city's first display of gas-lit buildings.

Whenever a town was large enough, it built gasworks and laid the gas mains along the busier streets. By 1900 about a hundred towns were lit or partly lit by gas. While the tall, round gasometer might appear to be a tawdry industrial sight, it was also a source of pride and a symbol of progress. Kyneton, a stopping place on the road to the Bendigo goldfields, was the first inland town to make its own gaslight, and a local newspaper in May 1858 praised the gas plant as if it were a town hall or grand statuary. The gas was at first expensive. In Melbourne and Brisbane the engineers insisted on making gas mainly from coal imported at high cost from England. In contrast Kyneton was more frugal and at first made gas mainly by heating eucalyptus leaves. Its gumleaf gas, when burned in the street lamps, gave off a favourable light.

To supply gas to streetlamps and houses called for an expensive grid of underground pipes. Whenever a parliament passed a law creating a new gas company, it permitted the con-tractors to dig to their hearts' content. Thus a law of 1860, in licensing a Mr Tuck to light the towns of East Maitland and West Maitland with gas, specifically empowered his labourers to 'dig and sink trenches and drains and to lay mains and pipes' and put stopcocks, syphons and plugs in any park or footpath. While the first gas mains were being laid, a provincial town in extreme weather consisted of ribbons of mud or dust.

In the main streets gas burned behind a tall glass bowl

set on the edge of the pavement. The lamp stood tall, partly to shed light but also to prevent a vandal from snuffing the flame. Each night the gas was turned on by a travelling lamplighter who, carrying a light on the end of a pole, set the gas aflame. In the morning, just before sunrise, he snuffed the gaslight. In some towns the lamp-snuffers were milkmen who extinguished the light while on their way to deliver milk to houses. Lamp-lighting became a common occupation. The city of Sydney in 1897 had 154 lamplighters, and additional men must have worked in the outer suburbs where the oil lamp still burned.

To the first spectators, the streets seemed ablaze with dots of light. Light is relative: it comes from the eyes as much as the streetscape. To a gold-rush migrant who, for some decades, had read at night by the light of a candle, or had driven a horse and buggy by the light of an oil lamp, the gas lamps in country towns were spectacular. They were also conspicuous because at that time no telephone or electricity poles ran along the streets. The only pole to be seen was the gas lamp, made of wrought iron and of pleasing design. Long after telephone and electricity poles arrived, every pole in a busy street was simply called a lamp post.

The gaslight was seen as a preventor of crime. Who but a brazen thief would dare pick a pocket or hit a stout citizen on the head in the glare of such an incriminating light? The gas lamp initially was a warning: 'we are watching you'. Some of those who were impressed by Sydney in the late 1840s singled out 'the blaze of gas from the splendid and glittering shops'. For those young people who, reared in the interior, did not set foot in a city until the era of gas, the dense traffic and the lighted streets were doubly dazzling: 'The different sorts of people, the carts and carriages, buggies and drays, pony-carriages and spring-carts, all jumbled up together; even the fruits and flowers and oysters and fish under the gas-lights seemed strange and wonderful to us.' Cities did not become equated with 'bright lights' until the era of the gaslight.

Sydney, viewed from Darlinghurst at nightfall in the 1880s.
In the era of gaslight, even the streets of the inner suburbs
were not brilliantly lit.

First used in streets, gas was then connected to wealthier houses and later – as it became cheaper – to small houses. There the gas was used mainly to give light. It proved to be more convenient than candles and oil or kerosene lamps, with their dimmer light. To clean the greasy glass in the old lamps had been an arduous daily task in many households. Gas ended that task.

Live theatre became, above all other institutions, the home of gaslight. When the big Theatre Royal was opened in the heart of Bourke Street in Melbourne, it was lit by sixteen chandeliers, in each of which gas flames were burning. In the 1860s the new Prince of Wales Opera House in Sydney displayed a fine chandelier with more than 130 gaslights burning: the light was not dazzling enough, and two more chandeliers were quickly installed. On a warm night a theatre was turned into a hothouse by the burning of so many small fires. Moreover they consumed oxygen and made for a feeling of drowsiness. The gas flames that served as footlights were a hazard to actors and dancers. In Sydney on 20 December 1872 a ballet dancer grazed her dress against the footlights, and the dress caught fire. She died three days later.

The opera houses, far more popular than today, welcomed gaslight. When Melbourne held fewer than 200 000 people, its two opera houses were far larger than the elegant opera house that today delights Sydney. Being in no small part a social promenade, opera houses remained alight with gas during performances. The strong gaslights were also appreciated by the spectators who bought the small booklet setting out the words of the opera. Throughout a performance there was much reading of the printed word, and much moving of lips by those pretending to sing along.

The singers usually stood at the very front of the stage, close to the bright footlights. As the footlights burned gas, they virtually placed a curtain of hot rising air between the singer and the audience. At times this created visual effects that slightly distorted what the audience saw. Many singers preferred to walk through this barrier of hot air and sing from the very edge of the stage, leaning slightly forward. Some critics complained about this practice; but Harold Love, a historian of Australian opera, sympathised with the craning singers. He explained that 'a moment's reflection will show that no artist with respect for lungs or eyes would have wished to enter the band of hot, fume-laden air directly about the burners'.

At first glance, most singers and actors should have welcomed the coming of electric light and freedom from hot fumes. But many were in two minds about the innovation. The celebrated Nellie Stewart, seeing electricity illuminate the stage for the first time in 1883, was disappointed by its cold, harsh light. She decided that the gaslight, for all its defects, was kinder to the face, giving 'an atmosphere of warmth and naturalness'.

Electricity: the Time is Here

Electricity at first showed little sign of replacing gas as a way of illuminating houses and streets. Electricity had novelty: it still lacked efficiency. It had been first used in Sydney as early as June 1863, when, to commemorate the birthday of the Prince of

Wales, a battery of 100 'wet cells' worked an arc lamp at the summit of the observatory. Every visitor marvelled at the 'extraordinary brightness' of the light: it made gas seem dim.

In 1878 in Sydney the urgency of completing the Exhibition Building persuaded builders to set up an electric arc light so that work could continue after sunset. At the Melbourne Cricket Ground on an August evening a year later, a major match of Australian Rules football was planned, with the aid of what was called 'the stream of electricity'. A crowd of at least 8000 paid to attend and an even larger number attended but did not pay. The light was neither bright nor even, though a white football did aid the players and spectators.

In 1882 a small power station supplied electricity to the Redfern railway station, which became Sydney's first public place to be permanently lit by electricity. In the same year, in Melbourne, the government astronomer, R. L. J. Ellery, disowned his recent prediction that electricity still belonged to the future: 'I must now recant – the time is here.' The harbour dredge worked at night with the aid of an electric light, while the opera house changed its lights from gas to electricity. Surprisingly, the audience was now said to suffer from headaches. Meanwhile the public library resolved to install incandescent electric lamps, to avoid the excessive heat of gas lamps and the damage done by gas combustion to the leather binding of books.

It was a small town in New South Wales that decided, ahead of any Australian city, to light its streets with electricity. Paying a big sum to a Birmingham firm, Tamworth installed its streetlamps in 1888. Eager farmers sometimes stayed in town long enough to see the magic of the filament lamps before driving home along dark roads by horse and gig. In the next decade, scores of towns stretching all the way from Broken Hill to Launceston installed electric lamps. Launceston harnessed hydroelectricity for its lamps, but most power stations produced electricity by burning coal.

Sydney, well served by gas, was late to illuminate its streets with electricity. It waited until 1904, by which time electricity was used to power trams and suburban trains. Soon small boys were saying they hoped to become, not a locomotive driver or mechanical engineer, but an electrician. In wealthier homes an electric kettle was sometimes tried. So far, however, there was no sign of the common electrical appliances of the 1930s – the electric refrigerator, electric stove, electric radio and vacuum cleaner. Only the electric kettle gave a taste of the future.

Tinderbox and Matchbox

One invention was so simple that it rarely appears in a list of useful inventions: the box of matches. This new way of lighting fires was a boon to those travelling in the bush, living on the diggings, running a household or smoking a pipe.

Even in 1850 many of the cooking fires lit by people in the countryside started with the striking together of flint and steel. The European version of the Aboriginal way of making a flame, the spark was created through friction. Every traveller worthy of the name had to carry a piece of hard English flint and a strong pocket knife or other object made of quality steel. People about to make camp on a cold evening felt anxiety until the flint and steel were rubbed together with a sharp 'nick nick' sound, and the first sparks appeared in the darkness. In the eyes of some, the sight of those little sparks was 'the most wonderful thing in creation'.

The sparks fell into a small tinderbox – usually manufactured in the English black-country town of Wolverhampton – and ignited a tinder consisting of carbonised fragments of cotton and lint. With the aid of a little puffing, the tinder began to glow. Into the glow was gently thrust a sulphur-tipped splint or 'spunk' of wood, which quickly caught alight. The flame was applied to the paper or dry bark which served as kindling for the fire.

To spend a cold night without a fire was a painful experience in the bush. Therefore the metal tinderbox was carefully carried in the driest part of the bullocky's dray or the horseman's pack. The difficulty of lighting a fire in very wet weather was increased because dry kindling was not as easily obtained then as now. Scraps of paper were scarce, for in 1850 most households did not buy even one newspaper in a week, and the typical newspaper held only four or eight pages. Wrapping paper was also rare.

At one time every child knew this slow, roundabout way of making a fire. This cumbersome activity, long forgotten, lives on in daily speech. 'Tinder dry' is still the expression used to describe land which is especially vulnerable to bushfire. While the tinderbox seems to us a tedious way of making fire, it was attractive to Aborigines. They were eager to accept a gift of this fire-making equipment and adept in using it.

Travellers making a long journey far from town sometimes carried a 'burning glass'. When the sun was hot they held the glass against inflammable material – perhaps dry grass or paper – and focused the rays of the sun until smoke slowly began to rise. A gun was sometimes used to create a fire. A small amount of gunpowder was inserted and above the barrel, loosely arranged, was a small piece of cloth or other tinder. If the gun was pointed into the air and fired, the rag rose into the air, alight or smouldering. The advice was firm: 'You must pick it quickly up, and then fan or wave it into a flame.'

The striking match first appeared during the heyday of the squatting movement. Thin and flat, and tipped with a small head of phosphorus, it was first manufactured on a large scale in Vienna in 1833. In little factories the head of each match was dipped in a hot solution in which white or yellow phosphorus was combined with chlorate of potash and other chemicals: the exact mix was often a secret that the owner of the factory carried in his head. Those Australians who first used these imported matches were delighted by how easily a flame could be produced. Struck against a wall or a rough book or a piece of wood, the match created a flame. Generally they were called Lucifer matches, though sometimes they were known as Congreves or Instantaneous Lights.

Lucifer matches endangered the health of those who made them. In Europe those workers who actually dipped the matches into the phosphorous mixture sometimes caught an ailment called 'phossy jaw', which led to the removal of part of their jaw by a surgeon. In Australia the buyers of imported matches were also at risk. Those who carried matches in their pocket soon learned that a few matches, rubbing against each other in the box, could suddenly catch alight.

The first version of the match we use today probably appeared in Australia in the 1850s. Called the 'Safety Lucifer Match', it was less likely to ignite while sitting in the tin. As the white phosphorous mixture was no longer on the wax matchstick but on a special striking surface, the match could only burst into flame when removed from its packet and struck against the striking surface, which was normally fixed to the side of the container. A 'safety match', which was not likely to ignite itself accidentally, could be packed safely in a flimsy wooden matchbox instead of a fire-resistant tin.

The matches were brittle. In exasperation a person would take a clump of matches and hold them tightly so that the chance of striking a light was higher. As a large box of the newfangled wax matches cost the high sum of about half a crown in 1860, the expense of striking a light could be high. When one of these fickle boxes reached an old pioneer named 'Parson' Tom, living on the inland side of the Blue Mountains, and he tried to light a candle, two boys 'heard him strike every one of those matches, and finally go to bed in the dark'.

The cheap, portable match was one cause of the increasing use of tobacco. Smoking a pipe in the era of the tinderbox had been largely an evening activity, indulged in at the fireside, where a light was readily available. Few smokers could be bothered going to the trouble of making a flame from flint and steel each time their pipe went out. The safety match was handier.

Safety or wax matches became more reliable and cheaper. In the big Australian cities by the 1870s the itinerant match seller was a common sight. At first children were probably the main match sellers but by the late 1880s 'beery old men' and beggars had taken over the trade. In a busy city street a shopper could hardly walk more than a few steps without hearing the cry, 'Wax matches, penny a box'. Most buyers of matches in the street were men who smoked pipes. Compared to cigarettes, a pipe was gluttonous for matches; and a vigorous pipe smoker could easily use a box of matches in a day.

By the early 1900s, Sweden was the busy maker of matches for our market, packaging them skilfully by printing on one side of the box a map of Australia, a pair of kookaburras or a kangaroo. In a Swedish attempt at a joke one brand of matches was labelled 'The Cricket Match'. The side of the box depicted a cricket or grasshopper holding a cricket bat. Matches were mostly sold in boxes of sixty, and the flimsy box was re-used by children. Tens of thousands of ladybirds, crickets, grubs, worms and other imprisoned creatures were taken to primary school in a matchbox – sometimes on a bed of cotton wool – by small children, for 'nature study'.

3

ACROSS THE SEAS

Australians travelling to Europe now expect the aircraft to depart at the advertised time and land about twenty or twenty-four hours later. In the heyday of the sailing ship, however, the idea of fixing an hour of sailing was unthinkable. Again and again passengers boarded the ship only to wait a day or two, the winds being unfavourable or the cargo slow to come aboard.

In 1866, Kate Fowler resolved to travel from England to Queensland to marry a man she had not seen for four years; and when she boarded the barque *Alfred Hawley* in the Thames, her hair was in long ringlets, and her portmanteau carefully packed. Like thousands of young women, she had resolved that she would keep up a brave heart 'in those long, long, months when I am cut off from friends on both sides of the globe'. Her heart soon sank. Her ship was towed by a steam tug to the open sea where the winds were so unfavourable that for six days the ship had to anchor, the wind buffeting her, the rain pelting down, and the coastal town of Deal not far away.

All passengers, in the days of sail, knew that the voyage to Australia would be long. They were advised to make painstaking preparations. Wealthier passengers bought a host of items including a cabin lamp and maybe 3 kilograms of wax candles to provide light at night or on those stormy days when they would be confined to their dark cabin. Many also bought a looking glass, camp stool, and a washstand where they could freshen-up with cold water each day. Humbler passengers might buy a washbasin, a water can, a drinking mug and metal dinner plate. For assisted migrants – and many women and children travelled without charge – the government provided the cooking and eating utensils.

A weekly ration of food was given to each passenger. Single women, for example, received 3.25 pounds of meat, 3.5 pounds of flour, 2.5 pounds of biscuits, 2 pounds of potatoes (or an equivalent in preserved vegetables), 1 pound of oatmeal, and 1.25 pounds of sugar and treacle. In addition they received raisins, rice, suet, butter, plus pepper, salt and pickles. To each passenger came a weekly allowance of tea and coffee. A child under the age of twelve – other than a baby – received a half-ration of food.

For children the rules were often strict. 'With a view to the prosecution of health and cleanliness during the voyage', their hair had to be 'cut close' before they were allowed to board the ship. Presumably head lice multiplied during a long, congested voyage – unless firm precautions were taken. At night the families usually stayed together, but single men slept at one end of the ship and single women at the other. Beds were generally bunks but in some ships hammocks were widely used, especially for adults.

As soon as a migrant ship sailed, the passengers were formed into messes, each of six or eight persons. Collecting their rations daily from the ship's store, they ate at set mealtimes – once they had ceased to be seasick. The baker took the flour ration from each group and baked bread in a large oven, handing it out three times a week.

Before 1850 nearly all the sailing ships, when possible, called at ports in order to take on fresh fruit and vegetables, meat, firewood, water and other supplies. As most ships were at sea for at least a hundred days, and many for 150 days, these ports of refreshment were vital. The frequent visits to Cape Town help to explain why so many of our flourishing plant pests – the boxthorn, capeweed and Cape tulip – are natives of South Africa.

The Hazards of Icebergs

In the 1850s fast clippers entered the route, and they called at no intermediate port. A captain's mission was to harness the prevailing westerlies. On most voyages no land was seen all the way from the south coast of England and Ireland to the south coast of Australia. In crossing the southern Indian Ocean, they were far from help. The westerlies were strong and the waves could be mountainous. In exceptional months icebergs drifted nearby, endangering the fast clippers that normally sailed on through the night, with all the speed their sails could harness.

At Circular Quay in Sydney the tall sailing ships were eagerly inspected by an admiring audience on Sundays and weekdays too.

The fear was that in such wild seas and winds the ship, at night, might come so close to an iceberg that there would be no hope of changing course in time.

Early in the morning of 28 February 1855, at 48 degrees south, the sailing ship *Ocean Chief*, on a voyage from Liverpool to Melbourne, encountered heavy snow squalls. At 4 a.m., close to dawn, the crew saw a large ice island only 4 miles away. The huge block of ice chilled the morning air: the temperature on the deck fell to a mere 30 degrees Fahrenheit. On the following day, in a gale so fierce that the mainsail was torn apart, icebergs were visible on both sides. For several days the scenes were dramatically recorded in the ship's log: 'tremendous heavy sea . . . most terrific squalls . . . Ship rolling most horrible'.

In most of the large immigrant ships, in any given week, a few women would be approaching the end of their pregnancy. In this rolling ship, three days after the sighting of the first iceberg, the captain noted, 'Mrs Jarvis safely delivered of a fine son'. On the following day, with the ship pitching drunkenly into a head sea, the captain saw 'another large iceberg under the bows, white like marble'. It was possibly in sight of this iceberg that another mother gave birth to her child.

Meanwhile, in tamer seas far to the west, Captain Hewett was eating breakfast in the sailing ship *Cambridge* when he heard a shout coming from outside: 'Ice ahead.' He hurried onto the open deck. It was thick weather – 'as thick as a hedge', said the captain – and the poor visibility heightened the ship's danger. Around noon the sky cleared, and the ship was virtually surrounded by icebergs.

In the same strip of ocean in the same month, the *Ralph Waller*, within a fortnight of reaching Melbourne, hit an iceberg. The bow was damaged, and water gushed in, filling the hold to a depth of 5 metres. The pumps were worked for more than three days and nights before the ship was finally safe.

Another fast ship was already on her way to Melbourne. The *Guiding Star*, built in Canada only two years previously, held the highest classification awarded by Lloyds of London to a colonial-built ship. She carried four officers, a surgeon, and sixty men whose ability to handle the sails aloft had been recently tested by the authorities. Five weeks after leaving Liverpool she was observed by a passing ship to be well south of the equator, and heading for the roaring forties where, unknown to her captain, icebergs were adrift. The crew and passengers in the *Guiding Star*, all told, numbered 546. They were not seen again.

The practice of sailing to Australia by way of the Cape of Good Hope (though not within sight of it), and sailing back to Britain by way of Cape Horn, persisted until the advent of the more powerful steamships and the opening of the Suez Canal. Thereafter steamships followed exactly the same route to and from Australia. At Ceylon or Alexandria or other ports, passengers bound for Australia might chance to meet those who had recently left Australia, but such meetings were rare. They were most likely to happen in the Atlantic Ocean where the outbound and homebound routes sometimes intersected. On windless days near the equator two sailing ships might briefly be lying within sight of each other, and occasionally a boat could be rowed across the still sea to a neighbouring ship in order to gather verbal news and newspapers. In the stifling heat the sailors would row back, carrying perhaps a recent newspaper from Boston, Sydney, Cape Town or Calcutta.

In windy weather the ships might exchange news while quickly passing one another. A chance encounter could be a wonderful experience. Passengers remembered it as long as they lived: the first sight of sails in the distance, the unknown ship coming closer, the numerous guesses about her nationality and destination, and the asking of that crucial question: would she pass within shouting distance? Sometimes the other ship came so close that faces could be seen on the deck, with even a glimpse of a shawl-wrapped baby held aloft in a passenger's hands. For half a minute, in that eternity of ocean, the two ships might come within shouting distance; and each captain would speak through a trumpet and call out the name of his ship and destination. Every passenger on deck would be silent because any noise, additional to that of the sails and creaking timbers and splashing waves, made the trumpeted voices difficult to hear. If by chance the parting ships remained a little longer within earshot, loud-voiced passengers would shout across the water.

In the language of the sea such an episode was known simply as 'to speak a vessel'. The phrase was to speak, not speak *to*. It was part of the everyday language of Australians in the second half of the nineteenth century, when so many people had crossed the wide ocean by sailing ship. It is little wonder that the verses of Henry Wadsworth Longfellow, who had often crossed the north Atlantic, were recited in Australian school-rooms and on concert platforms:

Ships that pass in the night, and speak each other in passing;
Only a signal shown and a distant voice in the darkness;
So on the ocean of life we pass and speak one another,
Only a look and a voice; then darkness again and a silence.

Today these verses are largely forgotten, the experience they captured having ceased to be part of a people's memory.

When a sailing ship reached port, her master and passengers were questioned eagerly about vessels they had 'spoken'. In the era before the telegraph and wireless, the latest information held commercial value to merchants expecting cargoes from a distant port; and the newspapers printed brief details of those ships met by chance on distant oceans. When a large sailing ship was lost at sea, the last sentence in her obituary would be the observation that she had been last 'spoken' in a certain latitude and longitude. So fell what Longfellow called a darkness and a silence.

On some voyages the craving for news was met by a newspaper, which one or two passengers edited as a hobby. Found in recent years on the dusty top shelf of a second-hand shop in New Zealand was a newspaper that had been published during an 1862 voyage of the famous iron steamship *Great Britain*, from Melbourne to Liverpool. The ship had called at no port and 'spoke' only a couple of vessels but gleaned from them no news. Such a ship was like a modern space capsule, but totally out of touch with outside society. The news of importance came from within the capsule itself – from the whims, friendships and jealousies of the people thrown into each other's company. A long voyage in which hundreds of passengers were confined was a kind of floating keg of gunpowder, and some of these ship's newspapers set fire to the keg. The news that people aboard must have read with zest consisted of snippets which to us mean almost nothing:

Dropped in the Saloon of the 'Great Britain', several very valuable H's. The finder will be rewarded upon returning them to their proper place.

Here, one assumes, was a gold digger or squatter of rough manners and ungrammatical speech, returning in triumph to what he called 'Ome.

In 1866, when the three-masted clipper *Lincolnshire* approached the equator, several passengers began to produce their *Observer*. Henceforth, every Saturday, the passengers could read about the ship's dances and theatricals they had attended, glance at humorous notes on the ship's menu, read miscellaneous nonsense and scan a few sentences from the captain on the exact distance covered each day, the stars visible at night and the direction of the winds.

Ships' newspapers were usually written with pen and ink, and possibly the circulation of a typical paper was only two, the first copy being for the saloon passengers and the second for all the other passengers. Copies of these newspapers, thumbed scores of times in the course of the following days, rarely survived. But sometimes the proud editors, when their ship reached her final destination, carried the sequence of ten or twelve handwritten issues to a printer and paid him to set them in type and quickly bind them as booklets. So they became a keepsake for those passengers who, thrown together for so long, knew at the voyage's end that 'our company will disperse, probably to meet no more'.

Scent of a New Land

Many passengers hated the long voyage, the bouts of seasickness and the absence of privacy in the cramped quarters. The most cheering words came near the end, 'Land Ho!' Shouted by a sailor when the Australian coast was seen in the far distance, the words electrified passengers. Some passengers who had rarely been seen on deck during the voyage now appeared in their finest clothes. Mothers held their babies aloft in the hope that they would see the land where they were likely to spend the remainder of their life.

In certain months the new land invisibly announced its presence to approaching ships. It gave off a distinctive odour; and passengers far out to sea – even beyond sight of land – suddenly caught the smell of raw earth or perhaps of blossoms. 'We are near Australia,' said sailors, nearing the end of one long voyage, 'Can't you smell the flowers?' On some voyages, passengers discovered the scent for themselves, and the discovery was all the more pleasant, being unexpected. One passenger, 90 miles from the first sight of Australia, opened the scuttle in his cabin and to his amazement sniffed the smell of a hayfield, though on second thoughts the smell was rather more spicy and exotic. Like several others aboard he recalled the well-known lines from *Paradise Lost* that told of the scent blown by the north-east winds 'from the spicy shore of Araby the blest'. Another scent sniffed by passengers long at sea was the smell of woodsmoke coming from bushfires. The scent of the new land was to become faint in the era of steamships with their pervading coal smoke.

At the port of disembarkation, few rules were imposed, and landing documents were not required. Normally firearms, knives and gunpowder could be carried ashore. Passengers could land freely with pet parrots in cages, dogs on a rope, and a wealth of animal products that today would be confiscated.

Quarantine was loosely imposed. In 1832, after cholera had raged in Europe and Asia, the governor of New South Wales tried to prevent infectious diseases from entering. If the Sydney pilot learned that an overseas vessel had come from an infected port, or that passengers and crew had died from infection during the voyage, he now had the power to place the incoming ship in quarantine. The ship was ordered to fly at the head of the main topmast a flag warning other ships and rowing boats to keep away. The warning flag was yellow and white, and measured 'six breadths of bunting', according to the new regulations. When it was taken down at night it was replaced by a large signal lantern.

The dreaded yellow-and-white flag was not seen often. The captain of an incoming ship was especially wary of quarantine, because he was compelled to anchor in an isolated bay and, if so ordered, unload the passengers' possessions so that they could be 'opened and aired'. During that delay he earned no revenue for his ship and had to feed passengers and crew. In inspecting such ships the colonial officials were not always vigilant. Until a new law was passed in 1853, many incoming ships reached the main wharves and moorings in Sydney and unloaded passengers without undergoing adequate inspection. But a few officials were strict, even stricter than the law demanded. In Fremantle in 1851 the ship *Anna Robertson* was placed in quarantine for fear that whooping cough might go ashore and infect thousands of Aborigines, who possessed no immunity.

The slowness of sea travel served as a form of quarantine. The ocean was Australia's main barrier against infection. Passengers who boarded an Australia-bound ship in Scotland with an infectious disease – in its first stage but still undiagnosed – were likely to show outward signs of the infection before the long voyage was over. When the ship reached Australia the crisis might be over. Infection was more likely to arrive, undetected, in the shorter voyages from China. In 1881 Sydney suffered an outbreak of smallpox, and forty people died. While the longer voyage served as a barrier to the spread of infections, the ship herself, with crowded quarters and sometimes the absence of vitamins in the food rations, could be the chief incubator of infection. The *Ticonderoga* lost 165 passengers when typhus and scarlet fever raged during the long voyage to Melbourne in 1852. Half a century later, in an era of improved hygiene, seventeen Australians soldiers returning from the Boer War died in the one troopship. In 1914 and 1915, some Australian soldiers setting out for overseas ports died of infectious diseases in troopships.

The Seaway Through Suez

Steamships were as important to Australians as the coming, more than a century later, of the jumbo jet. The mail steamer dramatically cut the length of the voyage. Usually it followed a route through smoother seas. It required coal and so it used ports of call, which, for passengers, broke the monotony of weeks at sea. It was safer than a sailing ship.

The first steamship to arrive with immigrants was the *Chusan* in 1852, the second year of the gold rushes. Like all steamships of that era, she relied heavily on her sails and used her engines only when the winds were light or unfavourable. During the following two decades other steamships entered the Australia–England route but they were not yet dominant.

The Suez Canal was a boost to steamships. It was especially designed for European steamships travelling to and from Asia, East Africa and Australia. At first it was narrow, its dimensions being closer to those of a large barge canal. After being widened, it was used regularly by mail steamers, and by the 1880s it was part of the main passenger route to Australia. It was shorter than the traditional routes, and took advantage of the coaling ports spaced at frequent intervals across the Mediterranean Sea, the Red Sea and the Indian Ocean. It was a revolution in travel.

Perhaps the most reliable passenger ship of the 1850s had been the *Norfolk*. Her average passage between Melbourne and England was just under ten weeks – remarkable for a sailing ship. Three decades later the days spent in the average voyage between London and Melbourne was almost half that. Moreover additional days could be saved by wealthier passengers. Leaving London one week after their ship had sailed, passengers along with mailbags sailed in the ferry from Dover to Calais, then went in the fast mail train across France, through the Mount Cenis tunnel, and past Turin and Bologna. At Brindisi, the ancient Roman port near the southern heel of Italy, they boarded the Australia-bound steamer, which was waiting for them.

The mail steamer obeyed something quite unknown to sailing ships: a timetable. When a dignitary set out for Australia, his likely time of arrival was known, and a massive welcome could be prepared. When in 1873 Dr Roger Vaughan, the new co-adjutor archbishop, approached Sydney Heads, crowded vessels were there to greet him with flags, cheers, and waving hand-kerchiefs; and when his ship berthed at Circular Quay maybe one third of the Catholics of Sydney waited for a glimpse of him.

Sailing ships still offered advantages. Their fares were cheaper though their amenities were simple. They were also cleaner. In contrast, in a fast steamship a frequent complaint of passengers who strolled in spotless white clothes along the decks was that they were spattered by black coal, soot and cinders spewed from the ship's tall funnels.

As the steamships regularly had to take on coal, and as the coal was carried slowly aboard by a crocodile of human coal-carriers, the ships had to stay a day in various tropical ports, thus enabling passengers to make excursions. Whereas those passengers who left Australia in the 1850s usually saw no port during the whole voyage to England, those travelling thirty years later called at Adelaide, Albany, Colombo or Galle in Ceylon, Aden in the Red Sea, Suez and Port Said in Egypt, Naples or Brindisi in Italy, and Gibraltar or Malta, before reaching their destination in England. The voyage had become a way of sight-seeing as well as travel.

A voyage in the P & O and Orient steamships was like a long holiday for the passengers who could afford the first- or second-class saloons. They enjoyed, by 1890, more amenities than a millionaire could obtain at sea one generation previously. Before boarding a ship they packed their cases and trunks as if they were embarking on a holiday. Following the detailed advice of the shipping lines many men took aboard their two dozen handkerchiefs, their five suits of clothes – including evening dress and cricket flannels – and numberless other items. Women paid a porter to carry to their cabin a variety of leather hat boxes and shoe boxes. Lavender water, tooth powder, toilet soap and a box of 'Tamar Indian Lozenges' – a help in easing constipation – were in the luggage of the well-prepared traveller. For sightseeing they carried umbrellas, field glasses, opera glasses and special smoked-glass goggles which they could wear on deck when sparks were flying from the steamer funnel. As the richer passengers made a point of leaving the ship in Italy and then going by train to England, they were advised to carry from Australia a 'railway rug' to cover their legs. And should men take razors for shaving? Yes – 'in case there should not be a pleasant barber on board'.

In 1890 the new steamers of 4000 to 6000 tons were luxury hotels compared to the floating boarding houses of old.

Whereas a long walk on the deck of a fast clipper had been impracticable, the ship being so cramped, now passengers could stroll along the promenade decks, wearing rubber-soled shoes if the deck was wet and slippery. In the smoking, writing and drawing rooms they could sit in wide leather chairs and hear in the distance the sound of a grand piano or organ. The grand rooms were heated in cold weather, and hot baths, heated by steam, could be ordered daily, an electric bell summoning a steward to the cabin. A cow, pigs and hens were no longer carried on deck in order to provide fresh food because now refrigerated compartments supplied meat, milk and eggs.

To travel in third class was to have access to few amenities. The largest ships of the Orient Line, which by the 1890s was setting the pace on the Australian route, carried a total of about 300 passengers in the first and second classes, but crowded another 500 into the third class. There, passengers spent much of their time below the deck, because in cold or rainy weather they had no shelter while sitting in the open air. In many steamships the passengers had to wash their own cutlery, cup and plate after each meal. While the main meals were filling, no morning or afternoon tea was available, and so the passengers carried their own tea, condensed milk, sugar, tins of potted meats and biscuits. Even then they had to win the favour of the cook in order to be able to fill their iron pannikins with hot water.

Passengers who wanted hot water were advised to send on their behalf a small child, a small bribe or a pretty woman. In contrast the ships of a Hamburg–Sydney line that catered

In the era of steam the British mail steamer calling at Glenelg in South Australia was almost suffocated in its own coal smoke and the smoke blown from the funnels of tugs, lighters and ferries.

solely to third-class passengers offered them electric light, vent-ilation and bathrooms (but not too many), and placed mothers and their children in a special compartment rather than a dorm-itory. Of course the present-day passengers flying 'steerage' or even first class in a jet aircraft bound for Australia are infinitely more cramped than those in the old-time steamship. Fortunately the flight lasts less than one day and one night. Someday our descendants will marvel at the squalor and congestion in which we flew across the world.

The third-class quarters in the latest steamship, while miserable to many passengers, were a long jump ahead of a humble berth in a sailing ship. The steamship voyage was twice as quick. The new refrigeration enabled fresh meat to be supplied, water was plentiful, and the diet was more varied. Electricity, replacing the lamp swinging overhead, enabled passengers to read or play cards on those wet days when they could not walk on deck.

In 1890 steamships left England for Australia about three times a week. Most of the ships passed through the Suez Canal but once a month a steamship left for Tenerife, Cape Town and Hobart – on her way to New Zealand. Another route to Sydney was by ship to New York, train to San Francisco, and ship by way of Honolulu, Suva and Auckland.

Decade by decade, voyages across the world during peacetime became safer. Insurance offices knew the risks of the voyage in the 1850s. In that decade not more than one in every 100 passengers who crossed the world carried an insurance policy on their life, but those who did hold a policy knew that they had to apply for permission from their life office before they could embark. Without such permission their policy was forfeited. The statisticians of the life offices, having carefully calculated the risks of sea travel, imposed a surcharge on any Australian customers making a long voyage. Indeed Australia's largest life office called a special meeting of directors in 1859 to discuss whether they should insure a banker about to sail to Mauritius and live in that tropical climate. Ten years later, such was the improvement in safety at sea, the special tax on long voyages was removed.

In some years not one ship was wrecked on the sea lanes between Australia and England. But just when the oceans seemed safest, strange news began to reach Australian ports.

A new passenger and cargo steamer, carrying 212 passengers and crew, had disappeared from sight. The *Waratah*, of 9300 tons, had brought migrants to Australia, and on her return voyage was last seen in heavy weather on 27 July 1909, steaming along the most southerly tip of the South African coast between Durban and Cape Town. She was not equipped with the latest novelty, the radio, and so no distress signal was heard on the nearby shore. No wreckage was found. The most extensive searches discovered no lifeboat, no lifebuoy. A search vessel travelled 18000 nautical miles without finding clues to the missing ship. Here and there on the walls of Australian churches and public buildings can still be seen tablets or brass plates with the name of a passenger and the words, 'Lost in the *Waratah*'.

Whenever a ship was lost or overdue, Australians feared not only for the safety of the passengers aboard. They also privately wondered whether letters they had written or letters written to them were aboard: ships carried all the overseas mail. The real lifeline between Australia and the outside world was the handwritten letter, and only merchants and government officials kept a copy of the letters they wrote. A private letter lost was most probably lost forever.

4

LETTERS, CAMERAS AND
THAT MAGIC WIRE

The letter, decade by decade, grew in importance as a conveyor of news. The increase in letter-writing was aided by simple inventions. The quill pen, made from the five outer feathers of each wing of the goose, had largely given way to the cheap steel pen, of which hundreds of millions annually were made in Birmingham in the 1850s. The fountain pen already existed but was an expensive novelty. The writing of letters called for the frequent dipping of the steel nib in the well or bottle of ink. Most people dipped their pen with the kind of slow deliberation also used in the lighting of a pipe. If they were not careful the ink flowed too freely and formed a blot or a chain of tiny splashes on the paper. Children just learning to write could not be entrusted with ink: it was likely to splash onto their clothes and soil their fingers. To blot one's copy-book – the book where the art of writing was practised in school – was such a common occurrence that the phrase was transferred to every facet of daily life.

There speedily arose a remarkable system of international postage. The cost of sending letters to the far side of the world fell away and then fell again. As more people learned to write and read, they used the postage network more confidently, though spelling often gave them difficulties.

Many of the early letters passing between Australia and the British Isles had travelled partly on the honour system. A letter from the far side of the world was often delivered in the hope that the recipient would pay all or part of the cost of the postage. In New South Wales at first most customers did not have to prepay their postage. But by 1840 the posting of a letter from the river port of Maitland to London incurred a succession of fees. Ten pence was charged for the short sea journey to Sydney, another three pence was collected in the ship and another four pence when the letter reached London. There still remained the highest charge of all – fourteen pence, to defray the postage from London to Ireland. No wonder that poor people, even if literate, rarely wrote letters. Many who did write letters waited until a friend was about to return to their home town: the friend could personally deliver the letter without charge. In each decade the postage was to become cheaper, and the postal service faster and more reliable.

An Australian wishing to send letters abroad, by the time of the gold rushes, first had to buy postage stamps; and they did not always stick to the letter. Each colony printed its own postage stamps, with the typical stamp displaying the face of Queen Victoria. Western Australia, more adventurous, often displayed the swan on its postage stamps, but for many years it was a European and not a native black swan. In 1896 the Tasmanian government, even bolder, depicted landscapes on its stamps. A year later the New South Wales government, determined to be adventurous, printed three special stamps to celebrate the diamond jubilee of the reign of Queen Victoria. The two and a half penny stamp, alas, was judged by a panel of stamp collectors to rank with the world's ugliest.

More and more Australians learned how to write. A sheet of writing paper became cheaper as a result of paper-making machines devised in the United States. Initially most writers of long-distance letters were careful to waste no skerrick of space on the sheet of paper. They continued their sentence to the very edge of the paper; and then they turned the paper on its side and wrote another sequence of sentences – as if nothing was already on the paper. Finally they turned the paper upside down and wrote in the same frugal manner on the other side. This artifice defies our sense of order. At first glance such a letter, usually on unlined paper, seems like a gabble of handwriting, and virtually a crossword. In fact it is not difficult to read the first or horizontal sequence of sentences and then to turn the paper around and to read the vertical lot of sentences running in the opposite direction. This method would have been more readable if typewriters existed. But this machine did not become common, and then only in the smarter offices, until the 1880s.

The longing for letters from Europe was acute: it was more than a longing, it was an aching feeling that even the latest letter did not quite satisfy. Rachel Henning, in March 1855, noted that she longed for letters from 'home'. But when a letter did arrive she felt homesick after opening it and digesting its news. The typical overseas letter, she observed, 'makes me feel miserable for at least a day'.

In this era of to and fro, many of the letters reaching Australia found no recipient. In Liverpool or Bristol letter-writers did not realise that a friend had already moved on to another Australian town or gold rush. The practice of addressing letters to a central post office rather than to a specific street or suburb in Australia did not necessarily help in finding the recipient. As a result, piles of unclaimed letters grew taller at nearly every large post office. Most colonies set up a special office, known as the Dead Letter Office, to handle such letters. In Queensland, as late as the 1880s, the government took the trouble to advertise each of these dead letters in its official *Gazette*. The unclaimed Queensland letters were returned, after a month, to the address of the writer. The unclaimed letters from overseas were returned after twelve months.

Travelling Inland

To travel from one Australian city to another in 1860 was mostly to travel by coastal ship. Those travelling inland went on horse-back, on foot, or in a horsedrawn coach. Bags of letters travelled with the passengers.

No land in western Europe was as dependent as Australia on the horse. The horse was absolutely indispensable in most regions, even at the ports. A far higher proportion of Australians than Britons knew how to harness, saddle and ride a horse.

In remote or rugged parts of the continent, whether in Queensland or Tasmania, packhorses carried mailbags and supplies.

Newcomers marvelled at the ease and daring with which many Australians, both women and men, handled horses. Horse races drew large crowds. A township without a racecourse, or land set aside for one, was a rarity. In the cities the yards where horses were displayed and auctioned were the equivalent of second-hand car yards today. An auction of horses enticed crowds of spectators and a few potential buyers. The theft of horses, like that of cars today, was also on a large scale. An old horse, however, was unlikely to be stolen, for horses were said to be 'finished' when they were eight years old.

On country roads and farms the new breeds of sturdy draught horses were increasingly seen. They were replacing the slow bullocks. It is a sign of the strong but now forgotten regionalism that different breeds of draught horses were favoured in different areas. For years the big Suffolk Punch was the favourite in the Hunter Valley, the Shire horse in Tasmania and the heavy Schleswig horse on South Australian farms. By 1914 the noble Clydesdale was becoming the favourite across the country.

Those who did not wish to walk could travel in the horse-drawn coach, if they could afford the fare. By 1860 a network of coaching routes was beginning to crisscross the settled districts of eastern Australia. In the heyday of shallow gold-winning on the fields of Ballarat and Bendigo, when each of those fields held close to 30 000 people, the coach was the fastest means of public transport. Even the middling-size gold town of Castle-maine sent off four stage coaches a day to Melbourne, which was more than 100 kilometres away. In fine weather, when the road was firm, a team of six horses – exchanged for fresher horses at wayside hotels and stables along the way – enabled passengers to reach Melbourne in about eight hours. The largest inland coach, built to serve Ballarat just before the first railway arrived, was said to carry sixty or seventy passengers. Some witnesses said it could carry over eighty people, of whom twenty-eight sat in high rows of four, their heads exposed to all weathers. The coach, garish in red and gold, was called The Leviathan. To see twenty-two grey horses drawing such a heavy, high coach was a wonderful sight. The driver, however, was less impressed because his whip could not reach the leading horses, so far ahead of the coach did they run.

Sitting in a coach on rough roads was an ordeal. The coach offered neither heating nor cooling, though in one sense it offered heating because it jolted the passenger from side to side. In small coaches four passengers sat inside, facing each other, while the other four passengers rode high. If the coach was full, leg room was cramped. Legs could not be stretched and arms could not be waved freely about until the coach reached one of the wayside inns where the horses were groomed or changed and passengers were fed. A few of these Queensland stops were long remembered for their appetising food. Who will ever forget, wrote one traveller, Mrs Loder's meals of roasted goat, home-made bread, prickly-pear jam, and hot scones spread with butter made from goat's milk.

Cobb and Co was the celebrated coaching firm and the carrier of the royal mail on a grand scale. Founded on the gold-fields in 1854 by a young American with a large moustache and a slight limp, Cobb and Co met competition from the advancing inland railways by also moving further and further inland. The interior of Queensland was its last stronghold. Bumping along inside a high coach, some passengers felt a version of the sea-sickness they had experienced on the first days of their voyage out to Australia. Most of the regular passengers must have been delighted when in 1912 three motor vehicles were bought by Cobb and Co.

Passengers, almost without exception, preferred the steam train to the horse coach. In the twenty years after the opening of the first railway in Melbourne, in 1854, a few trunk railways slowly pushed their way inland. Then began a frenzy of railway-building.

To travel in a train called, at first, for a new alertness.

Passengers did not realise how dangerous it was to project the head outside the window in order to gain a closer look at an approaching tunnel. Hints for Australian travellers who had not previously been in a train were drawn up by the Rev. Canon Wilson. The following advice was not always listened to:

- Always alight on the *platform* side of the train.
- Try to avoid, if possible, travelling in express trains.
- Avoid making a train journey during foggy weather.
- Select a carriage in the centre of the train.
- Do not try to enter or to leave a moving train.
- Beware of putting an arm or a head outside the railway carriage.

The first lines of railway had expanded into a network by 1890. If in that year it had been possible to fly in a balloon across eastern Australia, the pilot would have seen, scattered below, hundreds of temporary railway camps, each one a small huddle of tents and huts of the gangs who were building the embankments, quarrying the cuttings and laying the sleepers and rails. In 1890 the two longest inland railways extended as far as the river port of Bourke on the Darling River and the small settlement of Williams Creek, which lay west of the dry expanse of Lake Eyre. Another railway, built by Chinese labourers, was extending south of Darwin to the goldfield at Pine Creek, in the hope that, in the unknown future, it would reach faraway Alice Springs. In 2003 that railway is close to completion.

Two populous and many lesser regions of the mainland were not linked by railway to Melbourne, when in 1901 it became the first capital of the new Commonwealth. The settled districts of Western Australia were still separated by a vast arid plain from the east. Until the railway crossed that plain in 1917, all travellers – with the exception of a few hardy overlanders – had to go in ships. Far north Queensland, another important region, remained isolated even from its own state capital. In 1917 the residents of Cooktown, Charters Towers, Cloncurry, Cairns and Townsville could travel south to Brisbane only by a combination of ship and railway.

Even when remote regions were linked at last by railway, the movement of trains was often impeded by a break of gauge. Across Australia was a chain of busy railway stations where passengers had to leave their train and carry their own luggage across the platform to a waiting train that would run on a track of different width. Kalgoorlie, Port Augusta, Terowie, Hamley Bridge, Ferntree Gully, Albury and Zeehan were among those stations.

Virtually every railway line in the land carried passengers as well as goods and livestock. In every town that owned a railway station, the arrival of the day's first train – some stations received only one train – was the event of the day. The mailbags and the bundles of city newspapers arrived in the goods van at the rear of the train. Visitors to a town mostly arrived in the train. The stationmaster, with his ornate uniform and distinctive cap, inspected and presided over their arrival, the loading and unloading of the mail and other luggage from the goods van, and the final slamming of carriage doors and the blowing of the official whistle or waving of the all-clear flag.

In remote towns at which the only train arrived near the middle of the night, a surprisingly large crowd tended to gather on the platform, rubbing hands and stamping feet when the night was cold. Among the prizes brought by the night train were the city newspapers and mailbags. This special meeting place in the town's daily life was lost when the motor car began to compete with the passenger train.

Many people did not use the railways. John Shaw Neilson, farm labourer and poet, who spent much of his life labouring on the wheatlands of the Mallee, had little wish to travel on the railways in which other Australians rejoiced. His mother's own experience was a warning. While ill with typhoid she was conveyed to the Bendigo hospital on a hot day in a dawdling goods train, an ordeal that perhaps hastened her death. Neilson himself was aged thirty-nine before he set out in a train to make his first visit to a capital city. Fortunately, while there, he consulted an oculist who prescribed a pair of reading glasses which enabled him to read if the print was large and the light was bright. Like many others, his mind travelled mostly on the printed page. That inky carpet conveyed more people than did the railway, steamship, horse and pushbike.

The Restive Telegraph

The letter, though aided by steamship and steam train, was eventually outpaced by the telegram. It was a long contest, and the letter was not invariably defeated, even in an emergency.

The first electric telegraph line in Australia was laid

between Melbourne and its port in 1854. It was simply a wire held aloft by a succession of wooden poles. From one end of the line an operator could send a message to the other end with almost lightning speed. If the message had to travel 500 kilometres, however, it had to be repeated or reinvigorated at telegraph stations along the way. There was one hitch: sending even a short message was expensive. Only important messages, only short messages, were sent by telegraph. At first the telegraph lines were confined to the south-east corner of the continent, and connected only the main towns and cities.

Initially the messages sent along the wires were impeded in certain weather. As the Sydney telegraph office reported on 29 August 1859, the wires 'were seized with an unaccountable fit of restiveness'. It was almost as if they were on protest: 'they did not altogether refuse to work, but acted irregularly'. On that same day Australia's main telegraph line – newly extended all the way between Sydney and Melbourne and Adelaide – was affected by strange delays and a fuzziness in the messages received. The appearance in the sky of a majestic aurora australis perhaps caused the irregular working of the wires. In compensation the sky at these times was a sensational sight. The keepers of the lighthouse at Cape Otway reported that it was like the opening of a scintillating lady's fan made of bright colours. In Adelaide brilliant red and white streamers could be seen in the night sky. At the same time an arc of light, with a red brilliance embracing the 'whole heavens', was watched with wonder around Ballarat. Then the magic departed from the sky, and telegraph lines again conveyed messages with their customary smoothness and speed.

All the telegrams sent from Britain to Australia arrived first at the cable station in the small township of Darwin, and were then keyboarded across the continent.

In the 1870s a new telegraph line crossed the continent in a south–north line to Darwin, where it joined the line to Asia and Europe. Another crossed the Nullarbor all the way to Perth. Telegraph lines, wrapped in protective cables, crossed the bed of the ocean to Tasmania and also to New Zealand. In 1893 a cable was laid on the seabed to New Caledonia, in 1901 to Durban in South Africa and a year later to Vancouver.

Meanwhile the procession of wooden telegraph poles passing through the countryside was vulnerable. Occasionally the tall poles collapsed, the wood having been eaten by white ants. In storms the wind or falling trees pushed down the poles and broke the wire. In floods the poles were swept away, in bushfires they were burned. On such occasions the line ceased to transmit – until such time as the telegraph repairers arrived. On the rare occasions when the cable on the bed of the sea was cut suddenly by accident or had been slowly corroded, the telegraph line could be inactive for weeks.

Everywhere, the local post office was the home of the telegraph apparatus. These offices were known, for decades, as post and telegraph offices. When a telegraphic message reached its destination, it was written or typed out on an official sheet of paper in the post and telegraph office, and then the paper – the telegram – was placed in an envelope and delivered to the intended recipient. From the 1890s the bicycle was used to deliver the telegram on the short, final leg of the journey to the front door of a shop, factory or house. The price of sending a telegram became cheaper but the arrival of a telegram was still an uncommon event in most Australian houses as late as 1900. A typical house probably did not receive more than one telegram a year. Often the telegram carried the news of a death.

People who lived in a remote place could still receive telegrams. They came by wire to the nearest telegraph office, were written out, and waited there in a sealed envelope – maybe for one or maybe for six days – until the mailman was leaving for the homestead to which the telegram had been addressed. In the bush, however, a sympathetic postal employee would often circumvent the rules and make efforts, if the telegram was important, to pass it on to the recipient. If he heard of private horsemen or a family in a buggy setting out in the direction of the distant homestead, he might entrust them with the telegram.

As a telegram was dear, people thought twice before they decided to send one. In 1887 in suburban Sydney a woman whose child or husband had suddenly died would think carefully about which relative, if any, should receive the sad news by telegram. If the relative lived in Perth the sending of the telegram – consisting of a mere ten words – would cost a total of three shillings. A message of twenty-two words would cost six shillings, which was perhaps equal to her husband's daily wage. If the relative lived in Victoria or rural New South Wales, a pithy message of ten words from suburban Sydney cost only one shilling. If the message had to be conveyed by a telegraph cable passing under the sea, the cost was much dearer.

The same pithy message, telegraphed from Sydney to Ballarat for a charge of one shilling, would cost almost 150 shillings if it were sent to an address in the British Isles. In essence, a payment equal to three or four weeks of a labourer's wages was required to send the humblest personal telegram to the far side of the world. Therefore the chances were strong that no telegram would be sent. Instead a mother in Dublin would hear of a death in the Australian family when, some seven weeks later, there arrived in the post an envelope in her daughter's handwriting, with a black band around the border. The black band conveyed the first hint of what had happened. At least the handwriting of the daughter, visible on the envelope, showed that she herself had not died.

A simple international telegram seems absurdly expensive until one notices the route it followed and the elaborate organisation needed to keep open that route. Between Sydney and Dublin ran a long wire, passing through telegraph station after station, each of which had to relay the message. Each Sydney telegram went by way of Melbourne, Adelaide, Alice Springs and Darwin, with numerous intermediate stations in between. It crossed the bed of the sea to the Indonesian archipelago and then by land and seabed on to Singapore. Sometimes the message took ten hours to travel that far. The few words in the typical message were then tapped on to Penang and so to the Indian telegraph stations at Madras and Bombay, crossing over land or travelling under the sea. From the British port of Aden on the Red Sea, the words crossed to the Suez peninsula and overland to the Mediterranean Sea, where they went along the seabed to Malta, Gibraltar, and so to Lisbon, before finally coming ashore at Penzance in Cornwall. When the few words reached Dublin, a messenger boy was ready to deliver the telegram to a suburban home. There, the telegram, being unexpected, would be opened nervously.

If there was a blockage along the way or if the wire was accidentally cut, then the telegram had to flow by an emergency route, sometimes through coastal China and Siberia and the Baltic ports. Important overseas news despatched to newspaper offices in Australia came by the same long routes. As the newspapers were busy users of the telegraph, they received bargain rates. But even the wealthier newspapers sent or received only urgent and headline news by international telegraph.

Here Comes the Mail!

The arrival of the overseas mail ship at major ports was eagerly awaited. At the main post offices, flags were flown to indicate when the bags of overseas mail had been sorted. On the clock tower of the general post office in Melbourne – the building still stands – a blue flag was flown when the fortnightly or monthly mail steamer, on her way from England, was reported to have reached the first Australian port of call, which was the isolated harbour of Albany in Western Australia. Until the 1890s the port of Fremantle was not visited by English mail steamers. A red flag was flown from the Melbourne GPO a few days later, after the mail steamer was reported to have reached Adelaide.

About one day later a white flag at the Melbourne GPO announced that – according to the latest telegraphic news – the mail ship had passed Cape Otway and therefore, in the space of not many hours, would enter Port Phillip Bay. Then a white flag, bearing the letter 'H', would announce that the ship was at the Port Phillip Heads. Inner-city mothers eagerly awaiting a letter from the British Isles, or merchants wondering when a special cargo would arrive, closely watched the flags on the post office tower. At night the blue flag was replaced by a blue light, a white flag by a white light. When the ship reached Melbourne and the mailbags arrived in horsedrawn carts at the post office, yet another flag was hoisted. At last a red pennant announced when the mail had been sorted. As most white Australians had close relatives in the British Isles, the mail steamer served as an umbilical cord. When it arrived, and did not bring the expected letter, the disappointment was deep.

Each capital city flew its own flags to signal the approach, stage by stage, of the overseas mail. In Brisbane in the 1880s a white ensign was raised on the flagpole at the observatory to signal that the European mail, coming by way of Indian ports and the Torres Strait, had reached Cooktown in the far north. In Sydney citizens keeping an eye on the general post office could tell at night by the colour of the lights that the mail steamer from San Francisco had reached Auckland. At the town hall in Perth a white and red pennant was the signal that the mail was being unloaded at Albany, though it still had to undergo a journey of two and a half days in the mail cart before it reached Perth. Alert children in the main cities knew what each postal flag signified.

By the late 1880s the delivery of mail within the bigger cities was frequent. In central Sydney each shop and office received four deliveries a weekday, the first letter-carrier leaving the Sydney post office at eight in the morning and the last at 4.30 p.m. Launceston received four deliveries a day, but Hobart had to survive on three deliveries. Even the central streets of Perth, when it was a small town, had three deliveries a day. In the Sydney suburbs the letter-carrier – not yet officially called 'the postman' – walked along each street in the morning and again in the early afternoon. People who posted a letter at the general post office only fifteen or twenty minutes before the letter-carriers set out on their morning rounds to the city streets could confidently expect a reply through the post before the day was over.

In the remote parts of New South Wales, far from a railway, the mail came less regularly. Thus Khancoban, in the mountains close to Victoria, received the mail only once a week. In outback Australia some towns, as late as 1880, waited even longer for their mail delivery. In Western Australia, so sparsely settled, the wool and pearling ports facing the Indian Ocean received a delivery of mail less than once a month. On the day when the steamer from Fremantle was about to arrive, there was a quickening of daily life in Carnarvon, Onslow, and the pearling ports of Cossack and Broome.

When the steamer called in again, on her return passage to Fremantle, the pulse rate of the town quickened. Farewells were made to people about to go on leave. Letters, begun a week

In the faraway townships and even in Sydney, large numbers of people called regularly at the post office to collect their mail. Many of the letters – eagerly awaited – were opened as soon as they were received.

ago and set aside, were completed with many hasty dips of the pen into the inkwell. Storekeepers made up their long list of orders to merchants and suppliers down south and hurried their letters to the post office. No telegraph line reached these remoter ports until the late 1880s.

In contrast, on the other side of the continent, the tropical port of Cooktown, lying almost as far north of Brisbane as tropical Cossack lay north of Perth, enjoyed fine communications. Twice a week it could send mail by steamship to Brisbane, though the steamer made slow headway because it called everywhere along the way. Cooktown not only had the advantage of standing by a busy sea route – it also had an eighty-bed hospital, four wharves, and a resident bishop who, under the grand title of Bishop of Maximianopolis, presided over a vast diocese of tropical islands. The bishop, if bound for Rome, could even board the British India mail steamers departing regularly from Cooktown to the Torres Strait and South-East Asia, where he could then transfer to a mail steamer bound for the Suez Canal, Italy and England.

After the first outline of a railway network was built, the inland terminus of each railway served a radius of a dozen or so coaching services. On some days at least 10 000 coach horses were probably on the roads. Even in 1900 many remote towns such as Birdsville, Cloncurry and Wilcannia could be reached only by the mail coach. It was a vital but expensive mode of transport.

Throughout the land the writing of letters was more important in 1900 than ever before. More and more people could read and write; postage was cheaper; and few houses owned a telephone. Indeed the letter was much more important as a means of passing on news and knowledge than it is today.

The first set of distinctive Commonwealth or nationwide stamps was not placed on sale until January 1913. Depicting not the king but a kangaroo standing on a map of Australia, the new stamp was seen by many critics as being disloyal. At the end of the year the critics were appeased. A new penny stamp virtually imprisoned King George V in a halo of blossom.

Craving for a Newspaper

A city newspaper achieved only a small circulation at the time of the first gold rushes. Each copy was relatively expensive. Its quota of news was small, except when a ship had just arrived with the latest British newspapers, many of whose news items were copied word for word. The paper carried advertisements, not news, on the front page; no photographs and – except on rare occasions – no illustrations. As late as 1850 a large minority of Australians could not read, and that diminished the potential readership. Many of those who could not read heard the news only when read aloud by friends in the evening.

The post office in many towns was the news centre, not only because letters were opened there and sometimes read aloud, but also because many newspapers were opened and read there. When in 1860 a small post office was opened in the rural village of Canberra and entrusted to the village black-smith, he was permitted by his customers to open and read the newspapers that arrived in the post. Only two daily newspapers arrived regularly in the post – one addressed to the Anglican clergyman and the other to a local squatter. When the servants from each of these households arrived at the post office to collect their mail, including the newspapers, the blacksmith–postmaster no doubt informed them of any sensational or vital item of news he had just read. As the blacksmith himself subscribed to the weekly *Illustrated Sydney News*, he was a mine of information in his own right and was probably the main source of Sydney and even British news for the majority of local people.

My surmise is that the typical Australian reader, as late as the year 1870, was reading a second-hand newspaper rather than one bought that day, straight from the press. Powerful concessions were offered by post offices in most colonies to enable newspapers, new or second-hand, to be posted cheaply to another address. In Tasmania and New South Wales, and perhaps other colonies, a local newspaper, new or not more than a week old, could be posted free of charge to a rural address within the same colony. Even the posting of Australian newspapers to England and the posting of English newspapers to Australia was relatively cheap. To send a heavy newspaper from Sydney to London cost one penny, whereas to send a lightweight letter and envelope cost six pence. Therefore the temptation was strong, when preparing to package and post a newspaper to a friend, to write on the newsprint a short personal message: this was much cheaper than writing a letter. To prevent this ploy the post office refused to deliver a newspaper on which even a few letters of the alphabet had been inked by hand.

Newspapers passed through the mail in huge numbers. The New South Wales post office in the year 1886 handled thirty million newspapers compared to forty-three million letters. In sheer bulk and weight the typical Australian mailbag, carried on the back of the postman, must have been dominated by newspapers. One reason why the sales figures of Australian-printed newspapers were not large was that a huge volume of British newspapers arrived each month. In some mail steamers there arrived three times as many copies of British newspapers as individual letters.

Both the British and Australian weeklies were available at the mechanics' institutes and other libraries that sprang up in most towns in South Australia, Victoria and New South Wales, especially from the 1850s. These homely institutions had a lending library, sometimes consisting of up to 1000 'serious' books, and also a reading room where local and British news-papers could be consulted. The most famous litigation in the British Isles in the half-century between 1850 and 1900 was the Tichborne case. A Wagga Wagga butcher, pretending to be Sir Roger Tichborne, the lost heir to a wealthy English estate, had gone to London in a bold, indeed brazen, attempt to prove that he was the heir. The butcher probably first gathered crucial details about the Tichborne family – details enabling him to pose as their long-lost son – when he read a copy of the *Illustrated London News* on the table in the mechanics' institute at Wagga Wagga.

The tradition of the recycled newspaper persisted. When the Chicago newspaperman W. D. Boyce travelled by train through the Victorian countryside in 1921, he heard cries and shouts as the train passed slowly, without stopping, through small railway stations and over level crossings. Turning to a friend for an explanation he was told that people were crying out the words, 'Paper, paper'. It was explained to Boyce that Australians far from the cities craved the latest newspapers, and that their cries were often answered by passengers who, having finished reading their own copy, opened the train window and tossed it to those starved for news. Thirty years later the cry could still be heard when up-country trains passed by.

By the 1880s the main Australian dailies, especially the Melbourne *Age*, had large circulations, even by most European standards. The competition from second-hand British news-papers had subsided. The high literacy rate, high prosperity and increasing leisuretime of Australians also encouraged them to buy a daily newspaper. Sunday was the exception: the selling of newspapers on that day was banned in most colonies.

Those who could not afford a daily tended to buy a fattish weekly which printed rather than summarised the main news that had appeared in a particular daily newspaper during the previous week. The best-known weekly, for decades, was the *Australasian*. Published in Melbourne, it was the outrider of the *Argus*, a conservative daily which in its coverage, prose and tone was seen by many as the quality newspaper of the land. This weekly *Australasian* was probably the first nationwide news-paper – appearing almost two decades before the dynamic and flamboyant Sydney *Bulletin*, which is often seen by historians as the first national paper – and was read in places as diverse as the new sheep stations in the Gulf country of Queensland and the 'most secluded gold-fields' on the west coast of New Zealand. A literary paper, it serialised new novels. The correct time to plant cabbages and radishes in the kitchen garden was also gravely announced in its columns.

People who lived in country towns tended to buy, in addition to a city weekly, the local paper which was produced from the clanking printing press two or three times a week. Many towns of only 2000 people or so published two competing newspapers, with titles such as the *Echo*, *News*, *Bugle*, *Times*, *Mail*, *Independent*, *Eagle*, *Chronicle*, *Courier*, *Liberal*, *Standard*, *Telegraph*, *Miner*, *Grazier* or the *Advertiser*. Local papers were small and many carried the same advertisements, maybe for a cough medicine or a sewing machine, in exactly the same column year after year. Some were literary, and it was the little *Gundagai Times*, appearing every Tuesday and Friday, that expressed an early delight in the verses and stories of the little-known Henry Lawson, calling him a genius. Many of these small-town newspapers were spiced with the names of local residents who liked to see their achievements reported as makers of prize scones at the showgrounds, as pall bearers at a funeral, and as owners of a prize sow.

A few weekly rural papers claimed to circulate far from home. Thus the *Richmond River Express*, published only on Saturday and circulating in only a dozen or two towns and townships south of the Queensland border, cheekily claimed that it was available 'in all the Principal Public Libraries in the World'. But at the St Petersburg public library a foreign visitor who asked for the latest copy of this New South Wales rural weekly would have received a stare of disbelief.

Significantly, the early federal parliaments housed numerous country newshounds. Of the early prime ministers, J. C. Watson had been a newsprint compositor in New Zealand, Joseph Cook had been manager of a Lithgow paper, Scullin had been the editor of the Ballarat *Evening News*, while R. G. Menzies' youthful interest in politics stemmed partly from his uncle, Sid Sampson, a politician who had edited newspapers in the Victorian wheatbelt. To be a country editor, and to be curious about everything, was useful schooling for the life of a politician.

The Miraculous Photo

A photograph was an eloquent message. This new invention was almost as miraculous as the electric telegraph. Both made visible what had been invisible. Both inventions were products of the same decade, the 1830s. A Frenchman, Louis-Jacques-Mandé Daguerre, virtually invented photography. By harnessing the rising knowledge of chemistry and mineralogy he captured a picture on a copper plate that had been coated with silver. The photo was permanently impressed on the plate – an image of astonishing sharpness, ideal for portraiture. By the end of 1842 the Frenchman's art was being practised professionally in Sydney.

The camera was heavy, the taking of one photo was costly, and the chemical process consumed time and patience. By the mid-1850s there was a cheaper, wet-plate process, using a collodion plate. Copies could now be made of the original exposure or photograph. A husband and wife in their smartest clothes could visit a photographer and, for a shilling or two, have their likeness taken. Clear black-and-white copies – each pasted on a small oblong card, measuring about six centimetres by nine – could then be posted to friends on the far side of the world. By 1860 more than 130 professional photographers catered for the soaring Australian demand for portraits.

In a new country it was the more successful who wished for a photograph: it was a proof of their success. And so, during the slow-ticking seconds while the camera did its work, diggers stood immobile beside the very gold nugget they had found, shopkeepers stood still by the bride they had wed, and mothers in their Sunday finest proudly nursed their baby with a tight grip and prayed that she would stop wriggling – otherwise the photo would be blurred. Sometimes the nation's failures as well as successes were photographed. In the early 1860s the faces of the prisoners in the main Adelaide jail were captured on a wet plate.

Even with new techniques, the taking of a photograph might require as long as ten seconds. In that space of time the sitter might move slightly, or the hands might fidget, thus creating a slight blur or fudging. Initially the rich or the mighty, sitting or standing for their portrait, acted as if the camera was not present. They ignored its gaze and looked the other way. An early photograph, taken in Sydney in 1856, shows Stuart Donaldson, the first premier of New South Wales, along with his ministerial colleagues, all displaying side whiskers and longish hair, sitting impassively on three sides of a small table. Curiously the five men give the impression they had not previously met one another: each gazes in a different direction. How fashions gyrate! Eventually the photographer would gain his ascendancy, and all would obediently look at him and even smile when they had no wish to smile.

Cameras at first called for plenty of natural light. A photo taken out of doors at night or in a dimly lit hall was a blank. The camera called for stillness, and photographs taken at the top of a clock tower could be impaired by vibrations if the clock struck while the picture was being shot. Smoke rising briskly from a locomotive, or the sudden movement of a horse and cart, gave rise to a ghostly or fuzzy image. While much money could be made by photographing the busy streets of a city – migrants loved to send to friends at home the visible assurance that Australia was civilised – the main streets could not be photographed on a weekday because too much traffic was moving. A Sunday morning in summer, maybe one hour after sunrise, was preferable. It offered radiant light, silent streets, and clearer air because most of the workshops were closed and the wood fires in the kitchens – busy creators of smoke haze – had not yet been lit. Of course the horsedrawn cabs, the taxi of the day, were already waiting in line in the street for early churchgoers, but the horses stood still between the shafts and so could be captured by the wet plate. Likewise the few people on foot could be persuaded by the photographer to stand still for the half-minute while he focused and captured the panoramic scene. Action shots belonged to the future.

Portraying the goldfields was still a preserve of artists, especially the brilliant young lithographer S. T. Gill. But even artists called on the photographers for help. Photographs of street scenes were used by artists and engravers to capture the details, especially when they drew a scene onto a block of wood, stone or steel, from which hundreds of copies could be printed on fine paper or even in newsprint.

By the early 1870s the cameramen were reaching the smaller gold towns. Driving a covered wagon – in effect their travelling darkroom and laboratory where the wet plate could immediately be processed – they halted at schools, blacksmiths' forges, shops and mines. Beaufoy Merlin, an artist with the camera, caught a girl sucking her middle fingers in that moment when adult eyes were looking elsewhere; captured another child perched on a wooden rocking horse outside a slab-roofed cottage; and caught schoolgirls wearing white sleeveless pinafores over their dresses and light-coloured ribbons in their neat-brushed hair. His captives looked his camera in the eye: hardly one laughed or smiled.

The photographer himself died in 1873, his lungs probably weakened by his daily exposure to the potassium cyanide which was part of the wet-plate process conducted in his wagon. Nearly eighty years after his death, his negatives, all preserved on small sheets of glass, were discovered in a suburban back-yard in Sydney. They make a haunting record of the goldfields' daily life.

The idea of photographing native animals and birds was entrancing to nature lovers but not easily accomplished. Birds could not be depicted in flight: the result was a blur. To photograph a bird sitting on a nest in a tree was almost unattainable; the camera was too heavy and unwieldy to be set up close by, and no telescopic lens was available to entice, in effect, the bird closer. The shade of the leaves was also a barrier. The first Australian birds to be photographed with success were sitting seabirds. The sun shone brilliantly on the Abrolhos Islands of Western Australia when a photograph called 'Lesser Noddies Nesting' was snapped two days before Christmas, 1889.

Newspapers were slow to illustrate their stories and scoops with a black-and-white photograph. The weekly *Sydney Mail*, founded in 1860, was twenty-eight years old when it produced its first photograph – of a railway accident at the town of Young. Another twenty years passed before its parent newspaper, the *Sydney Morning Herald*, published its first photograph. The coarse-grained photo depicted the Great White Fleet, the pride of Washington, sailing into Sydney Harbour through a barrier of smokiness that could be attributed to the imperfections of the photographic process. While the news of the American fleet's arrival could be swiftly telegraphed, word by word, along the wires to Brisbane, the photo had to travel by train. To transmit along the wires an actual photo or engraving was a dream for the future.

Ingenious technicians, advised by scientists, rebuilt the camera in nearly every decade. The new dry-plate process made photography less of a technique for itinerant chemists, because the picture no longer had to be processed immediately. The new magnesium powder enabled photographs to be taken, with a flash of brilliant light, at night or indoors. The cheap Kodak camera, devised by an American, George Eastman, spawned the amateur photographer. The novel movie camera arrived in time to snap the Melbourne Cup of 1896 but it was too expensive to be placed in the hands of anyone except a professional photographer. Ten years later most Australian adults had never seen a movie, and those who did see one experienced the excitement for rarely more than ten minutes. Of course they heard not a sound, unless a piano or violin was played as accompaniment: the movie was silent.

The Telephone – Can You Hear Me?

In theory the telephone enhanced the importance of word-of-mouth. But it was a sluggard of an innovation. It was available in a few shops and offices in several Australian cities by the end of 1880, but for decades it was of trifling importance compared to the telegram. An American invention, the phone was at first simply a commercial mouthpiece. A crucial disadvantage was that it could not readily use the existing telegraph wires that snaked across Australia. A whole new system of overhead lines was required. Moreover the telegraph wires went only to a central office in each town, whereas each phone subscriber required the installing of a procession of tall poles to carry the wires along the street to the office, shop or bank.

The first telephone exchange was opened in 1880, in Melbourne. The telephone directory listed forty-four subscribers, mostly business houses. At the central switchboard, young women were employed to manually link each subscriber who wanted service. The automatic dial-your-own phone lay far ahead. The women stood up while they worked. In the offices and houses a phone was usually attached to a wall, and so most phone conversations were conducted by people who stood while they spoke. At first they could speak only to people in the same town. The few Townsville offices with a phone in the 1890s could speak only to people down the street, and Perth subscribers spoke only to other Perth subscribers. The sound was not always clear. 'Hello, can you hear me?' was the question, shouted rather than spoken, that often began the early conversations. The question was like the coo-ee, repeated a couple of times from both ends of the line.

In the first telephone exchanges the female operators stood while they worked. In the few offices that owned a telephone, the manager also stood while he talked.

For years the phone wires did not link distant cities. Even Melbourne and Sydney were not connected by telephone until July 1907. Adelaide joined the interstate hook-up in 1914. It is a reasonable guess that at least half of the Australian soldiers who enlisted to fight in the First World War had not once spoken on a telephone.

The Boot and the Tyre

In the dozen years before the First World War, was the glamorous telephone or the humble bicycle the more valuable invention? For the average Australian the bike won hands down. It was valuable because it was soon everywhere. Moreover it supplemented the shoes and boots that were, for decades, the main form of transport.

As a cart horse or riding horse was expensive, more people walked than used a horse. On the inland routes to the goldfields a small army travelled by foot. Carters on the long inland roads also walked. Not often did they ride – unless they were tired. People travelling on foot carried their possessions on their back. Occasionally they would pay a carter, going in the same direction, to carry their pack and hand luggage while they themselves walked beside the dray. Sore feet were a common complaint. Boots wore thin and, being expensive, were stitched or patched up until no cobbler could possibly repair them again. When boots were wearing thin, the soles and perhaps the toes were stuffed with newspaper. A few travellers greased their boots every so often but the colonial opinion was that this merely let in the rain.

Hundreds of thousands of Australians of all ages were capable of walking long distances when the need arose. Many rural children walked miles to school, and home again. Women living far from the nearest shop might walk for an hour or two to reach it. Long walks were deliberately planned, sometimes to see the countryside and sometimes as a test of personal endurance. Thus in 1882, young George Morrison began to carry his heavy swag from the port of Normanton on the Gulf of Carpentaria by way of Cooper's Creek and Wilcannia to his home at Geelong College. He covered the 3300 kilometres in just over four months. He saw not one kangaroo, though he crossed country where today they can be counted in the tens of thousands.

Many men, when jobs were scarce, spent each week working at a mine or sawmill some fifteen or more kilometres from their house, and they looked forward to returning home for weekends. They did not pale at the weekly prospect of walking for two or three hours after a heavy Saturday at the mine, spending twenty-four hours with wife and family, chopping the firewood for several hours, and then trudging back to their workplace on the Sunday evening so as to be ready – after a night's sleep – to labour away the next morning. Farmers and their horses often walked 22 kilometres a day while ploughing, and a few more kilometres in other tasks. Some postmen walked long distances. Similarly a female servant felt stiff and sore in the legs after a day of walking up and down stairs and corridors, sometimes carrying a large bucket of hot water.

A labourer named Joseph Jenkins often walked up to

30 kilometres a day in search of his next rural job. After tramping on metalled roads for several days in succession, and carrying all his possessions in his swag, he recorded grievances in the remarkable diaries he kept for a quarter of a century. In May 1871 he complained justifiably: 'I find my present swag three times too heavy for travel, and too light to meet the bitter cold mornings.' Presumably he could carry only one thin blanket or at most two. His swag, weighed down by his working tools, weighed up to 40 kilograms. An inventory of the items carried in one swag of that era is revealing. A Riverina labourer named Donegal Jim, after committing a sexual assault on a woman near Ballarat in April 1876, was carefully described, along with his possessions, in a police 'wanted' advertisement. His swag contained two of those heavy hammers used for stone-breaking, a bluish tweed suit, a black cloth dress coat and trousers, a white shirt with studs, and that fancy footwear known as 'tommy-dodd shoes'. This was described as a small swag.

To those who travelled long distances, in city or country, the bicycle was almost a miracle. Even in 1918 it was more important than the motor car in everyday life. Admittedly the pushbike had a running start, having been invented before the motor car. It was fairly cheap to buy and incredibly cheap to operate, being worked by muscle power. As late as the First World War more personal messages, written and verbal, were probably conveyed each day by bike than by phone.

Bicycles had become fashionable near the end of Queen Victoria's reign. The invention of the pneumatic tyre by John Boyd Dunlop in Ireland in 1887, with its superiority to the solid rubber tyre, gave a boost to cycling. The new tyre was like a cushion when travelling along a rough road. At the same time cycling became more popular because the bicycle, with two wheels of the same size, replaced the penny-farthing with its tiny rear wheel and awesomely high front wheel. To fall from a penny-farthing was to risk breaking an arm, leg or wrist. Rightly, the latest bike was called the safety bicycle.

These new bicycles were very light. The owners, when riding in difficult terrain, could easily dismount and carry the bicycle across a rough or sandy stretch of track. The steel frame of the bicycle had the advantage that it was simple and strong. Perhaps the weakest part of the machine was the front forks: they were easily broken. The spokes on the wheels were also fragile, and a hard stick could fly up and break a dozen spokes in an instant. Even the pneumatic tyre was fragile. A nail left on the road, a thorn, or a sharp-edged rock could puncture the tyre. Some cyclists riding long distances no longer put air in the tyres: they were too peppered with holes. Instead they stuffed the tyres with dry grass, and rode on, as best they could.

By the early 1900s the cycles had many uses. They were relished for picnics and excursions. Post offices used cyclists instead of the horse and van in the task of emptying the letter-boxes. Many postal cyclists rode 20 000 kilometres a year. Shearers – and there was an army of shearers – rode a bike when they had to move to a new shearing shed. In the bush their bicycles were often heavily loaded with a tuckerbox, blankets, loaded sugar bags and a water bag carrying at least a litre of water. One journalist likened such a bike to an overloaded towel-horse. Many clergymen found the bicycle useful when they wished to visit members of their flock. Many men rode a bicycle to work and a few children rode a bicycle to school, and the butcher's boy pedalled to collect orders from customers. Women rode specially designed bikes and, as affirmed by the popular song 'Daisy, I'm Half Crazy', some rode on a bicycle built for two. Called a tandem, it was relished for picnics and excursions.

A few adventurers toured Australia on bikes long before there were rideable roads between the capital cities. In 1894, Mrs E. A. Maddock of Sydney rode from Sydney to Melbourne in nine days, a remarkable feat because the Hume Highway in places was so pocked with holes that the rider had to dismount. Young men wishing to travel between Western Australia and the eastern states, in the era when no railway crossed the Nullarbor, pedalled their way. The more popular route, favoured by tail winds, was from west to east. Even today jet aircraft make much faster times on their route when helped by the westerlies.

In the countryside, for the purposes of business travel, the bike was an asset. Over a journey of 40 kilometres in flat terrain the cyclist could often beat the train, especially if the train had to stop at all stations. The main goldfields of Western Australia were tailor-made for the cycle. Coolgardie and Kalgoorlie were discovered just when the first pneumatic tyres reached Australia. At first the expanding network of gold towns owned no railways, and no made roads. Water was scarce, and this favoured cyclists who, on the road, consumed far less water than a horse and driver or rider. As the terrain of the goldfields was flat, it was ideal for cyclists. The Coolgardie Cycle Express Co became well known for its fast courier service, using cyclists to carry letters and other packages from town to town and to outlying mines.

Bikes in Australia were not counted by official statisticians. In contrast, horses were counted almost to the nearest neigh, even if the calculating of their numbers was not as exact as the statistician pretended. Cars and trucks were easily counted, and motorbikes too, because owners had to pay a licence fee. To ride a cycle, however, required no licence and no payment of tax, and so a bureaucratic reason did not exist for totalling the tally of bikes. The total, though never calculated, must have reached at least 200 000 by the year 1900. And cycles continued to multiply. Twenty years later, when cars were about to increase noticeably, they were still far outnumbered by bikes.

Decline of the Horse Teams

The First World War marked a dividing line for transport. The largest population of horses – maybe 2.5 million – was perhaps reached near the end of that war, after which the decline was rapid. In the outback, the camel, whether carrying a load on its back or pulling a heavy wagon, was just past its peak of importance. And the railways, in the total length of tracks open to traffic, were close to their peak, with the suburban railways and tramways still expanding.

Those noisy engines of change, the motor car and the aircraft, were parading themselves. The future was theirs but their impact on everyday life was not yet profound. In 1918 no daily air service linked Melbourne and Sydney. Those motoring between the two cities, especially during heavy rains, were still seen as adventurers, and tales of their journey, their breakdowns, and where they stopped each evening, were listened to with intense interest. The whole country held the ratio of about a dozen motor cars and trucks – and some 500 horses – for every 1000 people. Only a tiny fraction of adult Australians had yet driven a car or motorbike, or if they did sit at the wheel they drove illegally or only for a few metres. Maybe half of the population had either not sat in a motor car or – if they did taste that noisy experience – had only travelled a short distance.

Many motorists carried their petrol in tins. They also carried water, for the radiator was likely to boil. They carried spare tubes and tyres, for punctures were frequent. Petrol stations or 'motor garages' were rising here and there, but the petrol bowser was a novelty. If motorists planned a long journey into the far interior they arranged for a horse or bullock team to carry tins of petrol to the halting places they planned along their route. Cars had already crossed the continent but their journey was slow. The first drive from Adelaide to Darwin took seven weeks.

The horse teamsters at first were amused by their rowdy rival. They laughed when summoned to tow trucks from boggy patches of highway. They smiled when they observed how many cars, on a hot day, would break down while climbing a steep hill on a highway. Brand-new cars could give annoyance, especially if the driver did not understand elementary matters: to start a car was not always easy in the era before the automatic starter was invented. When a hotelkeeper collected his new T Model from the tropical port of Burketown in 1918 and set out for his home town of Camooweal, he suffered the humiliation of having to be towed for three days by a team of draught horses that pulled a loaded wagon as well as the faulty car. Soon, however, the heavy-horse teams were to vanish from the roads, though not yet from the ploughed paddocks.

5

COO-EE, BELL AND SILVER TONGUE

The coo-ee was to the ear what the Southern Cross was to the eye. Both are vital signs of how an earlier generation viewed this land. The prospect of becoming lost in the bush worried many Australians, especially those who lived in the interior. Soon they learned how to cry 'coo-ee' in a piercing, arresting voice.

The cry was uttered as if it was two separate words, the *coo* being prolonged and the *ee* being shouted with almost a sharp jerk. The shrill coo-ee carried long distances, and was more penetrating and vibrating than a deep shout. On a still night the sound of a cry might carry as far as 3 kilometres. In contrast the normal English mode of calling to someone in the distance was 'hollo', a word which does not have the commanding force of the coo-ee.

The coo-ee was the Aborigines' invention. Perhaps they brought to Australia a version of it some 50 000 years ago, or perhaps they developed it in more recent times. The journals of the white explorers sometimes recorded this strange cry. Thus, in 1870, the explorer John Forrest was close to the cliffs of the Great Australian Bight at Eucla when a coo-ee was heard. An Aborigine in his party, Tommy Windich, was the first to hear the cry. After answering with his own coo-ee 'a good many times', wrote Forrest, 'we were surprised to see two natives walking up towards us, unarmed'. The two Aborigines were soon joined by another five, 'all entirely naked, and every one circumcised'. That night the seven visitors enjoyed companionship and the novelty of cooked damper before huddling together to sleep by the campfire.

The Coo-ee: an Early National Anthem

White Australians began to teach their children, in the interests of safety, how to coo-ee. The call became as important as a bicycle helmet is today. The novelist Marcus Clarke wrote a short story called 'Pretty Dick', which was widely known by the 1880s – perhaps because it caught the widespread and intense fear of being lost in the bush. He described how a seven-year-old boy was lost in western Victoria. Hearing a horseman in the distance, the boy began to shout coo-ee, and soon the search was over.

The coo-ee, when successful, was like a two-way wireless. It was answered by the hearer with his own coo-ee, which in turn evoked a reply. It became a useful shorthand signal for bushmen searching separately for straying horses. When one finally located the lost horses he coo-eed to announce that the search was over.

A cry for help, the coo-ee was also a greeting. One of the first of the consciously nationalist calls, it was perhaps the first national anthem. In some public places in London the Australians' confident coo-ee was the equivalent of the singing of 'Waltzing Matilda' at Earls Court a century later. In 1847 the Australian pastor John Dunmore Lang recorded an anecdote of how a party of native-born Australians, strolling through London streets that were strange to them, were accidentally parted from a friend while negotiating a whirlpool of traffic in Fleet Street. One of the tourists had the bright idea of shouting out a coo-ee. It rose above the clatter of the traffic; and 'the well-known sound, with its ten thousand Australian associations' was at once recognised by the missing friend.

At about that same period, Australians attending a show in London suddenly observed, to their delight, some friends seated on the far side of the theatre. They called 'coo-ee'. At once there arose from the gallery the voice of an Englishman. He called aloud 'Botany Bay!' Already some Londoners felt the need to put down visiting Australian larrikins.

Even before the gold rushes the word coo-ee gained another meaning. It was a rough measure of distance and degree. A footrunner of little ability, a shearer of little skill, was colloquially said to be not even within 'coo-ee distance' of the champions. Henry Lawson observed how a horse or bullock teamster would travel an additional half hour by twilight in the hope of camping for the night in the vicinity of a welcome hotel or shanty:

And I mind how weary teamsters struggled on
>   while it was light
Just to camp within a cooey of the shanty
>   for the night.

The coo-ee became an early expression of what was later called mateship. It was a greeting between those who believed that they had something to share. When in 1902 the singer Nellie Melba returned in triumph to Melbourne, her native city, she was welcomed at the railway station by a crowd from her old Presbyterian Ladies College. The girls in unison simply called 'coo-ee'. By then the coo-ee was almost the national war cry. Therefore it was favoured by Australians visiting England. At a test match their coo-ee would be heard: it was a precursor of the Mexican wave but more patriotic, more divisive.

Then, like all fashionable chants and slogans, it fell from favour. Australians became more urbanised. A child in the modern era was less likely to be lost in the bush. While many children living in the countryside in the 1930s and even later were still taught how to coo-ee, the cry was as much a cultural heirloom as a potential means of saving a life. In the 1960s one stockman recorded that in his own lifetime he had never heard anyone in the bush call out coo-ee, except perhaps in fun. But in hilly districts it was still used by some families as a useful form of communication even after the mobile phone became common.

Cattle Bells and Church Bells

While the coo-ee might have saved lost children, the bell more often saved lost animals. Many bullocks and horses, while on the road, wore bells. When at the end of the day they went out to graze, the sound of their bells pointed to their whereabouts, and they could be rounded up in the morning. On the road to the Palmer goldfield in north Queensland in the 1870s as many as four teams of bullocks would travel together, pulling wagons or drays loaded with supplies; and with an additional herd of spare bullocks following them, well over 100 working bullocks might be allowed to wander at nightfall in search of food and water, after the teamsters had pitched their camp. 'Most of the bullocks wore heavy bells strapped around their necks and the noise was anything but entertaining', wrote one observer. He found it hard to sleep while all those bullocks were nearby.

Blacksmiths created, for their customers, sets of bells with distinct sounds. So the owner of the bullocks or horses could identify, by the note of the bell, which were his own wandering animals. The bells made by Robert Mennicke, a blacksmith at North Wagga, were celebrated. He was a Stradivarius of the clanging bell. Some of his tenor bells, made from German metal, were said to be audible nearly 10 kilometres away when the night was frosty. Another bell whose sound carried far was the creation of a Welsh-born blacksmith living in Queensland. Called the Condamine bell, it could be heard far away. Those working bullocks which carried Condamine bells were more easily found.

Explorers in the vast interior were careful to hang bells around the necks of their horses and bullocks. Camped at night in parched country, explorers had to allow their animals to wander in the darkness, so that they could find the scarce feed and maybe the chance pool of water. More than once the sound of a bell saved explorers from disaster. Major Peter Warburton and his camels, on an arduous trek, were exploring the land between Alice Springs and the tropical coast of Western Australia when his party began to suffer from starvation and thirst. An Aborigine named Charley went alone to search for distant water and, returning in the darkness, might have been lost if he had not 'caught the sound of the bells attached to the camels' necks'. Of course he instantly shouted a coo-ee. In Warburton's journal on 5 November 1873 appeared a grateful tribute to the courage of Charley and to 'the guidance of the Almighty'. To the maker of the humble camel bell there was no tribute, but he had helped to save their lives.

Even the grazing cattle on many of the smaller properties carried bells, especially if the property was poorly fenced. One of Adam Lindsay Gordon's popular verses, first published in a Melbourne sporting paper in 1865, describes the cattle bells:

> Hark! the bells on distant cattle
> Waft across the range,
> Through the golden-tufted wattle,
> Music low and strange;

Cattle bells, as distinct from bullock bells, were heard less frequently a generation later. Though the population of cattle was many times larger than in Gordon's era, the 'tinkling sound', as he called it, was rarely heard. The fence and the cattle dog partly replaced the cattle bell. The horn of the motor truck partly replaced the bell of the bullock.

While some of the message carriers attracted the ears, others attracted the eyes. The lighthouse was a message carrier – a warning to passing ships that a dangerous reef or headland lay nearby. If a ship struck danger, and the lives of crew and passengers were at risk, a night-time plea for help could be made by setting off fireworks. On Boxing Day 1855, the large clipper ship *Schomberg*, her long voyage from Liverpool to Melbourne almost over, ran onto a reef only 300 metres from the western Victorian coast. Rockets were fired into the sky, blue lights were burned. A small coastal steamship, attracted by the signals, rescued the passengers. Half a century would pass before the Marconi wireless or radio would enable a ship in distress to signal more effectively for help.

The steeple or tower bell was the 'coo-ee' of a town. As few people carried a watch or portable clock, they needed bells to tell them the time. Many churches installed a bell in the belfry or on a post near the front door, and it was rung shortly before divine service as a reminder to members of the congregation. Many schools rang a bell, though bells were too expensive for the typical bush school. On the main railway stations a bell was rung to warn passengers that the train was about to depart; Ballarat Station owned a large bell which during the Second World War was souvenired by troops bound for north Africa. In many mansions a handbell summoned the servants to the

131

dining room or sitting room. Ships struck their bells, and mines too. When Australians Rules football began to attract crowds a bell was rung to sound the end of each half or each quarter. Even on the Melbourne Cricket Ground, as late as the 1940s, a large bell was rung by the football timekeepers. People learned to distinguish the sound of each of the various bells they heard in the course of the week.

Any town of vigour employed a bellringer who, day and night, strolled along the main streets to announce important events. A bellman was useful in an isolated town where a newspaper appeared only once or twice a week, and was especially useful in a new town where the informal avenues of gossip were not yet laid out. In 1861, on the goldfield of Kiandra, a storekeeper hired 'Tom The Bellman' to advertise that a customer owing money had disappeared. The bellman, as he walked through the town, announced that a reward of twenty pounds would be paid to anybody who found the fraudulent customer. Thirty years later the growing town of Perth employed a town crier who, wearing a belltopper hat and swallowtail coat, rang his bell as he passed along the main streets. In some towns a night watchman paraded after dark, calling in a loud voice the passing hours. Henry Lawson has left a haunting picture of the night when his baby sister Nettie was dying. Just as the watchman walked past the house with his familiar cry, 'Twelve o'clock, and all's well', the baby died.

In cities and many rural districts bells tolled for the dead. By 1860 a few of the larger city churches rang bells which, following the age-old practice, sounded fifty-five times if the

Every Sunday morning and evening, church bells summoned hundreds of thousands of people. Here, two of Australia's largest churches – the massive Independent Church and the Scots Church (background) – stood at what was then the most impressive intersection in Melbourne, the corner of Russell and Collins streets.

dead person was aged fifty-five, and rang in a certain way if she was a woman. Often, when a funeral procession moved from the house or rural church to the graveyard, a handbell led the way. In Wagga Wagga, according to Mary Gilmore, a dinner bell was borrowed for use at funerals. If a baby was carried to the burial ground, a very small handbell was rung.

Bells passed on information to the attentive listener. At a fire station a bell not only announced that a fire was destroying property but also announced the location of the fire. In Melbourne in the 1860s, six distinct rings of the bell announced that the fire was in the suburb of North Melbourne, five bells signified Collingwood, while other sounds signified distinct areas of the city. This enabled firemen to leave their homes and hurry to the fire.

Roll Up, Roll Up!

One of the traditional joys in everyday life is to be the dispenser of news, especially dramatic and pleasing news. In the nineteenth century every adult and articulate child had an opportunity to dispense such news and to hear the instant expressions of astonishment. Today the television, radio, press and email are so pervasive that most people hear of important events from a professional purveyor of news. This public announcing of the latest news is less intimate, less personal, though usually more accurate than news passed on in the form of breathless gossip.

In 1850 the main way of communicating news was not

through the media. Most adults did not buy or borrow even one newspaper in the course of a week. On the sheepruns a newspaper was a luxury and stale long before it arrived. In the cities most people did not buy a newspaper.

In the countryside and the smaller towns, word of mouth remained the urgent carrier of news. Crowds numbering several thousands were mustered largely by word of mouth. On the early goldfields, where thousands of men lived in close proximity, a burning topic would draw them together. Word that a public meeting or demonstration was about to be held would be conveyed verbally, aided by the beating of a drum or banging of an iron pot. 'Roll up, roll up' became a common call on the goldfields. It was heard almost everywhere at Lambing Flat, when riots against the Chinese diggers were organised in 1861. The same cry was later heard on the Palmer River diggings in north Queensland, where the Chinese could be seen in their thousands, and around Kalgoorlie where no Chinese were to be seen.

Even in a large town, the news that somebody had died was passed on more often by speech than by the printed word. Maybe half of the deaths and most of the births and marriages in 1870 were reported by no newspaper. That a citizen was to stand for election was first heard through the circuit of gossip. If a woman was knocked over by a horse and cart, if a strange infectious disease entered a nearby town, if an unmarried girl was pregnant, or if a new pastor was about to take over a congregation, the news was spread through conversation. Moreover it was usually spread in more detail than would appear ultimately in the local newspaper – if it appeared at all. The butcher's, grocer's, fishmonger's and such other places where people were waiting to be served – self-service being unknown – were newsrooms as well as shops.

A ship that arrived from an English port was the conveyor of the latest English news – of riots, parliamentary crises, new railways, deaths in the royal family, inventions, shipwrecks and wars. News in the overseas newspapers carried in that ship found its way – in the following week – into the local newspapers. But much of that news was carried ashore by passengers and passed on verbally. Other items of overseas news came in personal letters and were passed on by the recipient to friends. In the process of being passed on, some of the news was embroidered in order to intensify the drama. Gripping items, when they reached outlying shepherd huts, might have been passed on at least ten times.

People travelling on foot usually carried snippets of news and eagerly passed them on to listeners whom they met along the road. Countless lives were changed by these wayside exchanges of news. Thus in the 1840s, Isaac Westcott was working his farm near Geelong when a passer-by told him that Judge Willis was about to depart from Melbourne. Isaac, hoping to marry the judge's servant girl, hurried to see her, in fear that she might have already left with the judge's family. His proposal was accepted. Similar episodes altered the course of thousands of lives. When the gold rushes set in, and the roads to the diggings were crowded, information on the latest rush was eagerly sought from those returning. Word of mouth rather than newspapers supplied most of the news and rumours from the fast-changing goldfields. The importance of verbal news was increased by the unusual mobility of Australians. Many wrote a letter rarely or not at all. They themselves were the letter, the carrier of news.

The typical young man longed to be on the move. Whereas Americans in the last fifty years have been moving easily from state to state, Australians in 1900 were probably more migratory. The succession of gold rushes spurred them to pack bags and swags and to travel. The shearers were nomadic. Even the first generation of farmers was footloose. Most of the soils in Australia, unlike those in the United States, were deficient in nutrients; and after a few crops of wheat, many farmers set out in their drays and wagons towards virgin land. The high proportion of unmarried males in the population also made for mobility, facilitating the folding of tents and moving on. The depression of the 1890s, worse in Australia than in the United States, also forced people to move, especially across the bight to Western Australia and the stormy Tasman Sea to New Zealand.

A Sound of Powerful Voices

The voice remains the most pervasive of all means of communication. A century ago, however, it was unaided. There was no microphone or loudspeaker to carry a voice to a live audience, and no radio and television to carry it into homes. A book on Australian speakers and mass gatherings in the era before the

The open-air gathering where a strong voice conveyed news and opinions was common. As here, in Ballarat, mining speculators gathered daily to hear the latest share prices called aloud, and to exchange news and rumours.

microphone is urgently needed, and it will reveal much about our history of persuasion and protest.

It is remarkable how many people could hear or half-hear the speeches given by evangelists, politicians and miscellaneous voices of protest in the open air. When the goldminers at Ballarat were organising themselves against the government in the spring of 1854, mass meetings were frequent. On Sunday 22 October, 10 000 or 15 000 people were said to be standing near the speakers' platform. We know that platforms were often used at Ballarat because when, some five weeks later, the flag of the Southern Cross was flown for the first time, it was depicted in printed newspaper illustrations as flying from a flagpole just behind a speakers' platform.

When in August 1860 Burke and Wills prepared to set out from Royal Park in Melbourne – with their procession of big American wagons, drays, horses and pack camels – the curious and the excited gathered to farewell the first expedition to cross the continent from south to north. It was a Monday, and not a public holiday, but men, some in black top hats, and women and children flocked to the park on foot, in carriages and on horseback. Eager onlookers clustered around the animals, wagons and the heaps of supplies not yet loaded. The crowd must have been scattered over a large area, for wagons and livestock and supplies and the occasional small tent were placed here and there, and so an estimate of the attendance was difficult. Some said 10 000 spectators, some said 15 000, were watching.

At the hour of departure, the mayor of Melbourne mounted either a dray or a wagon – news reports differ even on such an elementary matter. Addressing 'this great crowd', he called for three separate lots of three cheers for those departing, and the *Herald* reported that the crowd hoorayed nine times, 'with all the energy and enthusiasm that are characteristic of popular assemblages'. Burke replied in kind. It is not clear from the reports whether he mounted the wagon and thereby enabled the crowd to see his face and gestures. While the reports of speeches given to large crowds rarely touch on the vital question – could the crowd of listeners actually hear the speaker? – the *Herald* left no doubt about Burke's speech. He spoke in 'a clear, earnest voice that was heard all over the crowd'.

Burke then mounted his white horse, his tall wide-brimmed hat easily visible, and rode from the park, leading his procession. He did not see Melbourne again. Eventually his bones were brought back to lie in the Carlton cemetery, only a short walk from the place where he made his farewell speech.

In Sydney in January 1888 a statue of Queen Victoria was to be unveiled in an open space near St Mary's Cathedral, and all the governors of the Australian colonies – and New Zealand and Fiji too – were expected to attend, for it was the centenary of the first British settlement in the land. On the appointed morning hundreds of policemen took charge of the site, and by eleven o'clock, when the official guests began to appear, the crowd was enormous. It was expected that more than 30 000 could assemble there, but in the end perhaps 50 000 or 60 000 attended. At the start of the ceremony the near-deafening cheers of the crowd virtually drowned out the sound of the national anthem being played by the brass bands. Lord Carrington, the popular governor of New South Wales, and at one time a member of the House of Commons, had agreed to make the main speech. Many people must have wondered whether he would be heard above the hubbub but he spoke clearly and, more to the point, briefly. According to one journalist, the governor 'raised his voice so fully that one-half of the crowd was able to hear all he had to say'. Irrespective of how many heard him, they applauded him 'to the echo'. It seems likely that at least 25 000 people heard him.

A few days later Carrington laid a foundation stone, and in the open air the premier, Sir Henry Parkes, first tried to address the assembled people, using both his deep and his falsetto voices. When he was hooted, he responded with the insult: 'Brutes, I should like to spit on you.' Carrington, who was a smiler rather than a spitter, and was alert to the fluctuating moods of an outdoors audience, jotted in his private diary that Parkes was hooted not necessarily because he was unpopular. 'The real reason was that they could hear nothing – I got on a table and had it pushed to the end of the platform and spoke to the crowd of about 3,000 people and got a tremendous ovation.' While maybe exaggerating his own success as an orator, Carrington was simply pointing out that public speaking in the era before the microphone was a special art, of which he was a confident practitioner.

During the first federal election in 1901, crowds gathered in the streets of many towns to hear politicians speak from the balconies of hotels. The largest reported crowd, in the coal port of Newcastle, consisted of 8000 people. In large rallies the people standing on the outskirts probably heard only an occasional sentence, but they felt that their presence gave moral support to the speaker and his cause.

In estimating the size of a crowd, speculation and some

guesswork are almost inevitable. A really large crowd is so infrequent that few police officers, political organisers and public speakers have the chance to develop the expertise needed to count the people present. At its peak a crowd does not last long; and so the time available for counting it is brief. Moreover police are too busy maintaining law and order to circle the crowd and estimate its size. We do know that it was possible in the eighteenth and nineteenth centuries for at least 30 000 people to hear, while standing in the open air, a skilled orator who was experienced in throwing his voice. If the people assembled in a natural amphitheatre, so shaped by the contours of the land as to improve the acoustics, even more could hear a speaker.

Speakers hoping to reach a large crowd had to be experienced or, less common, natural crowd speakers. As a rule they spoke slowly and articulated clearly each word: fast speech tended to be inaudible, except to those nearer the speaker. Their voice also had to carry – a high voice as well as a low voice is capable of travelling far. An argument was understood more clearly if it was repeated again and again, in different words.

It was possible to buy speaker's manuals that gave advice. The ancient Romans were skilled in oratory, and a few of their surviving books give advice in Latin on how to speak, on how to persuade. Teachers of elocution offered lessons, for a fee, in the big cities. During the First World War, Archbishop Mannix of Melbourne, a fine orator, was to receive lessons in the outdoors technique, for huge crowds came to hear him oppose the plan to conscript young Australians into the army for overseas service.

Alfred Deakin, who was three times prime minister, privately commented on his fellow politicians and their speaking methods. He was frank. Fortunately for his own reputation and friendships, his thoughts were not published until after his death. He is most revealing when discussing those speakers who delivered their message in big halls rather than in the open air. He thought that the face and head of the orator were an important part of his message. Thus Edmund Barton, who handed over the prime ministership to Deakin, had the gift of a fine head and beautiful eyes 'glowing like jewels in the ardour of his inspiration'. Barton's mouth, alas, was like that of a fish, though when he pouted, his piscine mouth changed to a shape that was rather engaging. In Deakin's eyes, the greatest orator was George Higinbotham, a Victorian politician who became chief justice. His head and face were superb, his voice was rich and harmonious, and his message was simple. In him Deakin detected what he called 'a holiness of purpose'.

Sympathy and empathy were vital in appealing to a crowd. 'Holiness of purpose' was Higinbotham's version of sympathy and empathy. In contrast Edmund Barton, on the platform, was unable to make the most of his eloquent head, jewelled eyes, finely sculptured features and the noble manner in which he delivered his sentences. His main fault was insuperable: 'He had comparatively little of the sympathy which keeps a speaker in touch with his audience.'

Another chord of sympathy between speaker and audience was fun. The very appearance of the Sydney politician George Reid invited laughter. Big and slow-moving, his stomach ballooning above thin legs, his Munich moustache almost out-growing his face, he seemed to be half asleep when listening to others, but he was quietly alert. The first premier of a colony to become prime minister of the Commonwealth, he spoke slowly, almost in a drawl. Sometimes a clown, he made his audience laugh at his opponents, laugh at those who interjected, and laugh at him. Even the dimmest understood what he wanted: he wanted their vote. 'As a platform orator he was un-surpassed', wrote Deakin.

The voice itself was crucial. Sir Charles Gavan Duffy, who had sat in the House of Commons before emigrating, was one of the most polished of Australian orators in the 1870s but his voice prevented him, in Deakin's view, from becoming a persuader on the platform, though the same speech, if read next day in the newspaper, was the most charming and fluent of essays. His voice, thin and squeaky, could also convey a harsh note which seemed to match his cold and calculating eyes. On the other hand, one of the first workingmen to sit in the Victorian parliament, William Trenwith, spoke with the force of a sledgehammer, but many listeners heard that loud voice as the mark of personal conviction. Deakin's own speaking voice was a light baritone and ringing with music. One of the finest orators of the British Empire, it was his 'concentrated intensity of conviction', even more than his voice and wit and vocabulary, that appealed.

The microphone was to become influential in the late 1920s. It revolutionised the art of speaking in the open air. Radio, too, became a forum for electioneering: its speakers did not need a loud voice. Radio permitted and encouraged the art of reading a speech in such a way that it seemed off-the-cuff. The old-time orator with a powerful memory was sometimes undermined by radio.

Hitherto the reading of political addresses had been frowned upon. In parliaments, the reading aloud of a speech from notes was banned by the speaker. In most spheres of life a formal speech was delivered without notes. When handwritten headings were used to aid the memory, they were few and hidden in the cup of the speaker's hand. Likewise in the typical church, the sermon was given with few or no notes.

A journalist reporting these addresses and sermons had to use shorthand to record them. In the days before the tape recorder and the scripted speech, the valuable art of shorthand was taught in business colleges. As an editor liked to publish every single word of an important speech – and the interjections, cheers and groans as well – a good journalist needed the skill of shorthand.

Those public speakers who felt uneasy at the idea of speaking spontaneously, with the aid of few or no notes, had a clear alternative. They could write out their speech and learn it by heart. Sir George Reid's father, a Presbyterian minister, learned by heart the two long sermons he delivered each Sunday. The unease felt towards a read speech was partly a matter of fashion. The preference for a noteless speech reflected the belief, held more strongly then than now, that a retentive memory was one of the hallmarks of a capable and well-trained mind. There was another reason for speakers shunning the use of notes, let alone a written script. In the heyday of oratory the speaker tried to look the audience in the eye all the time: that was probably the first rule of public speaking.

More and more women spoke in public, from the 1880s onwards. At first the idea of a woman speaking to a mixed audience in public, even on the most ladylike of subjects, was taboo. When the wife of a sea captain made a public speech in favour of temperance in the 1840s several interjectors taunted her with the cry, 'Where's your breeches?' The insistence of St Paul, that a woman should remain silent in the church, deterred women from preaching. One sect, the Primitive Methodists, sometimes allowed women preachers; and that more sophisticated sect, the Unitarians, caused a stir in 1873 when it appointed Miss Martha Turner as a pastor in Melbourne. When she visited Adelaide to preach, one of her female listeners was mesmerised 'by her exquisite voice, by her earnestness, and by her reverence'.

The first woman to address large Australian audiences in the open air was probably the British evangelist, Margaret Hampson, who made a national tour in 1883. Her eloquence and demeanour helped to halt the tide of disfavour towards female orators. A Melbourne religious weekly that announced magisterially 'we do not view with favour the spectacle of a woman addressing an audience of both sexes', conceded that Mrs Hampson was so impressive that an exception could be made just for her. More and more exceptions mounted the public platform. To prove that they were ladies, they wore hats when they spoke. The crusade against alcohol was their favourite cause.

One other outdoors 'voice' was increasingly heard at

weekends: the brass band. It was not often heard in 1870 but was widespread in 1900. In street processions, on sporting occasions, at civic funerals, and in the local bandstand on Sunday afternoons, the bands played. They were especially popular in the new mining towns and in the industrial suburbs, and wherever the Salvation Army marched. The music of a brass band travelled far on a still day. It reached its peak in that era just before the microphone, gramophone and radio – the instruments of amplification – were widely available.

Hats, Armbands and Other Social Rules

Just as the speakers in public meetings and churches tried to impress their audience, so the hosts in a thousand homes tried to impress their guests or make them feel at home. Their social rituals and rules were spread by word of mouth and often – not always – by example. The rules of the home were stronger than the rules of the platform, pulpit and open-air meeting. They regulated conversation and speech and much else besides.

In the 1880s one strong set of rules, largely unspoken, prevailed at the top of the social ladder. At least half of the population accepted many of these rules or tailored them without altering their style and spirit. At home, in the presence of visitors, most expressions of opinion were encouraged but if a topic under discussion led to intense and emotional feelings the host tended to close or divert the discussion. Of course if the host was in a lather of passion she – or he – might have the last word, even when one last word was clearly out of order.

The social *don'ts* formed a long list. Do not boast. Do not offend the religion of your guests. Do not pass on malicious gossip. Respect the privacy of your friends. Some of these injunctions were expressed in fine detail: 'No person should ever look over the shoulder of another who is reading and writing.' And do not be familiar. Please do not address someone you have just met, or have met only recently, by their Christian name.

Other rules – not so important as to be invariably respected – referred to dress and deportment. Men should not wear a hat indoors, nor stand with arms akimbo. Children should clean their boots – dirty shoes were taboo. An Australian social guide of 1885 said sternly and even optimistically: 'On entering a room, bow slightly as a general salutation, before speaking to each of the persons assembled.' Some rules required no edict, for the Bible implicitly seemed to support them. The phrase 'your Sunday best' emphasised that on Sunday both adults and children should wear their best clothes. One of the astonishing social changes of the last hundred years is that on Sunday nearly all people once dressed in their best clothes, whereas today most display their casual clothes.

Ceremonies and social occasions, weddings and funerals, obeyed rules which seemed as solid as rock. Jewellery was thus not worn by people while mourning the death of family or friends. But how long should their bracelets and necklaces be put to one side? 'The people of Australia', answered a guidebook in 1885, 'have settled upon no prescribed periods for the wearing of mourning garments.' The same book, called *Australian Etiquette*, advised a woman mourning the death of a brother or sister to wear black dresses and bonnets for two months and then for the following few months to brighten her clothes just a little, advancing in the last six weeks to clothes of grey, purple, white and violet. The English rules of mourning, like other social rules, were less rigid in free-and-easy Australia. It was observed in the 1880s that many 'gentlemen' chose to wear only a black band on the left arm and a black band around the hat while in mourning. As late as the 1930s there were families, especially mining families, who obeyed these old rules and rituals; and in Port Kembla some children wore black armbands to school for a few days after the death of a close relative.

German settlers in the Riverina tended to obey different social customs to those followed by the Irish in the potato townships of Victoria or the Jews in the main cities. A Cornish funeral in South Australia was not like a Scottish funeral in Brisbane. Sportsmen had their code of conduct, including an emphasis on fair play that was stronger in 1880 than half a century later. The outback had its own codes of behaviour, made mostly by men. Mateship was one of those principles.

All these competing codes of behaviour were like coo-ees and bells – they were calls for attention, attempts to reassure, or efforts to bind people together or even set them apart. What was said from the political platform or pulpit was reported every day in the press. But the social rules for each section of society did not have to be reported: nearly everyone knew them.

6

GOLD WATCHES AND SOVEREIGNS

Counting and measuring did not follow our rules in the nineteenth century. The pound weight and the pound note both reigned. Admittedly time was measured by hours and minutes but many adults could only guess the time of day, and few people carried with them a watch or portable clock. The metric system was rarely used, though the new Olympic Games, founded by a Frenchman in 1896, used that French-devised measure.

Wholesale soap, whether colonial or 'Sydney white' or best English soap, was sold by the hundredweight – that quantity being 112 and not 100 pounds. Tea was sold by the chest as well as by the pound weight. Gold was weighed on its own special set of troy scales; and so an ounce of gold was not of the same weight as an ounce of sugar. On the goldfields nearly every schoolchild knew that 12 ounces of gold, not 16 ounces, constituted one pound of gold. An ounce of gold could be further divided into 20 pennyweights: indeed one of the commonplace names in Australia was Pennyweight, whether Pennyweight Flat, Creek, or Gully. Butter, like gold, obeyed its own measurements. The 1854 edition of McCulloch's *Dictionary of Commerce* noted that the 'custom of allowing more than 16 ounces to the pound of butter' was strongly adhered to in some regions of the British Isles. When sold in large quantities in Australia, butter was usually measured by the English firkin, keg or cask. As each firkin or keg was exactly the same size, it served roughly as both a weighing and measuring device.

At the city market gooseberries were sold by the quart, as were milk and vinegar. Apricots, peaches and many other fruits now sold by the kilogram were sold by the dozen. At the Sydney wholesale market around 1900 the stone fruits and apples and pears were sold by the 'gin case'. The wholesalers of alcohol paid for their port at so much a pipe, and paid for sherry by the butt, and rum by the punch, and ale by the hogshead. Every apprentice in a wine merchant's shop soon knew that a pipe and a butt each carried close to 105 imperial standard gallons and that a hogshead carried just half of that amount. Beer had its own set of measures, and even the pots, jugs and glasses of beer sold over the bar had special names. In Sydney the tallest pot of beer was known as the 'Bishop Barker', the name of an Anglican bishop who was one of the tallest men in the city and – more to the point – a teetotaller. The anonymous drinker who coined that sly and witty title, a Bishop Barker, must have been delighted to see it spread slowly to every pub around Sydney Harbour and beyond.

At sea the fathom was used to measure the depth of water. Thus a navigator bringing his ship for the first time into Sydney Harbour was assured that the depth of water in the middle of the entrance through the Heads was at least 17 fathoms, a fathom being 6 feet. At the racecourse the furlong was widely used, 8 furlongs equalling 1 mile. The yard, being 3 feet, was universally used. A cricket pitch was 22 yards long, and cloth of course was sold by the yard at the draper's shop.

Certain items were counted according to time-honoured usage. Corks – whether for ginger beer or wine – were sold in lots of 144. In other words they were sold by the twelve dozen or 'a gross', whereas eggs were sold by the single dozen. Oysters were usually sold by the dozen, but in most of the expensive white-cloth dining rooms it was the practice to serve thirteen oysters on each plate, a tradition maintained in several of Australia's oldest dining rooms. To ask, incidentally, for half a dozen oysters was very rare until the twentieth century, when oysters became expensive. In saleyards the cows and pigs were sold as individuals but working bullocks were nearly always sold by the pair, as were geese and ducks.

In shops, some of the weights and measures then widely used mean nothing now to most Australians. Wheat was measured by the bushel: so too were such different commodities as shellfish and quicklime. But the bushel did not have the same unchanging meaning. In Adelaide, as in Dublin, malt was sold by the bushel of roughly 40 pounds, barley by the bushel of roughly 50 pounds, and wheat by the bushel of roughly 60 pounds. A bushel was more a measure than a weight.

Thus the barley was sold in a jute bag of a specific size, and wheat in an even larger bag. The bag took the place of the scales. Some of the items sold at what were called Hay and Corn Stores – every large rural town had one or two such stores – were weighed rather than measured. While wheat was sold in a special bushel bag, the bag was also weighed; and so it might 'go' 61 or 63 pounds to the bushel.

Flour was sold not by the bushel but by the pound. Each bag of flour weighed 200 pounds, which meant that a full bag of flour was not easily lifted from the ground and placed onto the tray of a cart. Bread was sold by the loaf, and for decades a loaf was legally defined as a 4-pound loaf. Baker's shops displayed a set of scales on the counter for the benefit of doubting customers.

In the cities of the 1860s it was usual to buy firewood at the price of ten shillings for a 'one horse load'. Firewood could also be bought by the ton. Various industries had their own ways of weighing or measuring a ton. Goldmines were diligent keepers of statistics, but 'one ton' of gold-bearing ore was not of the same weight on every goldfield. Old mining men still speak familiarly of 'the Bendigo ton'. On the Western Australian goldfields many mines measured their annual output in American or short tons, each of 2000 pounds, whereas other mines counted the tally in traditional British or long tons, each of 2240 pounds.

Such contradictions, to our eyes, come as a surprise. But even in measuring the time of day, people did not tell the time as we do.

Clocks and Whistles

Most adults in the first year of the gold rushes did not own a clock. Timepieces were expensive: they were not yet mass-produced. Most people who wished to know the time of day looked at the sun and estimated how far it had run its course. Rural work did not depend on the clock. In summer most people worked from dawn to dark and in winter they worked from dawn until a little after dark.

In towns the clock was more important. Banks and other offices were open for definite hours. Skilled tradesmen, if employees, were likely to work for definite hours. On the other hand, many domestic servants worked for nearly all their waking hours. The government usually did not regulate hours of labour in the 1850s – except those hours worked by its own employees or its own prisoners. To regulate hours of labour required the widespread possession of clocks and watches.

The erection of a public clock was a memorable event. In some towns the post office, town hall or a church displayed a clock, but the typical town in 1860 probably did not possess a large public clock. The cost of erecting a clock tower was heavy enough, and the clock itself was so expensive that to this day the towers of various public buildings possess a clock-shaped circle but no clock.

Many of the public clocks were unreliable. The first public clock in Melbourne easily jumped half an hour or, equally easily, lost half an hour. A large clock had to overcome the friction created by its own parts and by the resistance of air.

155

In a turret or tower clock the heaviness of the metal parts increased the friction. A strong wind also retarded the movement of the hands, while dust in the air during a hot wind affected the mechanism.

Soon a large city could erect a high clock that could keep time with accuracy. In 1872 Adelaide opened its new post office, a stone building with a tower 149 feet high – as high perhaps as a modern fifteen-storey building. The clock and the great bells imported from England and hung in 1875 sounded across the rooftops. Four bells sounded C, B Flat, A Flat and E Flat, while a big bell weighing nearly two and a half tons sounded the hour. The hour bell and the quarter chimes were said to resemble those of the houses of parliament in Westminster and could be heard on frosty nights almost on the outskirts of Adelaide. Unfortunately the face of the clock was not large enough, defying the rule that the dial should be 1 foot in width for every 10 feet it stood above the pavement.

So long as most people did not possess a clock, the sounding of the time by bells, guns or whistles was important. On the diggings in the 1850s a gun was fired to mark the beginning and end of the day's work. Such a warning was essential on shallow goldfields because on any one day the gold itself could be actually seen in many shallow holes. To prevent the stealing of gold, no miner was allowed to be present on the diggings before or after the legal hours.

The bell was heard more often than the time gun. Larger churches rang their bell to announce the hour of worship; and the larger schools rang their bells to summon the stragglers. The

*In Sydney's Pitt Street, as in so many other city streets, the high clocks
could be seen from afar by people who owned no watch.*

railway train and steamship blew their whistle to announce that they were about to arrive or depart. Steam was the sister of punctuality, and the word 'timetable' was coined in the new age of steam, in the late 1830s. The steamship, unlike the sailing ship, did not depend on the winds and so could depart on time. A steam train, unlike a horse coach, did not depend on the temper of the horses or the state of the road, and so could leave on time. Above all, steam engines in factories, mines and locomotives also provided a loud throat for announcing the time of day.

Every large mine and factory blew its steam whistle. As most manual employees lived within walking distance of their work, they could usually hear the whistle. In the era before alarm clocks were common, steam whistles often awakened employees. At Bendigo in 1900 the goldmines blew a loud whistle each morning at six to awake the miners in nearby cottages. The whistle was blown again at seven, to announce that the morning shift was beginning, blown at three to mark the start of the after-noon shift, and at 11 p.m. for the night shift. Each whistle had its own sound, and children living in such mining towns as Bendigo, Broken Hill, Kalgoorlie and Charters Towers, or in the factory suburbs of cities, knew the distinctive sounds of ten or fifteen whistles. The loquacious ones even played a tune. The New Moon mine at Eaglehawk, near Bendigo, could whistle 'Home, Sweet Home' and a few of the popular hymns. Even today, in some of the round-the-clock mining towns, the mine whistle is the substitute for the public clock.

The finest tower clocks, such as Ballarat's, not only struck the hour in loud, clear notes but also chimed on the quarter hour. The chimes of the clock at Bendigo were said to be so loud that in the adjacent Shamrock Hotel, the singer Dame Nellie Melba complained of broken sleep. The visibility of a tower clock was also aided by the lower height of rival city buildings. At night, however, it was not easy to illuminate a public clock clearly. As its hands could not be seen from a distance, the chimes and gong were important.

Accurate time was vital at sea. Indeed, the requirements of navigation were one of the spurs to the making of very accurate clocks. By 1860 both Sydney and Melbourne had an astronomical observatory which issued a public time signal for the benefit of ships' masters who wished to correct their chronometer. The chronometer was vital for determining a ship's longitude at sea; and an error in a chronometer could easily result in the captain, thinking he was far from land, running his ship aground in darkness or storm, with the loss of many lives.

In Port Phillip Bay the time signal was displayed on a small flagstaff atop a bluestone tower at Port Gellibrand, Williamstown: the tower still stands. At first a signal was flown but from the 1850s until 1926 a time ball was used. In Sydney the observatory at Flagstaff Hill gave a similar signal to ships. It dropped a large time ball once a day, usually at one o'clock in the afternoon, so that any captain within sight of the ball could instantly check the accuracy of his chronometer or fine maritime watch. Adelaide began to drop its time ball at Semaphore, by the sea, in August 1875. Most observatories adopted the practice of firing a loud gun once a day, usually at 1 p.m., to inform city people of the correct time. A daily time gun was fired in Hobart until 1927 and in Perth until after the Second World War.

Visitors who entered a large house in any town in 1860 would almost certainly see a large pendulum clock standing in the hallway or in the dining room. Often the loud slow ticking could be heard before the clock came into sight. In the towns a skilled tradesman or shopkeeper probably did not yet have a clock in the house. The small settler certainly did not possess a clock, and so the song of the kookaburra at sunrise was useful; the kookaburra was widely called the clock-bird, the settler's clock, the shepherd's clock, cocky's clock and bushmen's clock. Indeed, it was not often called a kookaburra, the term 'laughing jackass' being preferred.

By the 1880s house clocks, whose two hands were visible from every corner of the kitchen, had become cheaper. They ticked away in nearly every Australian house, as distinct from every hut. The whole way of life was bowing to the command of the clock. The drover's wife, the hero of the short story by Henry Lawson, lived in an outback house of a mere two rooms made of rough-hewn timber, and yet she possessed a clock.

In John Longstaff's fine painting *Breaking the News* – now in Perth's Art Gallery – we see a goldminer's wife preparing the evening meal. Crockery is set on the table, and a rocking chair stands by the wood stove in readiness for the weary husband. The handsome family clock ticks away on the mantelpiece. But there, at the doorway, miners can be seen, carrying a stretcher or flat door on which lies a corpse. Her husband, unknown to her, has just been killed in the mine. The clock on the mantelpiece points to five o'clock, the hour when most miners began their evening meal. John Longstaff came from the goldmining town of Clunes and he knew that mining – in the period that his painting depicted – was one of the few industries in which the hours of work were regulated closely by the clock. He highlighted the drama by bringing home the corpse at the very hour when the husband was expected home, alive.

The personal watch was less common than the household clock. Thus one of the items of casual conversation, in addition to the weather, was the time: 'Have you got the time, Missus?' a caller would say at the back door. 'What o'clock is it?' another would ask, along the road. Most people who wished to know the time of day simply looked at the sun and estimated how far it had run its course.

A Pocket Watch that Chimed

In 1860 only the wealthier people owned pocket watches, and a few owned a gold repeater watch, which was capable of playing chimes on the hour. The advantage of a repeater watch was that – in the era before a phosphorescent or illuminated watch face – its owner could ascertain the time in the hours of darkness. He merely pulled the string which allowed the watch to chime prematurely. So the owner, by counting the chimes, could roughly tell the time. Safety matches and electric light were to make repeating watches superfluous.

Men who had enjoyed luck on the gold diggings saw merit in buying a watch. It was an easy way to carry wealth and a pleasing way of displaying success. Such pocket watches, how-ever, were prized by the bushrangers. In the 1860s Dan Morgan confiscated a watch from the son of a pastoralist, and on the present-day Hume Highway he stole a watch from a bullock teamster returning from the Ovens goldfields. Ned Kelly and his gang stole watches, including one from the bank manager at Euroa.

Today a watch is nearly always a wristwatch, but then it was a pocket watch. Attached to a chain in a pocket or waistcoat, it was handled with care. At night, for the sake of safety, it was placed under a pillow or hung up near a bed. The typical watch was worked by a spring – a clock was worked by a pendulum – and had to be wound up carefully once a day. When withdrawn from the waistcoat, the watch did not reveal the time until the owner had opened the lid to reveal the clock hands. There was thus a certain amount of ceremony and pomp associated with the telling of the time. Likewise at a meeting, a business-man or politician, worried that time was being wasted, would silently reveal his concern by taking his watch from his pocket and opening it. A protest became more visible if the protester held up his watch and shook it, as if to say that his watch must have stopped.

Pocket watches soon ceased to be rare. One of the Afghan camel drivers who crossed arid country with Ernest Giles in 1875 dressed himself in fine satins and silks on reaching Perth, and displayed a silver watch in each pocket of his tunic. By 1890 an American watch could be bought for less than two days' pay. While a workingman might ponder for weeks on whether to spend his hard-earned money on a watch, he was likely, when he did make up his mind, to buy the cheap Waterbury watch. Its parts were mass-produced and therefore could easily be replaced by watchmakers.

One Adelaide watchmaker, in his advertisements of 1891, proclaimed the revolution in daily time-keeping. Fifty years ago, he said, only a rich man could afford a watch but now 'a timekeeper of some sort is positively indispensible' for every man. Very cheap watches, however, were unreliable. The cheap watch – later called 'a two-bob watch' – was to become the very symbol of unreliability.

Wristwatches, as distinct from pocket watches, were rare. Mrs Abraham Lincoln wore a watch on her wrist – perhaps a statement of fashion – at the inauguration of her husband as president of the United States in 1861; and twenty years later, wristwatches were common among women of fashion. A wristwatch, like a cigarette, was still primarily for women; and a young Australian voyaging to England in 1907 was astonished to see a red-headed Englishman with a watch on his wrist. In the First World War many Australian soldiers wore a wristwatch. Its advantage was increased when the luminous dial became common. It could be now consulted in the middle of the night, in complete darkness. The era would come when the watch did not have to be wound up every day, and so the large winding knob could be dispensed with.

Towards the end of the century the measuring of time was becoming sophisticated. Spectators examining new wares at the trade display at Melbourne's Exhibition Building in 1888 noticed a Bristol machine made for the specific purpose of clocking the arrival and departure times of workmen at factories and shops. By 1900, some of the older tradesmen who had begun life without a clock were now being awakened each morning by their own alarm clock.

In big factories the punching of the clock by employees at the start and end of the day's work was seen as a way of enforcing punctuality, but the owner did not always gain. Men now made sure that they dropped their tools punctually instead of staying on and completing a job. Furthermore trade unions opposed this impersonal way of treating employees. In the railway workshops in New South Wales in 1917, the workmen went on strike when punch cards were introduced, and the strike, lasting for eighty-two days, eventually dislocated the state.

That Australia legislated for the hours of labour of many people in the era spanning 1855 to 1890 was a sign that clocks were becoming plentiful. Any law calling for an eight-hour or ten-hour day was abortive if the employers and employees did not know the time of day. After all, it was not sufficient that the employer possessed a watch. The employee also had to possess a watch, or be within sight of a public clock. If a workman was to be paid so many pence an hour, he had to be able to measure the hour as carefully as he counted the shillings in his pay.

Timing is now a vital part of sport, but it was more a curiosity in the 1860s. The winning time of a race might be recorded, but only to the nearest second. Fractions of a second do not appear in the winning times of most athletic events. The winning times of horses in the Melbourne Cup were recorded to the nearest second until 1872, when The Quack's time was officially recorded as three minutes, thirty-nine and three-quarter seconds. In the Sydney Cup, also a distance of 2 miles, the winner's time in 1872 was also recorded to the nearest three-quarters of a second. To time the winner of an important race down to a fraction of a second does not mean that any clocks were really that accurate. Possibly the timekeeper signified that the winning time was roughly halfway between the half-second mark and the second mark on his dial. In 1877 the winner was timed down to two tenths of a second, as were the winners in four of the following five years. This fine timing might have been an average derived from two watches which measured less precisely. But the fact that it was recorded so often suggests that a very accurate clock was employed. In 1877 the Melbourne watchmaker and jeweller, Thomas Gaunt, designed a fine clock which was installed in a tower at the Flemington racecourse.

The footrace that was to become the most celebrated in the land was first staged at the Victorian gold town of Stawell in 1878, and the winning time for the course of 130 yards was given as twelve and three-quarter seconds. Next year, with astonishing precision, the winner's time in the Stawell Gift was recorded as twelve and seven-eighth seconds. Another eleven years passed before the winner's time was again recorded to the nearest eighth of a second, which makes one suspect that the winner's time back in 1879 had been a compromise between two watches, one of which recorded thirteen seconds and the other twelve and three-quarter seconds. In the period between

The Melbourne Cup was a mirror of the increasing precision of clocks. The winner's time had previously been measured in seconds or half seconds, but soon the tiny fraction of a second could be accurately measured.

1903 and 1914, when watches were more uniform and more accurate, the winner's time was always recorded to the nearest one fifth of a second. At successive Olympic Games, the keeping of time became more sophisticated, and by the 1920s the winner's time was recorded to the nearest one tenth of a second. It would be timed to a one hundredth of a second in the 1950s when the electronic clock arrived.

Most traditional British games had been invented before the ownership of clocks became widespread. Thus in Australia in 1860 there was probably no category of sport that, like present-day soccer or rugby, was played in two equal halves. Such sports would have required the presence of a widely trusted clock or watch at every ground; and this was unlikely. Australian Rules football, an innovation of the late 1850s, did not originate as a game played in four equal quarters or even two equal halves. In the early matches, played over Melbourne park-lands, the teams changed ends only after a goal had been kicked: but a goal was not often scored. In 1870 it was agreed that each match of Australian Rules should be divided into equal halves, and fifteen years later it was divided into equal quarters. The pocket watch made possible these vital changes in the game's rules. Today in soccer the referee is still the keeper of the time, but in Australian Rules there have long been specialist timekeepers, one from each team, and a sophisticated way of measuring time.

Graeme Davison, in his masterly study of time, *The Unforgiving Minute*, notes that the attitude to time was one of the profound changes of the second half of the nineteenth century.

It happened so imperceptibly that it was not always noticed, even by people who were becoming enchained to their new watches. The clock replaced sunrise and sunset as the rough regulator of working hours; it began to flavour the reporting of events in the newspapers, giving them a new precision. Moreover all kinds of events and meetings were now arranged not for the hour but for the quarter-hour.

As the ticking of the clock was heard in more walks of life, scientists and surveyors tried to devise a common or standard time. Back in 1850 every region in Australia had followed its own time. I must confess that even after three decades of practice as a historian I did not know that each locality in Australia at one period kept a different time on its clocks. A hint of my ignorance came to me suddenly in the late 1970s, when, visiting the Greenwich Observatory near London, I saw a strange old timepiece which recorded not only London time but the time of several other English towns. Suddenly I realised that there was no national time in England in the early railway era.

Greenwich time was observed only in Greenwich and in those places due north, and even they did not call it Greenwich time: it was their time. Local time was the 'standard time', and there were as many local times as there were localities. The clock of every village church showed a different time. Local time – or rather the multiplicity of local times – held one clear advantage. In an era of inaccurate clocks it was possible, when the fixed stars were visible or when the sun was visible at noon, to determine and check the local time.

When the railways began to link the large cities of England, train travellers found the multitude of local times confusing. The first railway timetables were printed in England in 1839, and they showed in separate columns the local time and London time for each town along the route. Watchmakers in England issued, with new watches, a leaflet showing the differences in time between the main cities of the British Isles. A few clock-makers began to construct clocks that showed on the one clock face the different times of two or more cities.

The Quarrelling Clocks

In a country as small as Britain it was sensible to adopt one standard time, and by the 1850s the railways were adopting Greenwich time in place of local time. This initially created confusion, because each town now had railways time as well as local time. Finally, in 1880 Greenwich Mean Time – or railway time – became legal in Great Britain. Meanwhile in the United States, each separate private railway tended to adopt its own time for its own route, and so big railway junctions suffered chaos, with trains of each company departing according to different clocks. At St Louis the converging railways used six different times, and at Chicago three different clocks were followed, according to the platform.

In Australia each town in 1850 fixed its own time – according to the exact minute when the sun was directly over-head. As there were no railways, and as the coastal ships moved slowly, the multiplicity of local times created few problems.

Even towns within walking distance of each other followed a different clock. When it was noon in Sydney it was already two minutes past noon in Newcastle. In each of the following towns and cities the official clock lagged behind Sydney's time by a different number of minutes:

Hobart	16	Adelaide	50
Townsville	17	Port Pirie	53
Launceston	17	Port Augusta	54
Cooktown	24	Albany	133
Deniliquin	24	Perth	141
Melbourne	25	London	605
Portland	39		

In the late 1850s the opening of the first telegraph lines and railways made desirable a standard time that could be applied to the populous parts of each colony. Moreover the new telegraph was the ideal instrument for enabling each town regularly to set its clocks by the time of the capital city. Soon each capital city, at one o'clock on every weekday, sent a time signal along the telegraph lines, allowing each telegraph office to correct its clock. In Victoria the rule was strict: at three minutes to one o'clock, every telegraph operator had to cease tapping messages and leave the line clear for the transmitting of the time signal. The clock inside the post and telegraph office was thus the master clock for each town. Bankers, merchants, owners of mail coaches, clergymen, schoolmasters and all those who increasingly were expected to have an accurate knowledge of the time, could call periodically at the telegraph office and check whether their watch was reasonably accurate. For many of them an error of only five minutes did not matter: an hour did.

Even when schooling was becoming compulsory, and the schools had to open and close at a set hour, most teachers probably did not pay close attention to the clock. In January 1877 the inspector who supervised some 150 schools in the Ararat district in Victoria complained that many schools attended by farmers' children opened at arbitrary times. He noted, stern and punctilious man that he was, that the difference in time between two schools not far apart was often much larger 'than is warranted by the difference in longitude'. His comment suggests that local time was still kept in many rural districts.

Now that each colony had its own time, a written table (see below) was carried by businessmen who, travelling often, wished to know the exact time prevailing in each capital city:

CLOCKS OF THE COLONIES

When it is midday in Queensland, the time elsewhere is:

	Hours	Minutes	Seconds
NSW	11	52	43.1
Vic	11	27	47.7
Tas	11	37	13.5
SA & its NT	11	2	13.9
WA	9	31	

At every border town in Australia the clocks of travellers had to be adjusted. Thus those going from Albury to Wodonga had to put the watch back by almost twenty-five minutes. Travellers on the main railway between New South Wales and the Queensland border had to adjust their watch by seven minutes and seventeen seconds. Inside the mining town of Broken Hill, time was chaotic. Its residents set their clocks to local time. Its railway station, being linked only to South Australia, followed Adelaide time. The post and telegraph office, being an instrumentality of the New South Wales government, followed Sydney time. In Broken Hill the clock at the stately post office was always fifty minutes ahead of the clock at the railway station.

At last, time reformers began to raise their voices. They complained that Australia followed too many different times. Sir Charles Todd, who more than any man was responsible for building the overland telegraph linking Adelaide and Darwin to the outside world, believed that all clocks in Australia should keep the same time. Even Perth should adhere to the same time as Brisbane. As a South Australian he preferred Adelaide time as national time but was not dogmatic. In contrast most of the other reformers – especially those postal and railway officials who handled intercolonial traffic – saw merit in dividing Australia into those three time zones which make up the present-day Eastern, Central and Western time zones. This proposal was furthered by the bold attempt in the United States in 1883 to simplify its multitude of times. It agreed on four simple time zones, each one hour apart.

A serious attempt to create Australian time zones emerged from a meeting held at the Customs House in Melbourne in November 1892. At the suggestion of A. C. Gregory, a former explorer who served as surveyor-general of Queensland, the conference voted to introduce three time zones into Australia. Postal officials took up the campaign. Colonial premiers by 1894 were also in favour and each colony prepared the necessary laws.

A few politicians opposed the change. F. S. Grimwade, a Victorian politician and manufacturer, thought a bureaucratic thief was about to arrive and steal the people's time, throwing the rhythm of their days into chaos. He told the legislative council that he would not tolerate such a revolution in daily life. 'If a man', he argued, 'wanted breakfast at eight o'clock in the morning, as had been his habit, he would not get it until twenty minutes past eight.' Interjecting during the debate, he lamented that henceforth in Victoria 'people will be getting up at the wrong time every day'. Attempts to explain to him that he was perhaps the victim of his own confusion met with indignation. He was quick to remind his listeners that local railway passengers would be perplexed on the night when the clocks were altered. He pointed out that trains were scheduled normally to leave Flinders Street Station at five minutes and ten minutes past midnight. But 'if the clock, at the stroke of twelve, was altered to twenty minutes past twelve, what became of those two trains? How could passengers travel by them?'

On 1 January 1895 Queensland changed its clocks in order to adopt the new Eastern Standard Time. At midnight on Sunday 1 February, New South Wales put back its clock by about five minutes and Victoria put forward its clocks by about twenty minutes – or twenty minutes and six seconds, to be exact. To conform to the new time, Tasmania made a correction of eleven minutes. Now all districts in eastern Australia shared the time of day, and people travelling in the steamships between Hobart and Brisbane or on the new railways along the eastern coast no longer had to alter their clocks whenever they entered a new colony. South Australia and its Northern Territory continued to set their own distinctive time, except that Adelaide was now one hour, instead of twenty-five minutes, behind

At Albury railway station, passengers not only changed trains but changed time. Eastern standard time did not arrive until 1895.

Melbourne. In 1898 South Australia adopted its present time.

The concept of punctuality was increasing in importance but even in 1900 it was widely ignored. The priest driving his horse and gig sometimes arrived twenty minutes late at the rural church, and umpires arrived late at the football or cricket ground – or one of the teams arrived late. There was no thought of disqualifying the late team. Even steamships following a timetable could be held up by a strong wind or the train could be delayed by a cow standing on the line. The ever-present clock could guide: it could not yet command.

The Power of Sunday

In the era when many people lived isolated lives far out in the interior, they had more trouble knowing the day of the week than the time of day. As the work of every day except Sunday was the same, they could easily miss counting a day. Accordingly, primitive calendars were devised. One shepherd, living on his own for thirty years, used to take a piece of charcoal from his camp ashes and make a stroke on a piece of clean wooden board each day. When he had made six black strokes on the board he knew that the following day was Sunday. On Monday he cleaned the board so that he could begin counting the days again.

Another man kept two empty jam tins and labelled one 'This Week' and the other 'Last Week'. Each week commenced with seven pebbles resting in the tin called 'Last Week', and each day he would transfer one pebble into the other tin. The transfer of the seventh pebble marked Sunday. It seems quaint that people living in remote places could forget the day of the week, but even today, even in cities, such forgetfulness is known to occur.

Sunday was the distinctive day of the week. In 1850 it was the only regular holiday for Australians, whether convicts or free citizens. Fifty years later maybe three quarters of the workforce worked on every single weekday, though large and increasing numbers had a holiday on Saturday afternoon. Sunday was *the* day of rest.

England and Scotland, more than almost any other part of Europe, treated Sunday as a holy day; and the attitude landed here. In Australia almost every shop was closed on Sunday. In most of the cities the sporting events, unless held on private grounds, were banned on Sundays. The theatres were closed, and debate raged on the question of whether art galleries and museums should also be closed. The tendency was for Sundays to be regulated more closely as the century went on.

Hotels could serve drink on Sundays only to people who were designated, by the standards of the time, as long-distance travellers in need of refreshment. A ship about to leave for foreign ports did not sail on Sunday, except in rare circumstances. Real estate could not be sold on Sunday. Country trains were restricted on Sundays. In most colonies the publishing of newspapers on Sundays was banned, and indeed Melbourne, the federal capital from 1901 to 1927, must have been one of the few capital cities in the world to deny itself a Sunday newspaper.

South Australia and Victoria were the bastions of this Old Testament rule that the Sabbath should be honoured. In tens of thousands of families, all children's toys were put away on Saturday evening. In a host of houses, as little cooking as possible was done on the Sunday, and only certain kinds of books could be read on that day. A host of citizens refused to travel on public transport on Sunday. In Victoria there was an outcry when the governor made an unnecessary journey on a Sunday. While most religious leaders wanted a sober and contemplative Sunday, many other people thought that Sunday was the ideal day – indeed, for many it was the only day – to ride in the trams or the ferries, to stroll in the park, saunter along the esplanade, or enjoy a picnic.

In a large city, each Sunday morning had a special feeling. A hushed silence lingered. The hooves of few horses and iron wheels were heard in the streets. The street vendors were silent. No wood was chopped in the backyards. Shops were closed. By mid-morning the church bells were ringing, and families were walking to church. But Sunday afternoon was not so quiet. Even in Sabbath-abiding Adelaide in the 1880s a bright young journalist observed how the suburban streets came to life on a sunny Sunday afternoon: 'All the world and his wife in private carriages and buggies, carts and omnibuses, even on Shanks's pony, come away for an airing.' Sunday was a time for wearing the best clothes, and women especially liked Sunday.

Respect for the sanctity of Sunday was not merely a spiritual respect. It was widely accepted that a day on which no work could be demanded of an employee was a special privilege for a breadwinner who had worked energetically during the week. The principle of Sabbath observance is now looked back upon as an infringement of personal liberty – a denial of the right of people to do what they wished on a Sunday. The old-time Australian Sunday is understandably looked back upon, in Nellie Melba's exaggerated phrase, 'as a day of gloom and solemnity, in which no one might smile or hum a tune'. But at one time a host of people, including many trade unionists, saw the puritanical Sunday as a freedom, a respite from daily work that was much more demanding, physically, than the typical job of today. Moreover unionists and workers accepted that the day of rest had been won and upheld for them by the churches. The coming of the secular or Continental Sunday, especially from the 1950s onwards, reflected the churches' declining influence and also hastened that decline.

Meanwhile the Jews in Australia, as in many other lands for thousands of years, celebrated their own Sabbath. Busy in commerce, and often their own employers, they closed their shops on Saturday so they could attend synagogues. They printed their own annual calendars, because their counting of the years began some 3800 years before the time of Christ. In Hobart in 1853, and in other large towns, a locally printed Jewish booklet setting out the 'Days and Nights, Sabbaths and New Moons, Seasons, Holydays, and Fasts' could be purchased.

Another curiosity of the nineteenth-century calendar has been virtually forgotten. Nowadays the start of summer is usually accepted as the first day of December, and the start of winter as the first of June. It was not always so. Summer and winter each officially commenced three weeks later than now, according to early Australian calendars. Summer officially began with the year's longest day, and winter officially began with the shortest day. The other two seasons began at the equinoxes, when day and night were of equal length. Thus in 1859 the autumn in Tasmania began around 22 March and the spring began on 23 September: indeed, spring began at 6.14 p.m., according to the Tasmanian calendar printed for that year by William Fairfax in his *Handbook to Australasia*.

This precise dating of the four seasons had arrived with the settlers from Britain, but was inappropriate for Australia where in December the summer and harvest were far advanced by English standards. Many of the Australian wheat farmers had already harvested their wheat before that day when summer was formally declared open.

Sovereigns and Half-sovereigns

In 1850 Australia's major coin was the gold sovereign. It was equal in value to one English pound or 20 shillings. First minted in England in 1817, it replaced the gold guinea, which was worth 21 shillings or 5 per cent more. After the guinea ceased to be a separate coin, the word continued to be used in Australia until just beyond the first half of the twentieth century. Barristers set their fees in guineas. Doctors did not charge their patients 1 pound: they charged them 1 guinea. Private schools set their term fees at so many guineas. In city frock shops the dresses and hats of distinction were priced in guineas. The guinea conveyed a touch of class.

The specifications for the gold sovereign and half-sovereign were unchanging. The amount of gold in each sovereign was exactly weighed, right down to the weight of a strand of human hair. Each sovereign contained 123 grains of gold – imperial grains by troy weight. To be exact – and the master of the mint was nothing but exact – each sovereign contained 123.27447 grains. The half-sovereign contained exactly half that amount of gold, all weighed to the fifth decimal point. The sovereign was not just a coin: it was a storehouse of physical wealth. It appeared small but when held in the hand it was surprisingly heavy.

At first, nearly all the gold coins came out from the British Isles. They arrived in passengers' purses and luggage, and in the strongrooms of ships. But as soon as gold was being mined here on a large scale, the case for establishing a mint in Australia was overwhelming. Here was one of the world's great miners of gold, forced to send its own freshly mined gold on the long voyage to London. Having been minted into coins, it was shipped back to Australia. The insurance alone on this global transaction was high. So the Sydney Mint, a branch of the Royal Mint, was opened in April 1855.

Those who wished their gold to be turned into coins paid to the Sydney Mint a fee of less than 1 per cent of the value of the gold, and in return they received shining gold coins. Soon the Sydney sovereigns were circulating in Hong Kong, Ceylon and Mauritius. For two years Victoria tried to ban the sovereigns minted in Sydney on the grounds that the new mint should have been built in Melbourne. Eventually the Australian sovereigns circulated everywhere. Melbourne finally opened its own mint in 1872. Sydney and Melbourne each minted more sovereigns annually than did the mother of mints in London. In 1899, when the gold finds in Western Australia were spectacular, Perth opened its own mint. There, in a mesmerising spectacle, you can still see molten gold being poured.

The gold sovereign had a status and magic that no circulating coin and banknote possesses today. Elegant in design, bright when freshly minted, and almost lovable when cupped in the hand, it also was an ideal gift. When people were farewelled upon leaving their town or their profession, they were handed, when the speeches were over, a purse of sovereigns. The gift seemed just right. In contrast, to hand over a cheque as a farewell present seemed tasteless. Naturally, the best turf clubs announced that the prize for an important horse race would be 500 or 1000 gold sovereigns.

Most children boarding a country train carried only copper and small silver coins in their purses. A banknote was a rare possession.

The status of the sovereign reflected the fact that gold was the anchor of the financial system. If customers wished to withdraw their money from a bank, they were legally entitled to take out that money entirely in gold sovereigns. Whenever there was anxiety about the solvency of a bank, jittery customers would nervously appear at its door, take out their money in gold coins, go home, draw the curtains, and hide the coins. Thus in the autumn of 1885, when Britain and Russia were competing for influence in Afghanistan, and there were rumours that they might go to war and that the Russians might even raid Australian ports, some local depositors – especially elderly women – withdrew sovereigns from the local branches of the National Bank. Once the financial scare had passed, they redeposited their gold coins in the bank as if nothing had happened.

In shops the banknote was seen more often than gold coins. Each bank printed its own notes. Only in the rarest circumstances – South Australia in the early 1850s was an exception – did a government print banknotes. The public trusted these private banknotes and used them freely. Generally a banknote or cheque was more convenient, being hidden easily in the pocket or clothing, and so was preferred.

Never were banknotes so welcome as in the gold rushes of the 1850s. To the diggers the banknote was light and portable. A large sum of money in notes could be carried, rolled up and out of sight, or even sewn into the lining of a coat or trousers. A similar sum, carried in gold sovereigns, would have been heavy, and might attract the attention of potential robbers if the coins jingled noisily. Many banknotes became greasy, torn or tattered through rough handling. A few showed the stains of clay from mining shafts or soot from bush fireplaces. Curiously, in Victoria the peak circulation of these private banknotes was not in 1900, when the population was large, but back in 1859.

Each bank printed its notes in inks of different colours, in the basement of its head office. The paper, of high quality, carried a distinctive watermark so that forging of notes was difficult. Over time the notes became prettier and more elegant. Thus the National Bank's notes for Victoria showed a handsome woman holding a long-tailed lamb, its South Australian notes depicted a girl with grapes in her hair and a sheaf of wheat resting on her shoulders, while its early Western Australian notes depicted a stouter girl, with her hands resting on the head of an axe. The west in 1870 was still in its pioneering stage, as the axe-girl proclaimed.

Since a pound note was a firm promise by the bank to pay a gold coin to the person who handed it over, any note accidentally lost constituted sheer profit for the bank. Each year, thousands of Australian banknotes were lost. Men were drowned in swollen rivers with notes in their pocket, fires burnt down diggers' huts and houses where notes were hidden away, or passengers accidentally allowed a note to slip into the sea as they walked on deck. Of course the owners of these lost notes got no compensation. The inconvenience for the bank was that it had to make allowance for lost notes in its half-yearly balance sheet – just in case they were still in existence. Later the banks also had to pay a small tax on each of their notes in circulation.

Experienced bushrangers hoped that a bank, on the day

they robbed it, would hold more banknotes than coins. It was easy to make a quick getaway on horseback if heavy coins did not predominate. When Ned Kelly robbed the bank at Euroa in 1878 he needed a large sugar bag to carry away the gold and silver coins and banknotes. Again, when Ned robbed the bank at Jerilderie he used a sugar bag – it was the cheap kitbag of that era.

A defect of banknotes was that they could not be used nationwide. They were usually treated as currency only in the colony where they had been printed. Elsewhere a fee had to be paid, almost as if the note was the currency of a foreign land. B. A. Heywood, who visited Australia for the sake of his health in 1861, noted that even a Bank of England note which he carried from London incurred 'a heavy rate of exchange' when cashed in Australia.

Coins in the Hat

In Bourke lived a tall young man, bursting with generosity, usually grinning disarmingly, and often taking around his hat – a big cabbage tree hat – and collecting donations in the various hotels for someone in need. Known as The Giraffe, he was the inspiration for Henry Lawson's captivating story, 'Send Round the Hat'. Today it is not easy to understand parts of that story without appreciating the coinage of the 1890s. Sometimes a pound note or a half-sovereign was dropped by a well-wisher into The Giraffe's hat, but a host of lesser coins were also tossed in – coins so heavy that the hollow of the hat was almost worn out. The hat had been handed around for so many years 'that the crown was worn as thin as paper by the quids, half-quids, casers, half-casers, bobs and tanners or sprats – to say nothing of the scrums – that had been chucked into it in its time and shaken up'.

The story makes sense when one realises that the quid and half-quid were either banknotes or gold coins. The silver crown or 'caser' was worth five shillings, followed by the half-crown or half-caser. The names half-crown or half-caser – shorthand for two shillings and sixpence – were common in everyday speech long after that coin had ceased to be minted. When G. J. Coles, just before the First World War, opened his first low-price emporium in Smith Street in Collingwood, his slogan was 'Nothing Over Two and Six'.

After the crown and half-crown, in order of value, came the florin, which was worth two shillings. That coin was identical in size but not in value to today's twenty-cent piece. Then came the lesser silver coins – the 'bob' or 'deener', which was worth one shilling; the sixpenny coin, called a 'zac' or a 'tanner'; and the tiny threepenny coin, known colloquially as a tray, tray-bit, scrum, or thrum. Nearly all were British slang names: indeed, the 'deener' probably went back to the Roman coin, the *dinarius*.

The humblest coins were the penny and halfpenny. (The farthing or quarter penny, widely used in Britain, was useless in Australia after 1851.) Commonly known as 'coppers', these coins consisted of tin and bronze. They were rarely seen in Australian shops in the years between about 1852 and maybe 1858. In any case the inflation of prices was so high that one penny purchased almost nothing. It was normal for shop-keepers to give small change to customers in the form of a box of matches, priced at three pence, or a cheap cigar priced at one penny. Some shopkeepers began to make their own bronze tokens and hand them as small change to the customers. Perhaps there were 400 different kinds of such tokens in the pockets and purses of the people. They were so widely accepted that maybe three quarters of the total of copper coins in circulation in 1863 consisted of homemade tokens.

The teenage son of the bestselling author Samuel Smiles came to Victoria for the sake of his health, and in the late 1860s he worked briefly as a bank clerk in the prosperous gold town of Majorca. He recalled that rarely did he see copper coins in the course of his daily handling of money: 'I never had any copper in my pocket, except only a lucky farthing. Many asked me for it, to keep as a curiosity, saying they had never seen one since they left home.' In a typical day at the bank, the threepenny piece was the humblest coin he saw.

At times silver coins were also scarce. Dinted and defaced by intent or by accident, many were in use long after they should have been withdrawn from circulation. Tens of thousands were worn so smooth that the face of the monarch could no longer be seen. At last, in 1872, Britain began to supply Australia with new silver coins, even paying the cost of shipping them. In return the two mints in Australia served as collecting agencies for worn-out coins, which they sent to England to be melted down.

When the Banks Closed Down

The country was to pay a high penalty for its neglect of one aspect of money. The leading businessmen and politicians had long assured each other that the banking system was exceptionally safe: but a sparsely regulated banking system can never be entirely safe. Between 1875 and 1890 a few smaller banks did fail but none of the ten or so largest banks seemed endangered. But danger was there, especially when the economy sagged in the early 1890s. In April and May 1893 – months of severe depression – more and more nervous customers demanded their money in gold. The panic increased: at the doors of several Victorian banks small crowds jostled for admission. In danger of exhausting their supply of gold, and unable to import gold with the necessary speed, banks began to close their doors temporarily and reconstruct themselves.

The financial panic dinted public confidence in banks and in paper money. Banknotes were not completely trusted, though the notes issued by most banks were perfectly safe. In Queensland the government taxed the private banknotes out of existence and issued its own notes, calling them treasury notes. Guaranteed by the government, they soon became the only notes in Queensland's purses and pockets. An early £1 Queensland note eventually became a collector's item: one such note was sold for more than $200 000 in 2002.

After the creation of the Commonwealth government in 1901 it was only a matter of time before a common currency was imposed on the six different colonies. At last, in 1910, the

Commonwealth's treasury was given a monopoly on the issuing of notes. At first it borrowed notes from the old banks and simply printed over them. In 1913 it issued its own freshly designed banknotes. In every town, in every hotel bar, church meeting room and post office around Australia, the notes were a talking point because they were smaller than the traditional notes and less ornate. Their usefulness was increased because they now included a new ten-shilling note – the equal of the gold half-sovereign. At the other end of the scale the most valuable of the new notes was almost astronomical in price. It was worth 100 pounds, which was equal to some four months' take-home pay for a skilled labourer.

Gold coins were slipping out of sight. Customers no longer had a right to appear at the counter of their bank and withdraw their money in gold coins. At least they could call at the office of the treasury in Melbourne, the temporary national capital, and personally hand over new Commonwealth notes in return for gold coins. That right was soon withdrawn. The outbreak of war in 1914 further cut the role of gold coins. Soon they were curiosities and ornaments, hung on watch chains or necklaces.

Saving the Threepences

Savings banks, as distinct from trading banks, had been founded to help the poor acquire what was described as the useful 'habits of economy, industry and matrimony'. They failed to attract the savings of poor people. The first such bank, founded in Sydney in 1819, would not accept very small sums. Melbourne's first savings bank was open for only a few hours in each week. Many people who did save money concealed it in their own home. Gold coins were hidden under a floorboard or in a small cavity in the chimney: a mattress was another hiding place. If the house burned down, the gold would survive.

Maybe half of Australian families, as late as 1900, did not have an account in any kind of bank. Other institutions were the havens for money they saved. Indirectly, trade unions were savings societies, for they collected fortnightly or monthly payments from members, and used part of that money to provide social security. Also vital in the fostering of savings were life assurance offices such as the AMP Society and Colonial Mutual, and friendly societies such as the Australian Natives Association, Hibernians, Manchester Unity and IOOF. These offices helped families who otherwise would be unable to pay for the funeral if a relative died suddenly. A pauper's funeral was the ultimate in humiliation.

In the 1880s a few life offices made positive steps to encourage weekly savings. Their agents came to the back door at the same hour each week and collected the family's sixpence or shilling. By 1914 the AMP Society collected in this way the weekly savings of some 100 000 families. It is possible that this one society, under its various schemes, collected weekly, half-yearly, or annually the savings made by one in every six Australian families.

In some colonies, especially from the 1870s, people could take the money they had recently saved to the local post office.

A sum not less than one shilling could be deposited at any time. Those who wished to withdraw their savings had to give notice to the postmaster. Several days elapsed before the payment would be authorised and the money handed over the counter. When people had to transfer money to friends in a distant town, the post office offered the best and easiest means of doing so. The safe method was to send a money order or a postal note. The stream of postal notes mailed from the goldfields of Western Australia around 1900 propped up the income of thousands of homes in Victoria.

Others preferred to post an actual banknote. To lower the risk of it being stolen in transit, customers were advised by the post office to cut the note in half and send the first half in a letter. When they heard that it had arrived safely they should post the other half of the note.

'Save for a rainy day' was a slogan with which everyone agreed, in theory. The penalty, month by month, for those families who had no savings and who had suddenly lost their sole breadwinner, through injury or prison or death, was harsh. To be down and out in Sydney was almost as miserable as to be down and out in London. There was one exception: it was easier to keep tolerably warm in a Sydney winter.

Much private charity was dispensed by the Protestant, Catholic and Jewish churches. Members of their own congregations tended to receive first priority. Public charities imposed strict rules on those who received food rations and blankets. Curiously, in at least two colonies in the period 1860–1900, it was far easier for an Aborigine than a white person of working age to receive long-term charity from the government. However, nearly all charity had strings attached to it, and for Aborigines the strings were extremely restrictive.

In 1901, a revolutionary step – an old-age pension – was made available to a few thousand Australians. The wisdom of inaugurating such a pension was debated excitedly in public houses and general stores as well as in parliaments. Working people who had tried to save money all their life, and succeeded a little, were not eligible for a pension whereas their less frugal friends were eligible. In short the new pension, it was argued, was a long-term deterrent to saving and to self-help. On the other hand, the supporters of the pension argued that a nation had a duty to help those who, through their own fault or through forces beyond their control, lacked money to cope with old age. They argued that a welfare society would build social cohesion and foster fairness. Truth probably sided with both arguments.

At first those who collected the old-age pension were few, partly because few people lived to the age of sixty-five. The pensioners were also few because Victoria and New South Wales, which inaugurated the schemes, excluded a wide category of old people. Pensioners had to be poor. They also had to be long-time residents of their state; naturalised citizens; and of sound moral character, with no conspicuous record of crime and no record of having deserted wife or husband. The early pensions were not a right but were declared to be the repayment of a public debt to those citizens who 'during the prime of life, have helped to bear the public burdens of the colony by the payment of taxes and by opening up its resources by their labour and skill'. In 1909, the Commonwealth set up its own careful scheme to extend old-age pensions to every part of the country.

The movement towards a welfare state in Australia ran powerfully until 1914, but the outbreak of the First World War slowed its momentum. The war effort was expensive, and funds were needed to support the casualties of war. Much of this money might otherwise have expanded general social welfare. The war also inflated the price of nearly all goods and accentuated industrial conflict. So this long period ended as it had begun, with strain and signs of economic chaos. Whereas the strains of the initial years of the gold rush were tempered by high optimism, there was far less optimism in 1918.

PART TWO

The Black Kettle Sings

7

THE FULL TASTE OF MEAT

Some history books suggest that visitors a century ago were surprised the most by Australia's radical politics, particularly the secret ballot and the vote for most men. Visitors, however, were surprised less by the vote than by the meat. That every man could vote was interesting. That nearly every man and woman could eat meat at nearly every meal was astonishing.

In the history of England and France many of the notable riots were spurred by a dramatic rise in the price of bread, but in Australia in the half-century after the first gold rushes a food riot on even a minor scale was rare and it was more likely to be a meat than a bread riot. At the north Queensland town of Charters Towers in November 1872, miners who were protesting at the expense of beef actually tied ropes to the flimsy butcher's shop and pulled it to the ground.

The butcher's was one of the most common shops in Australia. Even a crossroads township with little more than a general store, blacksmith, school and post office was likely to have its own butcher. As supermarkets were unknown and as a delicatessen was a rarity, the butcher virtually had a monopoly on the sale of fresh meat. The typical small-town butcher killed his own meat, sometimes in a yard at the back of his shop or in a wooden slaughterhouse just out of town. As he had no ice and no refrigeration, the meat was quick to deteriorate in sizzling weather; and when the butcher's boy drove his horse and cart to the houses of customers he sometimes found that the meat was beginning to smell by the end of his delivery round. In a burst of hot weather the outside of the meat turned black, but many butchers believed that this meat was the tastiest.

During a heatwave the danger to meat was highest, and a butcher requiring a fresh supply would try not to slaughter his sheep and cattle until late in the evening when the day's temperature had fallen and meat was more likely to last. It was accepted that in summer the meat of a cow lasted longer than that of a bullock. In summer the meat might last three days: in winter, when nature supplied the refrigeration, it normally lasted about ten days.

Hundreds of butchers hung their meat on hooks in the open air. Flywire was not common, though an expensive, heavy meat safe could be made from sheets of perforated zinc. Refrigeration in a typical butcher's shop was still unknown as late as 1900; maggots were to be found occasionally in most shops. Moreover the meat when it arrived from the suburban slaughterhouse might be already flawed. W. Tyson Kendall, a young Lancashire veterinary surgeon, called at Melbourne in 1880 on his way to New Zealand and, learning that there were only four other vets in the city, decided to stay. He was surprised to find that at some of the suburban abattoirs one in every four head of cattle had tuberculosis. From time to time the cattle whose meat was chopped into pieces on the wooden block in the butcher's shop had fluke, hydatids and even cancer. The mutton, pork and beef that was the produce of infected livestock easily found its way into the shops. Anthrax, then called Cumberland disease, had appeared occasionally in herds of cattle. It was first reported near Sydney in the 1840s and made a dramatic reappearance half a century later near Geelong where a dairy herd, so Kendall suspected, had been fed with meal ground from bones imported from India.

Meat – a Way of Life

As Australia possessed more sheep than any other nation, it is easy to assume that mutton was the most popular meat. On sheep stations the mutton was virtually part of the wages. A labourer living in his own hut would usually receive a weekly ration of close to 6 kilograms of mutton, 6 kilograms of flour, and some tea and sugar. For migrants newly arrived from Scotland, one week's supply might represent more meat than they normally ate in half a year at home. At first some migrants wished for other food in place of so large a meat ration, but it was not long before they were contentedly eating three meals of meat each day and boasting of their good fortune in the rare letters they sent home. In the cities the butchers sold both beef and mutton, and by 1890 they were selling far more beef than mutton – except perhaps in Tasmania.

On the small farms, bacon and pork were an alternative to beef and mutton. The day when a pig was to be slaughtered was marked out in advance. The pig was usually given a smart hammer-blow on the forehead before it was killed with a long, slanting thrust of the knife. The removal of hairs from the carcass was a task in itself, calling for buckets of near-boiling water to loosen the tough hairs, and then the slow scraping away of the surface of the skin, often with the aid of the lid of an old billy. The curing of sides of bacon – the prized product – called for patience; and each day for perhaps a week a mixture of salt and dark sugar, with a dash of saltpetre and carbonate of potash, was rubbed into the bacon, with less frequent applications of the mixture in the second week. For the slow smoking of bacon hams, a cloud of thick, cool smoke was preferred. It was accepted that subtle flavour was given to the ham if twigs of ti-tree or melaleuca were added to the fire. Paddy Ryan and Dinny O'Dea and their kinsmen vowed that they cured the best ham and bacon. Maybe only 1 kilogram of pork and bacon was consumed in Australia for every 20 kilograms of other meats, but the homemade bacon that hung from the roof or sat in a box of bran inside kitchens in 1890 did not readily enter official statistics.

In 1890 the average Australian – including man, woman and toothless baby – ate a third of a kilo of meat a day. In Queensland, where official statistics were less reliable, the average person ate half a kilo of meat a day. In the country as a whole the typical family of four required, in the course of one year, the killing of one large bullock and eight small sheep for its own supply of meat. The average Australian ate more than twice as much meat as the average person in England and the United States, four times as much meat as the average German and French diner and – if the Italian statistics are reliable – twelve times as much meat as the average Italian. Here were the great meat eaters of the world. Of course the glut of meat had adverse effects. In 1863 a Melbourne physician, S. Dougan Bird, argued that too many deaths of children, especially children under the age of five, stemmed from 'overstuffing with animal food' and the onset of dysentery or gastric fever.

Meat was more than a food and more than an incessant topic of conversation: it was almost a way of life. To ascertain the name of a reliable butcher was one of the first wishes expressed by a newcomer to a town. Meat was eaten at every meal in many households. Meat was believed to be the vital source of stamina for the workingman who laboured for long hours each day. Accordingly, in those families too large or too poor, most of the meat was placed on the plate of the father in the belief that he would thereby be strengthened and so provide for his family – if not with meat, at least with bread.

It is impossible to appreciate the satisfaction that most Australians derived from plentiful meat without glimpsing the world they had left behind. In Suffolk in the first half of the nineteenth century most meals of farm labourers and their large families consisted mainly of bread and potatoes. When their families grew up, and there were fewer mouths to feed, they had a little money for an occasional meal of meat. But the money they could spare for meat was still not quite enough to justify a visit to the butcher. So families would combine their savings, buy a piece of meat, and share it. The poet Vincent Buckley, writing of families who escaped the mid-century famine in Ireland by emigrating to Australia, learned that fresh meat was one of their welcomes. Here, he wrote, it was their fate 'to forget the saints' wells and the music, and to learn the full taste of meat'. To know the full taste of meat was to be an Australian.

Why was meat eaten in such huge quantities? Part of the answer is that Australia's sweeping grasslands could feed huge herds and flocks. Another part of the answer, not so easily seen, is that distance favoured the eating of meat. Cattle and

Cheap meat could dominate the city menu only because cattle were driven long distances from the outback.

sheep could walk to the inland or coastal towns whereas grain, flour, potatoes and other foods had to be carted in drays at very heavy cost. Meat also tended to be cheap because there was no export market for the surplus cattle or meat. Admittedly, meat could be pickled or salted for export, but it usually acquired a second-rate texture and third-rate taste. Not until the shipping of refrigerated meat to London in 1880 did a large export market arise.

Most Australian butchers, in their aprons (made of leather and not of cotton), earned their money from orthodox cuts of meat. The novelty butcher, by any definition, was a rarity. The newspaper *Australian Israelite* in 1871 ran advertisements from three kosher butchers in Melbourne, but many Jewish families bought their meat and poultry from the ordinary butcher around the corner. Four decades later, few of the families worshipping in the influential St Kilda synagogue bought kosher meat.

Go-ahead butchers went out of their way to make delicacies and smallgoods. James Leggatt, who ran a butchery in Gulgong in the early 1870s, set up tables in the main street each Saturday night and sold joints, calf's heads, trotters, tongues and smallgoods to the miners. In the cities, from a little brazier on the edge of a pavement, salesmen sold pig's trotters, hot tripe, hot kidneys, brains and tongues, calling out their wares. These cheap foods, much more than the meat pie, were bought by those strolling the street a century ago.

The typical butcher sold tins and even kegs of dripping and bladders of pig's lard. He sold bones to housewives for the making of soup: tinned soup was still uncommon and packet soup was unknown. He sold flaps of mutton to old people, and plenty of lamb's fry, and especially the tripe for that popular dish of tripe and onions. Butchers also made their own saveloys, first boiling the meat to 160 degrees Fahrenheit, and then dyeing the meat with Armenian Bole, a kind of red earth from the shores of the Black Sea, and colouring the saveloy skin with old additives or coal-tar dye called Bismarck. The butchers also made their own sausages and cured their own corned beef. The popular corned beef, being salted, lasted longer than plain beef.

The earliest reference I can find to that revered delicacy, the hot dog, is in the mid-1850s when it was introduced to Ballarat by a butcher with Californian experience. He made his own saveloys (known as 'bags of mystery') and hired twelve lads with baskets to carry saveloys and bread slices to the crowded hotels. They were bought for a shilling each by what he called 'the pleasure-seekers of Ballarat'. When the cascade of red sauce first appeared is not known. The question may someday provoke a PhD.

During the gold rushes, imported English sauces were exorbitant in price. Even colonial brands were usually too expensive to squander on a saveloy. Then a pint bottle of sauce cost two or three times as much as a pound of prime meat: today the meat is much dearer than the sauce. At the great Intercolonial Exhibition held at Sydney in 1870 the only bottled sauces on display came from the Adelaide factory of Alfred Chance. He displayed nine dozen bottles of his prize chutney, mushroom ketchup, Prince of Wales sauce, and that Australian culinary overcoat of the future, tomato sauce. The judges at the exhibition ruled that Mr Chance's sauce lived up to his name. The tomato sauce – at ten and a half pence a bottle – lacked the flavour of a tomato. It was also too hot: above all it wasn't red. The heyday of the hot dog obviously lay in the future.

Tomato sauce and various chutneys were only some of the seasonings and spices that were added to meat. In 1863 John Pond, a Launceston grocer, being about to sail for England, sold his remaining stock at bargain prices; and his advertisement shows tins of Colman's mustard, ground ginger, French capers, caraway seeds, nutmeg, pint bottles of sauce and pickles, quart bottles of vinegar, and draught vinegar for those who arrived with their own billycan. In his shop could also be found coarse cheap salt and expensive jars of fine table salt.

Butchers formed a major industry. We know from the 1870 census that the electorate of Launceston, one of the dozen largest towns in Australia, gave work to a grand total of sixty-three butchers. Though a decidedly religious town, it held only one clergyman for every three butchers. A mercantile town, it held only one accountant for every five butchers. Moreover that tally of sixty-three butchers included only the owners of the shops and their skilled employees, and not the butcher's boys who drove the carts. Further down the list came the forty-eight publicans, the twenty-nine bakers, the twenty-three pastrycooks and confectioners and the eighteen grocers, all the way down to the three hatters and one wine merchant. In a large town the annual picnic for the butchers could draw quite a crowd because their families too were invited.

Meat was vital in the camp of the remote explorer. Some explorers set out with a small flock of sheep. When finally the mutton ran out they had to kill their camels and horses. In the 1870s, Ernest Giles, finding himself short of food while exploring between central and western Australia, turned his own horse into strips of smoked meat, having first erected a smoke-house by placing a tarpaulin over four stakes hammered into the ground. The smoked horseflesh was not fit either for a restaurant or an explorer's camp. At mealtime it had to be boiled and then pummelled with a hammer or tomahawk. The softened meat was then cut into small bits, coated with flour, and fried in the pan. Meanwhile, from the boiling of the horse bones, a little oil was collected. It too was eaten or used as cooking oil.

Roast Swan and Grabben Gullen Pie

While beef and mutton were plentiful, exotic meats were demanded by wealthy people in the cities. Men who were skilled with their guns hunted month after month, camping each night in a tent and sending game regularly to market. Quail, pigeon and the black duck won high prices. The stubble quail, a small plump bird which lived on the ground, was a favourite of hunters near Melbourne in the 1850s. Black ducks, with their exotic chestnut throats, were hunted between February and September, and a retriever dog fetched them from where they fell.

The black swan was another favourite when roasted, a pair of swans earning the princely sum of ten shillings in 1860.

A light-grey wild turkey, especially a mature bird, earned four times the price of a black swan. At the tables of the finest hotels the sight of wild turkey and magpie goose – its flesh was coarse – made visitors smack their lips. Already kangaroo tail was favoured as the main ingredient of a soup served in city hotels, while the kangaroo steak was praised as a poor person's venison. The selling of skins added to the profit of kangaroo shooters.

Maybe one third of a hunter's catch was lost through heat and persistent blowflies. Some of the newly shot ducks were 'a living mass of maggots'. Horace Wheelwright, a Victorian professional hunter, devised his own way of coping with blowflies. He carried on his back the kind of wickerwork basket used by fishermen, and he packed the ducks in successive layers of grass and ti-tree, just as if they were grouse shot on the English moors. At his camp the hanging of ducks in a high shaded tree, preferably where they could catch a fresh draught of air, seemed to thwart most of the blowflies. A little pepper placed in the mouth of each duck was said to preserve its freshness. Some city diners thought the native black duck, when cooked with flair, the tastiest in the world.

In the bush so many cooking pots, night after night, were full of native birds that parliaments eventually had to call 'halt'. Western Australia banned the killing of emu in 1894. From July to November, in some districts, it was illegal to kill wild geese, wild turkey, duck, quail, snipe, bronze-winged pigeons and a variety of other birds. Despite the law, the aroma of native birds could be smelled being stewed or grilled in the evening at dozens of bush camps.

Each region developed its own menu in native birds. On islands in Bass Strait the muttonbirds at nesting time were hunted in their hundreds of thousands each year by people of part-native descent. The young birds were smoked, and the eggs were collected, and in northern Tasmania these were classed as delicacies in season, decade after decade. The feathers also provided softness and warmth in the eiderdowns and pillows of Tasmanian hotels.

In many parts of Australia the flesh of the wombat, possum and emu were eaten, if nothing else was available. Possum was seen by most white people as third-rate meat, but in hard times they would gladly cook it. One dish, for the very hungry, consisted of a scooped-out pumpkin shell into which pieces of possum were placed alongside lumps of cooked pumpkin. In one region of New South Wales this roasted dish was referred to, slightly contemptuously, as Grabben Gullen Pie, taking its name from a small township near Crookwell. While many Aborigines still favoured their traditional meat, they were increasingly attracted to mutton and beef. Sugar, in their eyes, was even more tempting than mutton.

Rabbits, of British descent, could occasionally be bought in city markets in the 1850s. Their flesh tasted of the English meadows, and housewives gladly paid a high price for this taste of nostalgia. In 1859 the Victorian squatter Thomas Austin imported in a sailing ship from Liverpool some twenty-four live rabbits, seventy-two partridges and five hares. Released on to his sheep run beyond Geelong the rabbits flourished beyond all his dreams, but the price of their meat was still high. Within one decade the descendants of his rabbits had escaped his fences and entrenched themselves like an invading army in the rich soil of his neighbours' properties. Each year they occupied more and more of Victoria.

By 1870 thousands of pairs of freshly skinned rabbits were being packed in large wicker baskets and sent by railway to Melbourne where they were sold at the fish market. In Sydney for a few years, rabbits remained a luxury, being dearer than a pair of fowls. In the space of one generation, however, the rabbit, by spreading across the continent and multiplying prodigiously, ceased to be expensive. In this paradise of cheap meat, the succulent rabbit soon became the cheapest of all. In the history of the world, few other meats moved so swiftly from the status of luxury to that of all-too-common.

Hawkers made a living by knocking on suburban doors and selling freshly caught rabbits. By the 1890s the best known of these sellers, 'Yabba' Gascoigne, was hawking fresh rabbits in the Sydney suburb of Balmain on weekdays; and then on Saturdays, in neat clothing, he took his place on the hill overlooking the turf of the Sydney Cricket Ground. Commenting pungently on individual batsmen and bowlers with the same strong voice which shouted 'rabbit-oh' in Sydney streets, he could be heard on the far side of the cricket ground.

During the Depression of the 1930s, tens of thousands of families were to rely heavily on stewed or roasted rabbit. They caught their own, with traps or ferrets, and sold the skins and ate the meat. Most bush people could easily tell whether a newly caught rabbit was young or old. The hallmark of the old

An early rabbit trapper, pipe in his mouth, driving home with his catch in Victoria's Western District. The mother of nearly all rabbits was first let loose here.

rabbit, no matter how plump, was that its front claws had been blunted by constant burrowing.

Soon after the Second World War, rabbit fell from favour. People had the money to buy more expensive cuts of meat. And almost at the same time the disease of myxomatosis, spread by mosquitoes, decimated the population of rabbits. Rabbit meat, once relished, was now seen as tainted. Many people who when young feasted at least four times a week on rabbit would, in old age, not think of eating it.

Harriet Lane and Canned Meat

As Australia sometimes produced a surplus of fresh meat, there was an incentive to preserve it. In the 1840s the smoking of meat was well known as a preservative, but refrigeration was unknown and canning largely untried.

The canning of meat – a French invention – was pioneered in Australia by Sizar Elliott, a Sydney grocer. He read a little about the preserving process in Ure's *Dictionary of Chemistry* and conducted his own experiments. Eventually, in 1846, he cooked beef at high temperature in a pan of whale oil on a gas flame and tinned it. He filled and sealed tins of preserved beef, preserved mackerel and preserved carrots. When the tins were three weeks old he opened them for inspection. The tasters were pleased. In 1847, becoming bolder, he canned meat and vegetables, lamb and green peas, and oxtail soup.

One puzzle was how to seal the tins. Elliott partly cooked the meat inside his early tins and then funnelled in liquid meat stock through a small round hole in the top of the tin: a cover was then soldered over the hole. When the canning industry became firmly established, factories normally filled the open can with meat, soldered on the lid in one piece, and then left a small opening in the lid for the steam to escape while the meat was cooking. The final task was the plugging of this steam vent. Elliott's next difficulty was to find buyers. His own grocery must have sold few tins, for fresh meat was cheap as well as tastier. In theory the tinned meat was ideal for the long voyage to England – and a welcome substitute for barrels of salted beef – but the captains of English ships tended to shun it. American warships and whaling ships, calling at Sydney, proved to be his bravest customers, perhaps because settlers in the American west had already consumed tinned foods during the long westward trek.

Although Elliott arranged tastings for the sea captains and wrung from them signed certificates of commendation for his meats and soup, he was eventually compelled to abandon his little cannery. A few tins he put aside, almost as testaments to his faith. The last tin was twenty years old when it was opened at an exhibition in Melbourne in 1866. The judges, the courageous judges, tasted the meat and gratefully testified 'to its perfect sweetness and freshness'.

By then the canning of meat was flourishing. Ships often carried away boxes containing tins of meat weighing up to 3 kilograms. In London the meat was often judged to be overcooked or tasteless. Fortunately the sales of tinned meats boomed during the war between France and Prussia in 1870–71, and Australian tinsmiths earned the ducal wage of £5 a week simply by making the tins. Millions of tins of meat were now exported annually but the future lay with refrigerated, not tinned, meat.

To publicise preserved meat and mutton a Queensland firm

sent several casks in a P & O mail steamer to the port of Galle in Ceylon and back again. One cask was formally opened in February 1871 in Sydney, and the enclosed mutton was sent as a gift for the feeding of the poor. At the City Night Refuge and Soup Kitchen the cured mutton, by then some six months old, was placed in a big boiler and used as the base for the evening meal of hot soup. The manager of the refuge thought the meat contents of the soup were slightly more tender than the fresh meat they normally used, though this might have been a reflection of the poor quality of their normal meat. 'The whole of the soup and meat was consumed here at the one meal', he announced proudly. Several hungry customers were brave enough to ask for a second helping.

New ways of preserving meat were tested: some were based on smoking or drying, some on salting or spicing. From Bendigo came tins of kangaroo and other native meats. Formally opened in Sydney, these tins did not provoke the enthusiastic smacking of lips. A tin of wild goose was said in 1870 to taste of eucalyptus leaves. Tins of beef that were kept too long tasted strongly of sulphur or other chemicals. The sheer variety of tinned meats, however, was remarkable. From the Warrnambool Meat Preserving Company – founded in 1869 and in the hands of the receiver three years later – came tins of corned beef, ox tongues and ox palates, spiced beef, ox-tail soup, boiled beef, ox tripe, soup, 'preserved wild rabbits', sheep kidneys, sheep tongues, loin of mutton with bones, and boiled mutton without the bones. Jams, tomatoes and other vegetables appeared increasingly in cans.

Canned meat was not yet popular in Australia – except for

those settlers who lived far out in the desert or sailors who travelled far out to sea. Even on the ocean the tinned meat was often cursed. In May 1984 the London *Times* reported that a Scottish sea captain, aged ninety-six, had just visited the new maritime museum at Aberdeen where he reminisced about the food given to him when he was a young sailor. In his view the worst food was the tins of boiled mutton from Australia. These tins were nicknamed Harriet Lane. When asked why, the ancient captain explained that she was a woman of ill repute who, after a period as the mistress of two brothers, threatened to inform the wives about the dual affair. As a result she was murdered and cut into pieces. The tinned mutton, presumably consisting of small pieces of ill-tasting flesh, reminded sailors of her fate.

The Recipes of Mrs Wicken

Women migrating to Australia could only gasp at the frequency with which they were expected to cook and eat meat. One of the first guidebooks for young women setting up house was laced with instructions on the choosing and cooking of meat. Completed in 1891 by Mrs Harriet Wicken, who taught domestic economy at Sydney Technical College, it set out a list of 'economical dinners' for each evening of the week.

While Mrs Wicken prescribes a variety of hot vegetables and a pudding or sweet, meat is central to nearly all her dinners. On Sunday it is roast beef and Yorkshire pudding, and on Monday the beef is served cold with tomato salad, to be followed on Tuesday by a shoulder of mutton with onion sauce, and on Wednesday by stewed steak as well as meat moulded from the cold mutton of the previous day. By Thursday her happy family is ready for steak and kidney pudding, while boiled mutton and parsley sauce await the Friday, and rump-steak pie the Saturday. In her thrifty menus, hardly a scrap of cold meat and not even a meat bone is wasted. So for the Monday she recommends that the dinner begin with brown soup made from meat bones and for Friday it should begin with brown soup made from bones of mutton, while Saturday's dinner should begin with Scotch broth made from the liquor in which the neck of a forequarter of mutton has been boiled. As for the meat left over, it could be used to make rissoles, meat patties and rice cutlets for the odd breakfast and luncheon.

The only way to extract value from the butcher, announced Mrs Wicken, was to go personally to his shop and select the exact piece of meat yourself rather than asking him to deliver a cut he had chosen. In those days butchers were willing to deliver meat to the back door of their customers' houses.

In the last years of the nineteenth century a simple pattern could be detected in the ordering of meat. As most houses did not possess an ice chest they purchased fresh meat nearly every day. The man who, daily, delivered meat from his horsedrawn cart invariably received the most expensive orders on a Friday or Saturday, because these were the paydays for most employees. Thus an expensive joint of beef was usually ordered for the weekend roast. By Monday, however, money was less plentiful and so steak or sausages were likely to be

215

ordered. By Wednesday, when the money was running very low, boiled mutton was favoured by many families. By Thursday, tripe, lamb's fry or other tasty offal would be the favourite meats. In the butcher's shop the preparing of tripe was a major activity.

A one-time butcher's boy of the 1920s told me that his designated task, hour after hour, was to scrape away from the white tripe the black coating. Tripe – 'people either liked tripe or disliked it' – was eaten in large quantities, usually being served with cooked onions.

The big joint of meat, served hot at the main meal of the weekend, arrived cold at the next meal. Then the remnants were served as mince for a few more meals. By 1880 a housewife usually owned a simple, hand-operated mincing machine, made of heavy metal. Into the mouth of the machine were fed chunks of cooked cold meat, the handle was turned, and minced meat dropped slowly out of the other end. Those Australian newspapers which carried recipes – and recipes began to appear regularly in about the 1880s – devoted much space to the preparing and spicing of minced beef, veal and mutton. Thus the *Tasmanian Mail* in March 1886 sternly told its readers to slice up cold mutton, without skin or fat, and 'pass it through the mincing machine until quite fine'. The finely chopped meat was then spiced with pepper and salt and a little gravy, supplemented with milk and butter, and stirred in a hot saucepan over the stove. As a novelty, a little stewed cucumber was added by those cooks who faithfully followed the guidance of the newspaper. Some cooks liked to add to the minced meat chopped pieces of parsley, thyme and onion. Some cooks made the gravy with the aid of port wine and redcurrant jelly. Others squeezed a lemon or added a dash of mustard, perhaps adding a prayer for good measure.

In the large cities could be found a few early versions of what we would now call a delicatessen, though that word – coined in the United States in the 1880s – had not yet entered Australian speech. Such shops were a kind of halfway stage between cooking at home and eating in a restaurant. Adelaide had excellent shops that specialised in German sausages and other cooked foods, and indeed 'fritz' became a popular South Australian word for German sausages. Sydney had its 'Condy's London Ham and Beef Shops', in such prominent places as George Street and Bondi Junction. On a Saturday night in the early 1900s the customers would line up, sometimes four-deep, to select from the trays of roasted rabbits or fowls, pig's trotters and stuffed pork, or steaming haunch of beef, held aloft as it was carried from the rear kitchen to the busy shop. One young customer, recalling his visits to one of Condy's shops, vividly described tureens of freshly boiled beetroot and 'hams in their white paper', about to be cut into the thinnest of slices by an attendant carrying a long knife.

Pork ranked low in popularity compared to beef and mutton but by 1900 the demand was growing. The keeping of pigs went hand in hand with a boom in dairies, and pork became cheaper. In the larger cities arose pork butchers, who provided nothing but pork sausages, pork chops and other pork delicacies. Nearly all their sales were made after five in the evening, to people going home from work.

Fetch the Firewood!

Where was this annual mountain of meat cooked? In 1850 perhaps half of the dwellings in Australia had no kitchen. Men living in ones and twos in the bush, and married couples, cooked out of doors, or if they had a sizeable hut, cooked on an open fire at one end of the room. Many huts had huge fireplaces, running almost the width of the building. Cooking took place in pots and billies placed on or just above the open fire.

A camp oven was already a popular way of cooking. It was a small, portable cast-iron oven, very black after even a week of use, because it was usually planted within the open fireplace to make use of the hot coals, embers and ashes of the burning fire. Most stood on three short legs, had a flat base, and a lid shaped in such a way as to allow ashes and coals to be heaped on top. Bread could be baked inside, meat could be roasted, and a plum pudding could be cooked. It gave out a kind of music, especially when the lid was taken off – the sizzling reminded those with imagination of a hundred different tunes. Sometimes in village halls people would recite Edward Dyson's popular poem with its closing line: 'When the old camp-oven sings.'

Catherine Spence described the cooking of a fruit cake in a camp oven in her first novel, *Clara Morison: A Tale of South Australia during the Gold Fever*. 'It was twilight when she put the cake in the camp oven, and covered the lid with the hot red embers.' And then into the room came bearded men, one of whom observed her inexperienced way of cooking. 'You have not half enough of ashes in the hearth', he said. Picking up the iron tongs, he grabbed hot coals and arranged them close to the oven, thus preventing cold air from entering it. Clara thought the fire would be suffocated by his actions, but sure enough, she was mistaken.

Some wives preferred to select their own flour, mix their own dough and pay a local baker to cook their bread in his oven. Some sent their meat to the same baker for roasting. In North Adelaide in 1858 the wife of a draper regularly paid the baker to handle her roast. When the roasting was completed, the baker's boy usually delivered the dish of hot meat to the house. This reliance on the bakehouse, especially for the cooking of the Sunday roast, was a custom imported from England. Charles Dickens alluded to it in his novel *Martin Chuzzlewit*, noting that on Sundays many people carved their roast at 2 p.m. or later, for on that day the bakehouses did not open until noon.

In the larger towns a well-off family, living in a house of five or six rooms, usually had a separate kitchen in a small building a few footsteps from the back door. An adjacent room housed the female servant. In hot weather the heat from the kitchen fire, and the cooking smells, did not readily creep into the remainder of the house.

Clara Aspinall, reaching Melbourne in the late 1850s, spent three observant years there. Her first house, near the new parliament in Spring Street, was moderate in size with brick walls, a roof made of wooden shingles, a verandah to provide coolness, and a small garden with a grape-bearing vine clinging to the wall. The drawing room and dining room were large, one being about 9 metres long, while the three bedrooms were lofty but small. The kitchen, 'a miserable little kitchen', was entered by three doors, thus admitting unwelcome draughts and wind gusts in wintertime. Unlike most newcomers reporting on their life in Australia, she gave a description of her kitchen: 'The kitchen was just about large enough to contain an American stove, tables, and two good-tempered Irish servants.'

The main items in a typical kitchen were the fireplace; the big, roughly made wooden table in the centre of the room; the sideboard, which held the plates and more valuable items of cutlery and crockery; and the large clock. Perhaps a rocking chair stood near the wood stove. Such a kitchen is vividly depicted by John Longstaff in his oil painting *Breaking the News*, and in words by Henry Lawson. The typical bush kitchen, while large, was rough: its roof was of bark and its floor was made of earth and stamped firm. In Lawson's story of the loaded dog, the kitchen was superior, standing on stilts and protected by a corrugated-iron roof. But that was a kitchen belonging to an inn, and so it was a hub that embraced many tasks including the washing of clothes.

A stove, with black kettles and pans arranged nearby, was a novelty in the mid-1850s. About that time the Joyce family, running their sheep near Maryborough in Victoria, built a kitchen in which they installed the latest American stove, a sink for washing the dishes, and a rack on which to store the plates. A pipe conveyed fresh water into the kitchen. Alfred Joyce quietly boasted that his wife Caroline was now living in the lap of luxury compared to housewives who had to cook on an open fire, bake their bread in a small camp oven, and collect cooking water from a keg standing by the kitchen.

In most farmhouses standing on the interior of the Great

This English kitchen – with its large stove, its facilities for keeping the newly cooked food hot and its space for storage – was the dream of tens of thousands of Australians. There was one catch – you probably needed at least one servant to operate it.

Dividing Range during the years from 1860 to 1880, the kitchen – and usually the wash house – formed a separate building. Thus the drover's wife, as depicted by Lawson, lived in a main cottage, standing on stilts just above the earth, with a kitchen standing apart. Generally, less money was spent on the kitchen than on the bedrooms. It was considered tolerable for the kitchen wall to have chinks and small gaps in the woodwork – they let in the breeze.

By the final decade of the nineteenth century a new farmhouse was unlikely to possess an outside kitchen. Instead, the kitchen was now part of the main building. Why this change occurred is not clear. It is probable that by then most settlers were becoming acclimatised to the Australian summer. They accepted, inside their house, the presence of a wood-burning stove which emitted heat during the hottest hours of the day, in order to supply hot water for cooking, washing and other tasks. Moreover as families now feared the cold of winter almost as much as the intense heat of summer, they especially relished the warmth emitted by the stove on frosty or chilly mornings.

If people had to nominate the most important single item of equipment in the nation during the half-century from the mid-1860s until the First World War, most would have named the kitchen stove. It was a workplace, a tiny factory. It was the nerve centre of the home and, at times, the scene of high theatre when everything went wrong. The stove was the head of the household.

The steady transfer of cooking from an open fire to an iron stove reflected not only the increasing cheapness of stoves but also a change in social arrangements. When the Joyces installed their American stove, the majority of people lived in two main types of household. One consisted of husband, wife and children. As a family required a lot of cooking, baking and washing, the iron stove was a most efficient helper. A second kind of household, almost as numerous, consisted of one or two single men who lived in a tent or hut and cooked over an open fire. These men were often on the move, and a stove was not easily moved. A generation later, the numerical dominance of males over females in the total population became less extreme, and the married household became typical. So the iron stove replaced the open fire.

A stove in essence was an oblong iron box, painted black. Resembling a large cupboard, set against or built into a wall, it was capped by its own chimney of iron or brick and bottomed by a capacious oven. When at work – and in many houses it worked every day of the year – it gave off an intense heat. The handle of the door guarding the fire, and the handles of the oven, were so hot that the housewife required a piece of padded cloth or thick gloves or a long iron lever to open it. Little children playing too close to the stove burned their hands or elbows – but only once. The lesson was not forgotten. Curiously most stoves, when new, gave no impression that a fire was burning inside. The ironwork of older stoves, however, had an occasional gap or slit through which a dart of flame could be seen.

An all-purpose item, the stove did almost everything and did it cheaply. Usually burning firewood – except on the few coalfields, where the cheaper fuel was coal – it boiled the water for the tea, for washing the dishes, and for other household tasks. In most kitchens a large iron kettle – blackened by flames – stood on the flat top of the stove and was usually close to the boil. If a cup of tea had to be made quickly, the kettle was merely moved to the hottest part of the stove, where the water came to the boil in no time. The stove was used for frying, roasting, steaming or boiling. It was used to make soap and candles, jam and sauces. In households far from a bakehouse, the stove's oven baked the week's bread. Even the ironing of clothes depended on the stove, because there sat the heavy flatiron, gathering heat until it was deemed hot enough to press dresses, bows, shirts, and suits.

On a cold morning, the stove was the only warm spot, the door being left ajar so that some of the heat reached cold hands. Sometimes it was difficult to stand in front of the stove, after newly washed clothes had been arranged on a 'horse' or a set of wooden rails. When children came home from school, with their boots or shoes wet inside and out, the footwear was placed in front of the stove or sometimes, for a short period, inside the oven itself.

The early cast-iron stove, with its oven below, its hot-plate of iron on top and its chimney taking away the smoke, was made in the United States, especially in New York. Eventually hundreds of Australian blacksmiths and iron workers each made their own brand of stove. Called colonial stoves, they usually had a long working life. Moreover they tended to have room for larger pieces of firewood.

A fine servant, the stove was a harsh mistress. The lighting of the fire in the fireplace each morning called for a supply of dry kindling – strips of bark, old twigs, pine cones and thin splinters of wood. The task of setting and lighting the fire in the kitchen stove was much harder because wrapping paper was scarce, and newspapers were of few pages. The stove devoured a weekly stack of firewood, every piece of which had to be carried into the kitchen and placed in the woodbox or stacked neatly on the floor. It was the husband's task to chop enough firewood to keep the stove alight for fifteen or sixteen hours each day. If he was away, then the wife had to try her hand with the big axe, or maybe that little axe called the tomahawk. A wife skilled with the axe was often regarded in folklore as proof of a ne'er-do-well husband.

To tend the wood-burning stove required alertness. In the course of a day the housewife had to open the iron door dozens of times, and slide more wood onto the fire. If the wood was young and slightly green, the flames could easily stutter and finally the fire would go out, sometimes ruining the bread, pie, cake or pudding that was being baked in the oven. Likewise a new stove resembled a frisky horse – it had to be tamed. As temperature gauges were unknown, the progress of the roast, whether almost cooked or only half cooked, had to be measured by instinct or trial and error. The exact heat on the top of the stove was crucial to other cooking tasks. To bring to the boil a saucepan of fresh milk was a slow process on some stoves. Lo and behold, when the eye of the cook turned away for half a second, the milk would boil over and run across the hot surface of the stove. The smell of burned milk or burned porridge then permeated the house.

The stove called for a never-ceasing routine of work. At the day's end, or next morning, the ashes had to be cleaned from it and carried outside. Naturally the stove became grubby, and every now and then it had to be painted with blacking, and the inside of the oven had to be washed out with soap or a mixture of soda and water. The wood-burning stove was a tyrant. Moreover the main cooking utensils – the pots, pans, saucepans and big kettle – were heavy. Iron was the reigning metal, and the aluminium saucepan was unknown in 1900. Ten years later, the metal remained expensive and was not squandered on kitchen utensils.

Long after the iron stove became normal in a new house, many families preferred an open fire for their cooking. Francis Rawdon Hume, his wife Emma, and their many children lived on a sheep station on the Boorowa Plains in central New South Wales. Though Hume lived through an era of incredibly fast change he – unlike his wife – was wary of innovations.

Eventually the railway from Sydney came to within 25 kilometres of his property but he did not travel on it – he did not
even bother to go and see the trains. Splendid iron stoves came
on to the market, but his homestead did not welcome them. He
insisted that all food, apart from the bread which was baked in
a special brick-lined oven, be cooked on an open fire. When his
wife said the time had perhaps come to install an iron stove, he
replied: 'You're like all women – always wanting something new.'
Fortunately his wife had servants to do the drudgery.

In old age Francis Hume liked to sit by the open fire in the
dining room, even on summer days, with a pot of warm and
virtually stewed tea on the hob. From time to time he would fill
his own cup from the dark fluid in the teapot and pour into
a saucer a small helping for his tiny grand-daughter. She long
remembered the fireside ritual: 'The only word I could say was
"more", so I was always getting more.' Her own mother sometimes objected to this flow of dense tea, rich in tannin, to which
the old man responded with an appeal to his own experience:
'Don't talk to me: I have had fourteen children.'

In a country so large, no one way of cooking and eating
was universal. The shearers were a law unto themselves. As the
sheep-shearing season moved around the country, groups of men
assembled at each station for a week or two, usually camping in
narrow sheds with hardboard bunks along the walls. A full-time
cook prepared their meals, sometimes in the open air. Usually
he preferred to cook in the shed where all the shearers slept;
and the smell of his meals – mingling with the perspiration of
the men and the smell of the wool – lingered for an hour or

more. Australia's most successful union organiser, W. G. Spence, described these sheds or huts as they were before the 1880s – when his demands for change were heeded:

> The table at which the men ate their meals ran down the centre. The cooking was done in a huge fireplace at one end, with the oven at its side. When the cook wanted to grill chops he spread burning coals on the earthen floor in front of the fireplace and laid his gridiron – a frame about three feet square – on the coals, the smell of the burning fat filling the hut where the men had to dress and undress, eat and sleep, all in one room.

The fireplace at one end of the shearers' hut usually ran the full width of the building. Large buckets holding hot tea and coffee stood on the ashes. Near the fireplace were bags of flour and sugar, their tops wide open. The longish shed was like a makeshift restaurant, except that the local health inspector (if there was such man) did not visit it. Henry Lawson slept in a similar shed and described 'the unspeakable aroma of forty or fifty men who have little inclination and less opportunity to wash their skins'.

For decades, firewood was so cheap that it was used extravagantly in kitchens and roadside camps: indeed, in some years it was the largest single commodity carried by the Australian railways. Whereas coal was the main household fuel in many cities in western Europe, here the coal, being usually more expensive, was burned mainly in the kitchens of coal-mining towns and in nearby Sydney.

A Glance at the Gas Stove

In theory the gas-burning stove was a clean, simple alternative to the wood stove. Although Sydney possessed a gasworks even before the gold rushes, gas as a fuel was slow to compete. At the big trade fair held in Sydney in 1870, the official judges, admiring the gas stoves on display, regretted that they were not used more widely: 'In the heat of summer a kitchen fire is a nuisance, especially in a small house, and though often kept up all day is really only wanted for a few hours.' On the other hand the gas stove could be lit just when its heat was needed.

A gas stove was probably not cheap to operate. In addition there persisted, rightly or wrongly, a prejudice against food so cooked. The gas was said to flavour the food. By the 1880s this prejudice was falling away, and many city families preferred a gas stove, praising its cleanliness, simplicity, safety and the time it saved. But the overwhelming majority of Australian houses used firewood for cooking. Sydney in 1897 had a mere 7000 gas stoves, according to Beverley Kingston, who wrote a pioneering study of women and domestic work. She does not give an estimate for wood stoves but they probably exceeded 100 000 in that city alone. Long after 1900, on a winter evening, wood smoke coming from countless chimneys conveyed its aromatic scent to those walking along dark suburban streets.

In the capital cities the gas stove eventually became the normal cooker. In the countryside and small towns, the wood stove persisted, and its heat produced jam, sauces, cakes, biscuits and other manufactures. But many country women longed for

228

the day when they might retire to a large town and not have to light the stove every day of the year. For a few farms the kerosene stove was a windfall. It could be turned on and off on a hot day.

The large wooden kitchen table, regularly scrubbed with brush and soap and warm water, stood two or three paces away from the stove. Close friends and trusted neighbours were invited to sit at the kitchen table; but in a self-respecting household, the visitors of some social standing were led into another room – known as the living or sitting room, or 'front room'. A large number of houses, fully occupied simply for eating and sleeping, had no such room. But if there was a sitting room it was usually kept in a state of permanent tidiness, its door closed, so that unexpected visitors could be welcomed in style. There, on chilly nights, for the benefit of visitors, a fire was lit in the open fireplace. Soon in place was a back log, intended to burn throughout the evening. The expression 'back log' has now migrated to the workplace. Stripped of its fire it now signifies, curiously, a cluster of unfinished tasks.

On the hearth a long iron poker was at hand, ready to prod new energy into the fire. In some houses the end of the poker was allowed to lie in the red-hot coals until it glowed red. It was then dipped into a pot of beer or other liquid. The hissing and sudden rising of steam as the poker penetrated the beer was the height of conviviality. It was an unwritten rule that a visitor on no account should pick up the poker and prod or poke a slow-burning fire. As for kicking the back log with the boot, that too was deemed a discourtesy. The handling of the fire, the fiddling with it, was the privilege of the owner of the house.

The fire, whether in the kitchen or the front room, was a maternal spirit, almost part of the family that sat around it. It had a mystical quality. 'Can you see the faces in the fire?' old people would enquire of one another, because sometimes they observed that the flames and the silhouette of the burning wood took the shape of human faces. Nothing in the modern home – not even the cocktail bar or the backyard barbecue – has quite supplanted the household fire.

Firewood had a special place in everyday life. At one time probably ninety-five of every hundred houses and huts had access to cheap firewood, whether from nearby bushland or from fallen branches in their vicinity. In Europe the fuel, whether firewood or coal, usually had to be purchased; and often it was expensive. But as more and more of the poorer Australians lived in the inner cities, they could scavenge firewood only with difficulty. On winter nights some sat at home in their overcoat or went early to bed. It was possible to purchase a hot-water bottle, made of rubber, and fill it with boiling water; but such bottles were dear, rubber itself being still an expensive novelty.

8

DID EVER A WOMAN EAT MORE?

While ice was a luxury, bread was the anchor of daily life. The breadknife was more important than the knife of the butcher, surgeon and bootmaker, for the loaf of bread bought in a packet and already sliced was unknown in the nineteenth century. In most families the loaf – larger than the loaves now in fashion – stood on a wooden breadboard at the ceremonial end of the table. The head of the family cut the bread – thick slices for working people and thin slices for the genteel. Present at nearly every meal, the loaf of bread provided Australians with more energy than any other food.

It was appropriate that old-fashioned bread should appear on the new banknotes when in 1966 Australia changed from the pound to the dollar. If you look with a magnifying glass at the top right-hand corner of the $10 note that circulated for about a quarter of a century, you will see the weatherboard 'Times Bakery' which once served the gold town of Gulgong. In the small four-pane window, loaves of two kinds of bread are stacked. The banknote copies faithfully a photograph taken in 1872, at which time more than two thirds of Australia's bread was probably baked in commercial bakehouses. The remainder of the bread, including damper, was made in farmhouses, sheep stations, houses in the larger towns, and countless small ovens in mining camps.

Behind the Bakery Door

For the average family, bread possessed an importance which it now has lost. A sign of its importance was visible to all who entered a baker's shop. There stood a large pair of beam scales, and any customer who doubted whether the loaf was as heavy as the law demanded could weigh the loaf, using the metal weights which sat on the counter. If the loaf was under the legal weight, the customer could go to the police. But the fancy or French breads and rolls did not have to be weighed. The penalties for selling adulterated, underweight or wrongly labelled bread were so high that they could almost bankrupt a small baker. When eventually the baker ceased to be the main provider of daily food for the average family, the law ceased to watch him intently, and the beam scales vanished from his shop.

A common complaint in many families was that the bread they ate was stale. It is possible that in 1860 one third of the bread eaten had not been baked that day or even on the preceding evening. Many people ate their own bread and did not bake every day. On farms that were far from a town with its own baker, the custom even in the 1920s was to bake bread only once a week. On the seventh day the bread was dry and tough: 'it was like eating the sole of your boot'. As more and more people lived in cities, fresh bread became the normal experience.

Much of the bread eaten in Australia in the 1850s was made from imported wheat and flour, but as farmers increasingly moved to the dry side of the Great Dividing Range, the locally grown replaced foreign wheat. Flour mills, some driven by huge waterwheels, now dotted the countryside. Occasionally the flour gave off a distinctive odour, which found its way into the bread. Observant eaters were quick to notice that this local flour made a slightly sweetish bread.

The hallmark of 'good bread' was that it was white. A young Scotswoman living on the Daylesford goldfield in the 1850s wrote a memoir, *Old Days and Gold Days*, which emphasised the preference for white bread baked in brick ovens. 'The bakers,' she noted, 'were mostly Swiss, and they made excellent bread, light, white, and with a pale even crust.' The so-called soft wheats that were popular during the second half of the nine-teenth century produced a yellowish bread. In contrast some of the flour milled from wheat grown in northern Tasmania produced a dark, heavy bread. Guests who were handed slices of dark loaf were inclined to assume that they were receiving second-rate hospitality.

White bread contained the highest proportion of pure flour. This was an age-old preference. Indeed, cunning bakers, ever since the time of the Roman Empire, had added a little alum to the dough in order to whiten it. Australian laws banned the adding of alum. Such adulterated bread could be detected by

233

suspicious customers who heated a knife and thrust it into the bread. If alum was present, it adhered in small particles to the blade of the knife. The good loaf of bread, it was decreed, should not carry too much bran, which was one of the rougher and cheaper by-products of the milling process. Bread high in bran was known as 'household wheaten bread' and the crust was marked with a large letter 'H'.

There was an unending debate: was brown bread or white bread the better? White bread was more expensive. It was adored by those who could not afford it. Those who ate brown bread at nearly every meal were inclined to think that the pangs of hunger returned more quickly than if they had eaten white bread. Nonetheless there were nutrition experts who praised the brown loaf, noting that its gritty bits made it a fine laxative.

The ability of bakers to produce a very white loaf was aided by a new milling process. The old grinding stones used in the numerous small flour mills scattered throughout farming districts and big towns were challenged by a new Hungarian way of grinding and milling grains of wheat. In 1879 the South Australian firm of Duffield tried the Hungarian process in its flour mill at Gawler, using twelve sets of rollers made of porcelain. Eventually iron or steel rollers became normal, displacing the old grinding stones. South Australia was then the heart of wheat growing and its experiments were copied by other colonies.

The Hungarian process used less steam power. It was also cleaner, because in the words of the technology historian, Keith Farrer, it removed dirt from 'the crease of the wheat berry'. Above all, it was a more efficient sorter of flour from pollard and bran, and so produced a fine, whiter flour. The new milling process, however, could only go so far in improving the 'quality' of the first-grade flour. A new breed of wheat was needed. In the 1890s it was rare for an Australian flour to contain more than 8 per cent gluten or protein, whereas half a century later the new breeds of wheat, in a dry year, were to yield 13 per cent protein.

Until recently the bearded William Farrer peered out – with his high brow and small spectacles – from one side of the $2 Australian note. There can be no other currency in the world which has given such prominence to wheat and bread, though few Australians have observed this. Farrer, an English-born wheat breeder, lived on his farm near the banks of the Murrumbidgee, not far from the infant village of Canberra, and in the 1890s he tried to breed wheats suited to the Australian climate. He wanted a wheat that would be resistant to the rust that attacked the grain in moist summers. He also hoped to grow a wheat much higher in protein than the typical Australian wheat of his era. His 'great ambition', he is reported to have said, was to provide poor families with a new loaf that was far more nutritious than the old loaf. Much of the improvement in Australian bread was to come through experiments he initiated.

By the early 1900s the larger bakers were using new machines to supplement or replace human hands. The Tasmanian Bread and Biscuit Works used its own steam power for the new machines which sifted the flour, kneaded the dough, beat the eggs and neatly cut the biscuits. Its electric lights gave 'a most brilliant illumination' for the twenty-five people employed

*South Australia was once the granary of the continent, and much of the
nation's bread during the 1860s was baked from its flour.*

in night baking. Its factory made a variety of breads including a malt bread which was said to be appreciated by all who were prone to indigestion. It also baked bread rolls, scones, crumpets, muffins, those tough ship's biscuits that tested the teeth of sailors, and paper-thin wafers for Hobart gentlefolk to nibble. It was only natural that the owner of such a factory should, in the words of the *Cyclopedia of Tasmania* of the time, be 'esteemed by all who know him'.

While large city bakehouses advertised that their bread was superior, the small-town bakers disagreed. Some of their bread was praised universally – 'universally' being a radius of some 30 kilometres. Townsfolk would take a loaf of local bread as a trophy when they visited friends in another town. Many of these skilled local bakers had learned by trial and error how best to mix dough from variable kinds of flour. They had learned which of the local firewoods was best for heating the oven. Thus in the Victorian timber town of Gembrook, the baker burned silver wattle taken from the tall woodstack near his bakehouse. As he baked his bread in the early hours of the morning, the sweet aroma from his oven whetted the appetites of any sleepless people who lived nearby. 'I have never tasted better bread', wrote Genseric Parker, recalling the Gembrook bread just after the First World War.

Throughout Australia bread was still sold unwrapped, and the baker or shopkeeper handled it with bare hands. The idea of selling sliced bread lay far in the future. On nearly every meal table the breadknife and the breadboard held pride of place.

Damper and Porridge

At one time, maybe one in four of all Australian housekeepers or hutkeepers made their own damper or bread. Damper was a solid rather than an aerated bread. Bush cooks who owned no pots and pans simply prepared the flour by mixing it with water – and a little soda, a pinch of salt and perhaps some cream of tartar – on top of an old tin or a sheet of bark. Others mixed it on the surface of the oilcloth that, wrapped around the outside of the swag, normally kept the blanket dry. The mixture had to be of a certain moistness and firmness. When it was ready it was buried in a hollow, quickly scooped out of the hot ashes of the campfire, and more ashes and coals were heaped on top. A lump of dough so cooked was usually called damper. If sugar was added, and maybe a handful of dried fruit, it was more often called a johnnycake or brownie.

Even in the convict era this primitive method of making the simpler breads and pancakes was well established. Already the names damper and johnnycake were in use. But as the decades passed, a pattern of regional preferences for mixing and cooking flour and water was emerging. In some districts they baked a flat damper and in others they cooked a more rounded damper. In some regions they preferred small johnnycakes, which cooked quickly, while in others they baked in the ashes, with commendable patience, a chunk of kneaded flour. In August 1828 an item of news in the *Hobart Town Courier* described a wide fireplace in which the warm ashes concealed a large damper consisting of some 5 kilograms of flour. Such a dense loaf would make the heaviest of modern loaves seem small. Whatever its shape, taste and aroma the freshly cooked damper usually gave intense satisfaction to hungry people. Hunger, however, was the sauce which it often needed.

Capable bushfolk knew how to make bread even if they lacked the semblance of an oven. One method, common by 1900, was to mix a batter from water and a cup of flour, adding a teaspoon heaped high with baking powder and a little salt. The batter was arranged in a well-greased frying pan and the pan was placed close to the fire rather than on top of the coals. After the batter began to rise, the loaf was turned over so that the other side was baked. 'You can always tell when such a loaf is done by running a splinter of wood into it', wrote that popular writer on bushcraft, Donald Macdonald. 'If the splinter comes out perfectly clean, the loaf is done.' If the splinter stuck to the dough and was not entirely extracted, then that section of bread had to be eaten with care.

An earlier generation of bush cooks had shunned the use of baking powder or yeast. Sweepingly, they dismissed it 'as being very jackarooish', meaning upmarket and even pretentious. A true cook, they vowed, used only the simplest of ingredients and – in a pinch – could even dispense with a frying pan or iron pot. The secret was to improvise. Thus, by chopping a green thin bough off a tree, stripping away the bark and wrapping the wet flour around the bough, cooks could prepare a damper for baking. They simply held the bough above a hot fire and turned it like a spit, thus enabling the damper to be baked with speed.

Many children, at least in the cities and more fertile parts of the countryside, began the day with porridge made from oatmeal. Of Scottish origin, porridge was popular in the colder districts and especially those places where the Scots were settled. On the canefields of Queensland a porridge – made of maize and water – was widely consumed at breakfast by Pacific islanders. Molasses was often added as a sweetener.

Milk porridge was the superior version but not every family had access to milk or could afford it. Many families preferred to use stale bread, pounded with a pestle, instead of oatmeal. Some doctors insisted that the main food for children between the ages of three and seven should be crumbs of stale bread and a little loaf sugar in a bowl of milk – preferably straight from the cow. That milk straight from the cow sometimes carried tuberculosis was one of those unknown hazards of daily life.

While oats were grown in Australia, imported Scottish oats were often said to be superior. In some general stores people enquired of the oatmeal handed to them, 'Are you sure it is Scottish?' It was argued that Scotland possessed an adverse soil and climate (on this point they were not contradicted), that the growing of oats in such a soil was a triumph in the face of adversity, and that part of that triumph remained in the grain, ready to be imparted at breakfast time. As Pitman's manual on *Grocery* proclaimed, Scottish oats had to struggle against an adverse spring and rarely reached ripeness until late autumn: 'As adversity sometimes benefits mankind, so this long steady effort improves the oats. In other countries oats come with too much of a rush.'

Oatmeal was not only the basis of porridge. It was also boiled in water, allowed to cool, and then served as a drink. Thirst-quenching and energy-reviving, oatmeal water was especially favoured by those who harvested the grain on a burning day. Oatmeal was valued by most of the explorers. When Burke and Wills returned to their depot at Cooper's Creek they found, waiting for them, some 30 kilograms of oatmeal as well as sugar, flour and rice.

In the eyes of children, porridge sat at the bottom and cake at the top of the ladder of joy. In the early gold era the typical Australian rarely ate cake in the course of a week. By 1900 cakes and other mixtures of self-raising flour and sugar were a vital part of the eating week. The makeshift cake stall, in which homemade cakes were sold for a few hours in a street or other public place, was now a popular way of raising money for a church or charity. Cake was dispensed in large quantities to children on special occasions. When women entertained other women to 'afternoon tea', the plate of cakes ushered onto the table, along with the teacups, was a source of delight. Cake was still a luxury in many homes but it was to become more and more visible in the next fifty years. First a luxury and then a treat, and served only on Sunday evening, cake was eventually seen as a necessity in many households. Hundreds of thousands of men went to work with a cake, tart or buttered sultana scone wrapped up alongside their lunchtime sandwiches.

A full list of the homemade cakes widely eaten in Australia at the time of the First World War – all the kinds of teacakes, rainbow cakes, cream cakes, marble cakes, iced cakes, jam sponges, vanilla slices, rock cakes and others – would fill a booklet. The cheese, raisin, and other kinds of scones and pikelets would fill another half-dozen pages. Ways of making these cakes and scones differed widely. One determinant of taste was whether the housewife could afford to use butter rather than cheap dripping. Another determinant of the final taste was whether she could afford to use an egg or two. The highly skilled cook in a poor household could triumph even though she reluctantly used dripping.

Recipes for nearly all cakes were brought out from Europe. A few were local inventions. The lamington – its icing made of cocoa and vanilla butter and icing sugar – was almost certainly an Australian invention. The name came from Lord Lamington, whose term as governor of Queensland ended in 1901. A hallmark of this cake is the coating of dessicated coconut, and it could be that the coconut, being a fruit of warm climates, was more easily purchased in Brisbane than, say, in Adelaide around the year 1900. The pavlova cake arrived much later. It was probably a New Zealand invention of the 1920s, though it was launched in a more glamorous form and christened Pavlova, after the ballerina, by the cook at the Esplanade Hotel in Perth.

Before the end of the twentieth century the cake was to lose its exalted place on the special menu. What toppled the cake? It suffered from the rise of ice cream as an alternative delicacy. It suffered, too, from the rise of an alternative way of consuming sweetness: the drinking of alcohol at meals. The heyday of the cake also coincided with a period in which most people did more physical work each day and could easily absorb the sugar, butter and cream embedded in a cake. The iced cream cake flourished when diet charts and weight-watching were unknown.

A Sizzle of Frying Eggs

Mary Fullerton lived with her parents on a farm in east Gippsland, close to where the fertile plains bumped into the ranges. On a stormy night her father was sitting in front of the log fire, her mother was darning the holes in the socks, and all the children had just gone to bed. Suddenly the voice of a neighbour was heard above wind and rain: 'Are you in there, anyone at all?' The door was opened, and in she walked, her arms carrying a child, and water dripping from her clothes. She was welcomed, as were nearly all night-time visitors who called at isolated farmhouses in that era of few signposts.

The children of the house, awakened by the welcoming noises, were soon leaning on their elbows and peeping through a hole in the bark wall to see the excitement which Mary later recorded: 'The babe was laid temporarily on the sofa; his supper done. What a smell of bacon and a sizzling of frying eggs came to us, aching on our elbows! And did ever a woman eat more?'

This homely episode of the 1870s is worth a brief detour. The hospitality was unusually generous. Most farming families sold nearly all their eggs and bacon in the nearest town because they urgently needed the money. Therefore to present such an expensive meal to a neighbour was kindness itself. Eggs were often dear. Sometimes cheap in the 1840s, they soared to unbelievable prices soon after the gold rush began. As more gold seekers arrived in Melbourne, the price of eggs was multiplied by ten. There were months when a dozen eggs cost as much as 3 or 4 kilograms of prime beef.

In the distant outback, to request an egg at breakfast was to ask for a high surcharge on the bill. Sometimes the call for a cooked egg was an invitation to be laughed at. In Broken Hill, when the dazzling lode of silver was being unveiled, a newcomer arrived with the intention of setting up a makeshift boarding house. He carried supplies, including a dozen precious eggs. The landowner who provided the ground for the new boarding house saw the eggs and offered to accept them as payment. The deal was made. All but three of the eggs, however, proved to be rotten.

Initially there was scant knowledge of which breeds of hen were suited to Australian climates. Breeds no longer to be seen foraged for grain around rural cottages. Especially favoured as egg-layers in the 1870s were the silver-spangled and pencilled Hamburghs with their double combs. The name, given to them at a Birmingham poultry show, rested on the mistaken belief that they were mainly German in origin. Other Sydney breeders favoured the Cochin Chinas of various colours and those English birds, the Dorkings, known for their extra toe. In Sydney many prize-winning fowls lived in such inner suburbs as Randwick, Waterloo and Petersham, and even in William Street, in the heart of the city.

The British game hen, plump and with plenty of breast meat, was especially favoured at the dinner table. Along the Hawkesbury River these birds were bred partly for their skills in cockfighting, and their enlarged bodies – some of the cocks weighed more than 5 kilograms – gave the additional bonus that they were ideal for the table. The chickens of the species were lavished with praise at one Bathurst poultry show, their long and deep breasts yielding a wealth of meat 'of the much desired white or pale primrose colour'. For a time the local or colonial game was preferred over the British game at banquets, but in 1899 one Australian expert, George Bradshaw, protested that the local breed was being perverted at poultry shows by judges who insisted that first prize should go to those colonial game fowls with 'long legs and giraffe necks'. For the ordinary family, chicken as a meat was still a luxury and remained so even after the Second World War. Curiously, when chicken, frozen or fresh, became a cheap item at every supermarket, the exact breed of the chicken – once a cause of animated discussion among customers – was never mentioned on the label.

The primary goal in keeping hens was the egg. The game hens were poor layers. By the early 1900s the four main egg-layers were the white Leghorn, Langshan, Rhode Island Red and the black Orpington, which was an ancestor of that popular local breed, the distinctively named Australorp. Careful breed-ing produced one pleasing result for the housewife. Eggs were cheaper.

Stale eggs were far more plentiful than they are today. Some eggs had been laid in hidden nests by roaming hens, and found only when they were stale. Some eggs had been set aside by the farmer to wait for higher prices but had been kept too long. Therefore the sensible grocer bought his eggs only from agents or farmers whom he personally knew.

A grocer also learned how to tell whether an egg was stale or fertilised. Using the method known as 'candling', he inspected each dubious egg in front of a bright light. The bright light identified the fresh eggs – they were unclouded and almost translucent in the bright light. On the other hand a very large dark spot was visible in a faulty egg. The buyer of eggs had to beware, and that was one reason why, even in the big cities, many people kept their own hens in the backyard. Today, in contrast, most people hardly know the smell of rotten eggs.

A few Australian grocers adopted a novel French way of testing an egg. Placed in a bowl of salty water, an egg sank if it was less than a day old, and sank only just below the surface if it were three days old. It floated, however, if it were five or more days old. Before 1900 the Australian governments had little part in inspecting eggs or regulating their sale. The idea of placing a date on an egg carton was unimaginable because such cartons did not exist.

So long as the railways were few, the main farming districts could not quickly send their superfluous eggs to the coastal cities. Farmers driving their carts carrying farm produce to the nearest market town went along rough roads, and some eggs were smashed even when cushioned by chaff or bran. The sea transport of eggs proved cheaper. South Australia was already a busy exporter of eggs, for its farms lay near the coast. In 1865

Victoria received a total of 711 packages of South Australian eggs, each package containing maybe as many as 50 dozen eggs, packed in bran or straw. In that same year twenty-one packages of eggs arrived from Hong Kong, where very old eggs held a special place on the Chinese menu. By the 1870s Sydney's wharves were receiving eggs from small farms far to the north.

Eggs, when expensive, were a symbol of status. They might be displayed in a bowl in the kitchen, like those ornate stone eggs which people today collect on their foreign travels. Occasionally visitors to a struggling farm would be surprised to receive the simplest meal of bread and treacle while, in sight of the table, was arrayed a bowl of fresh eggs and a flitch of bacon. The hosts saw no contradiction between the frugal meal they served and the farm produce they displayed. The eggs were probably waiting to be sold on the next market day in the nearest town. And yet here and there, when gluts of eggs occurred, gargantuan egg meals were eaten. On a hot day in October 1901, at a cattleman's hut in the Northern Territory, the anthropologists Spencer and Gillen were offered a meal of cooked eggs. One ate six eggs, the other ate thirteen.

For a few months of each year, there were almost too many eggs. Farmers wishing to preserve surplus eggs in their cool cellar for as long as three months built wooden shelves on which small holes were cut to fit the curved bottom of each egg. The act of turning over the eggs every second day helped to preserve them. Alternatively eggs could be placed in a barrel and doused with a pickling mixture. Usually consisting of one part of salt, four parts of slaked lime and twenty of water, the mixture was said to

247

preserve eggs for almost one year. Another method was to store eggs in dry salt. Another was to grease them with butter or lard, place them on their side in a wooden box, and fill the box with sawdust or bran. During the annual glut, patented preservatives and ointments, such as Keepegg, were smeared by hand all over the shells. Such eggs were usually used in cakes and confections.

Slowly eggs became more abundant in towns and cities. The cheapness of wheat, pollard and bran was a boon, and the network of new railways enabled eggs to be carried quickly to the cities. But in each region there was still an annual tendency for eggs, in the space of a few months, to move from oversupply to scarcity.

Goose eggs were once popular, especially on the Victorian goldfields around Ballarat, Bendigo and Beechworth. Many towns set aside commons where geese and goats could feed at will. The grey Toulouse, white Embden and Amoy breeds of geese were adept at warding off predators, and their hardiness suited Australian conditions. They produced not only eggs but also the down which filled mattresses, while duck's feathers padded out eiderdowns.

The goose egg, weighing about three times as much as a typical hen's egg, was welcomed in some households, but was judged too rich by others. Geese were kept more for their meat than their eggs. Indeed, at Christmas the roast goose – stuffed with sage and onions and butter and served with apple sauce – was a British dish honoured for several decades in Australia, even in a heatwave. Eventually, as a source of meat, the goose gave way to the turkey.

The Mystery of Milk

Australia had so many cattle that beef was cheap. On the other hand, several cattle products, especially butter and cheese, were scarce. The reason for the contrast was that most of the cattle were bullocks, grazing on the poorer pastures inland and kept solely for their meat and hides. Dairy cattle in contrast were not plentiful until the 1880s when forest was increasingly cleared in the high-rainfall areas so suited to the lush grasses on which the milkers thrived.

At the time of the gold rushes there were few specialist dairy farms, and much of the milk came from single cows kept near the houses of farmers, squatters or city residents. In keeping with the summer practice in Europe, many cows were milked not in stalls but in open paddocks. Often the milking cows were picked from a wild herd of nondescript cattle and tamed in a variety of ways. According to one Tasmanian, they first 'had to be knocked down with a long pole and roped head and feet'. A Queensland cattleman remembers a wild milking cow being roped into a makeshift bail; her nearside back leg was tied so that she could not kick. 'I always found that even the wildest heifer, after a week or so, would walk into the bail of her own accord and gladly submit to being milked.'

The typical dairy farmer in the 1880s owned only a dozen or so cows, and his wife and children milked them by hand in ramshackle sheds with bark or shingle roofs. When the mud was deep around the milking shed in the winter and early spring, the first tasks on each cold morning were to scrape mud from the teats of the cow and then wash them, using cold water from a bucket. After the cows had been milked, the pails of warm milk were taken to the dairy and poured into dozens of shallow pans resting on the earthen floor. For some thirty-six hours the milk lay in pans while slowly the cream rose to the surface.

As the room was unguarded, mice or even snakes occasionally arrived and consumed part of the cream. 'The snakes', observed one early Gippsland farmer, 'were more cleanly than the mice.' For one thing the snakes did not drown themselves in the milk. Later the building of wide shelves around the log walls of a dairy enabled many of the pans to be removed from the earthen floor, above the easy reach of snakes. But mice had less trouble in climbing the shelves. When finally the cream lay thick in the pans, it was skimmed off with a perforated piece of tin. The cream was then dropped into a can or, more often, a butter churn. This age-old way of making cream, or rather letting the cream make itself, was challenged by that wonderful Scandinavian invention, the centrifugal cream separator, which was tried at Mittagong in New South Wales in 1881 and at Romsey in Victoria a year later. Soon farmers were buying hand-turned separators which quickly separated the cream from the watery skimmed milk.

By now much of Australia's milk came from the Shorthorn breed. She was a cow for all ages and all seasons. When her ample flow of milk was slowed by age, she could be sold to the butcher for her meat. Originating in the north of England, where she was sometimes called the Durham Shorthorn, she was increasingly known in New South Wales as the Illawarra

Shorthorn, being named after the river flats near Wollongong. Half a century later the Illawarra Shorthorn contained some Dutch Friesian blood. Friesian cows, incidentally, were known as Holsteins until that name was shunned as being too Germanic.

The brown and white Ayrshires were widely milked by 1900 but it is doubtful whether they equalled in popularity dairy cattle from the Channel Islands. Of those prized cows the Guernsey, with her rich yellowish brown and its white patches, was especially favoured while the plainer Jersey was a favourite of farmers who made butter. The typical farmer, however, milked a mongrel herd. A shrewd eye might even detect, in the same small cow yard, traces of Shorthorn, South Devon, Jersey and Derry in the assorted cows. The poorer of these cows produced such a thin flow of milk that today no farmer would dream of keeping them. In their day each had her own name, whether Daisy, Polly, Myrtle or Daphne. A Christian name became popular in the milking shed only after the name had ceased to be fashionable in the homestead.

Breastfeeding of infants was normal. Few babies were given solid food until the age of nine months. Surveys suggest that a typical child was still being fed at the breast on its first birthday. When a mother's breasts could not supply enough milk for her baby, no wet nurse was living nearby, and no cow's milk was available, the milk of the goat came into favour. Goats were much cheaper than cows. Diligent scavengers, and willing to eat thorns, flowers and dry bushes as well as grass, the goats lived off the land. In the streets and byways of a few Sydney suburbs in the 1840s, goats were allowed to wander freely until milking time. 'Woe betide the suburban garden whose gate is left for a moment unclosed', wrote one newcomer to Sydney. In an instant, goats poured in and nibbled sweetpeas, carnations, stocks and even roses until hardly a sign of the once-neat garden remained.

Officials who collected the animal statistics in Australia rarely bothered to count goats – they did not graze in large numbers. Kept mainly for their milk, the goats when old were killed for their meat. Goat's meat had a poor reputation, partly because the tough meat of the old goat rather than the tender flesh of the young kid was eaten. Early in the twentieth century an outback pub that served poor food was sometimes called a 'goat and galah', the flesh of that bird being equally tough.

In arid country a goat might supply milk. When no goats were on hand, sick children in need of milk might receive a few spoons of milk taken from a sheep. 'I even recollect', wrote Mary Gilmore, perhaps recalling the 1870s, 'a mare being milked', so that a nursing mother could have milk with her tea. Babies lacking breast milk and a suitable substitute were especially vulnerable and died in numbers that now seem unimaginable. In 1865 in Victoria alone the death statistics reveal that 111 babies died from a malady described officially as 'want of breast-milk'.

Goats were kept in the small outback towns founded by Cornish miners; and after these mining towns died, the beasts ran wild. Even today in South Australia, which was the favoured province of the Cornish, wild goats make their way across the bush and, with deft twisting of their long horns, wriggle through the strands of a wire fence and enter the better country, where they multiply. Each year, in some districts, wild goats are shot by the thousands.

In an era when the ice chest and refrigerator were unknown, the coolest place in which to store cow's milk was in a cellar. In the cities some cellars were excavated under the floorboards of houses. In the countryside, cool cellars were excavated close to the back door of the farmhouse; and the cellar might be half under and half above the ground, with a timber roof and a wisteria or other creeping plant to shade the roof. Most suburban cellars that survive are now called wine cellars, and their creation is often attributed to the husband's love of wine rather than the wife's need to keep fresh the milk, butter and eggs.

A glance at the milking practices of the largest dairy farm in the 1870s, at Bodalla on the south coast of New South Wales, hints at what must have happened on the less hygienic farms. Of the 1400 cows – Shorthorns crossed with the Ayrshire breed – about 400 were milked twice daily. The first milking commenced at 5.30 a.m., and before that the udders of the cows were washed. This hygienic practice was considered unusual. But here is the revealing admission: 'Water is provided in which the milkers wash their hands, dipping in the milk-pail being strictly prohibited.' In contrast, in many small dairy farms the milkers – whether child, woman or man – dipped their dirty hands in the milk and then rubbed them together, so that the hands would be clean.

Milk, hailed as the liquid of life and health, was also the carrier of disease. Many cows suffered from tuberculosis and other ailments, and the bacteria were carried in their milk. Typhoid was also carried by milk. Fear of infectious diseases made some families reject fresh milk and turn to condensed milk. A survey of the food habits of typhoid patients in the Hunter Valley in the period 1902–08 reveals that one in seven did not touch fresh milk.

Most householders were visited – sometimes twice a day – by a dairyman who came to each back door with his heavy shining can and ladled the milk into waiting billies or jugs. At times the milk was still warm, having come from a cow paddock only a few blocks away. Sometimes it was warm from the sun which beat down on the milk cart. The pasteurising of most of the drinking milk came after 1900, and was opposed initially by some doctors – in their view it destroyed vitamin C. Many customers were opposed to this busybody of a process because it dispersed the milk fat evenly, whereas the untreated milk seemed more appealing, with the cream resting on top. 'Where's the cream gone?' This cry of dismay often greeted the first deliveries of the healthier, pasteurised milk.

Raw milk now had competitors. The Swiss invented a mix of milk and flour that was especially recommended for premature babies. By 1906 Australia was said to be Nestlé's second-biggest export market for this infant food. The tin of condensed milk was already seen on thousands of dinner tables, next to the pepper and salt. This white, slow-pouring liquid was almost sickly in its sweetness. Some children wanted nothing better at Christmas than a new tin of condensed milk, all for themselves.

The Colour of the Butter

The price of Australian butter fluctuated sharply during a typical year. In the hectic years of the gold rushes, butter could be six times as dear in winter as in summer. Imports of European butter helped to iron out these fluctuations in price. Many hundreds of kegs, casks and tubs of English and Irish butter arrived annually in ships, 'Rose' being a popular Irish brand. The local dairying industry grew, and by 1890 most of the butter bought in Australian shops came from the local farms where it was made in a wooden churn. There were in effect at least 10 000 different brands of butter. By 1900 factory-made butter was more common than homemade butter.

The quality of the handmade butter ranged from first class to third class. A grocer buying such butter had to taste it himself or rely on a wholesale grocer who tasted samples from the keg, box or kerosene tin set out before him. He knew that if the butter was lumpy, the process of churning at the farm must have gone on too long. If the flavour of the butter was dubious he guessed that too much buttermilk had been left in the butter or that the cows had been feeding on Cape weed or other strongly flavoured plants, or that fermentation had occurred in the hot dairy.

Most city families had connections with the rural way of life. They tended to know that if butter was soapy, the dairy pail had not been washed with care, or that if the butter tasted flat, it had been stored in a damp, airless dairy. They knew when the butter had been salted imperfectly. Likewise if butter carried a strong taste of carrot, the cause was obvious. The farmer had added pulped or grated carrots to his pale butter in order to produce that strong yellow colour that was the hallmark of the finest butter.

To give butter a rich yellow colour, some Australian farmers used an additive known as annotto. Made from the seeds of a South American plant, it was mainly imported from Cayenne in square cakes which in colour were a strong orange-yellow. The formula for Gloucestershire and Cheshire cheeses allowed for as much as one ounce of annotto to each hundredweight of cheese. Many Australian farmers followed this formula. In 1885 the *Australasian* newspaper, in its guidebook for farmers, sang the praises of annotto, preferring it to crushed carrot because it did not flavour the butter. The rich colour of some pure Victorian butter also reflected the fact that in vitamin A it was superior to the Danish butter with which it vied on the London market, especially after the 1890s.

On some meal tables the butter was not very fresh. Farmers kept their butter until such time as they had enough to justify a trip to the railway station. Moreover many kerosene tins full of butter were hoarded, in times of low prices, until the price should rise, as it usually did in winter. Even in 1900 the typical grocer in Melbourne or Sydney did not have the means of keeping his butter very cool in summer. A preservative for the butter was therefore essential.

Most butter was salted. Salt was a way of adulterating as well as preserving the butter. The more salt that was added, the more water could be safely added, because the salt absorbed the water. *The Grocer's Companion* noted that the 'ordinary way of

THE HOME FARM

CHEESE ROOM

BREAKING UP THE CURD

Bega, operating some of the largest dairies in New South Wales, was an early home for the making of cheese and butter. In many districts the children milked the cows before they went to school and milked them again in the late afternoon.

adulterating butter is by adding a large quantity of salt'. Over-salted butter tended to have a flecked appearance, which experts would quickly notice even before the salty taste was in their mouth.

Increasingly the best butter was preserved in brine or liquid salt. A wooden cask was filled with rolls of fresh butter wrapped in linen, and brine was then poured in until the cask was full. It was a common sight in the general stores to see linen-wrapped rolls of butter, dripping with brine as they were removed from the cask, and surprisingly fresh after five or six months. There was one complaint: the butter nearest the side of the cask would be stained by the colonial timber of which the cask was made.

The normal container was a wooden tub traditionally holding 84 pounds of butter. As the tub itself weighed at least 11 pounds, a full tub was not easily handled. Another container of butter, known as the firkin, carried 56 pounds, packed tight. In the metric era a measure weighing 56 pounds sounds eccentric but that was exactly equal to half of one hundredweight. A light, square, wooden butter box eventually became normal, and the discarded boxes were used as kindling for wood fires in thousands of homes.

Butter was more widely eaten in the early 1900s than half a century previously. And yet butter was still too expensive for a typical workingman's family, and so was eaten only on special occasions or at just one weekend meal. 'Watch the butter!' was a common warning to children who spread their bread extravagantly. 'If you have butter on your bread, you can't have jam' was another rule, even in many middle-income houses.

The further outback you travelled, the less likely you were to find butter on a table. In the hot interior, even where the Coolgardie safe was the coolest place for keeping perishable foods, butter melted too easily. In 1909, the journalist C. E. W. Bean went to western New South Wales to observe the way of life, and in his book *On the Wool Track* he noted that 'butter was something of a luxury'. In the cooler months, however, a few of the wealthier shearers were beginning to ask their cooks to provide them with such luxuries as bacon and eggs on Saturdays and butter twice a week.

Butter's tenacious competitor, margarine, was invented by a Frenchman. Australia's first margarine factory was opened in 1885, and soon margarine appeared in grocer's shops under the English name of 'butterine' or under the misleading name of butter. It was usually made from butcher's fat, salt and skimmed milk as well as the vegetable dye, annotto. Bought mainly by the poor or by makers of low-priced cakes and pastry, it was cheap. The housewives of that era would have been astonished, had they lived long enough, to see margarine become the first choice in diet-conscious homes.

9

POTATO AND SPARROW

In the 1850s it was not always easy to buy fresh vegetables in Melbourne. The soil was said to be too dry, the summer too hot. Eventually parties of Chinese began to rent paddocks on the river flats and turn them into market gardens. From the river they carried water in buckets, suspended on poles, and irrigated their rows of young carrots, cabbages and turnips. They made it known that they would buy nightsoil from the city as a fertiliser, and their crops flourished. They were at work soon after sunrise, and returned to their hut and lit the fire for the evening meal only when the shadows were long. They carried fresh vegetables into the city, either in baskets suspended from a bamboo pole balanced on their shoulders, or in a horse-drawn cart.

By 1900 street after street in Sydney and Melbourne was supplied with vegetables and fruit by Chinese who knocked at door after door. Many of the fresh items sold in greengrocers' shops came from Chinese market gardens. In Sydney two kinds of tomatoes could be purchased, the dear ones, and the cheap ones grown by the Chinese and labelled as such in the Belmore vegetable market. A reluctance to buy the Chinese-grown product probably came more from the grower's use of human fertiliser than from an aversion to their ethnic background.

Chinese gardeners were important for a simple reason. In Australia land was cheap and plentiful, and so meat was very cheap. But labour was dear and scarce, and so fruit and vegetables, which required much labour, tended to be costly. The hard-working Chinese kept the cost down. It is even said that they grew most of the vegetables eaten in Australia by the 1880s and 1890s, but evidence culled from scores of scattered sources indicates that they were unlikely to have grown, in a typical year, more than one third of the vegetables consumed in the land. One crop they certainly did not dominate was the potato.

The Humble Spud

Nowadays in the supermarkets and fruit shops most potatoes on sale are already brushed or washed. In contrast, a century or more ago most of the potatoes on sale were lightly covered with soil. A connoisseur, by noting the red, black or grey soil on the potatoes, could usually tell which district had produced them. There was once a popular Australian phrase – 'a *clean* potato'. Someone who had never been a convict was often labelled 'a clean potato'. The phrase became part of daily speech, though it had to be used with discretion if an ex-convict was present.

The north-west of Tasmania grew fine potatoes even in the 1840s. Every visitor marvelled at the big potatoes uncovered by the diggers' long hand-forks. At times, however, the potatoes were left to rot in the rich soil. It was simply not worth the expense of digging and bagging them. Sometimes unsold potatoes were fed to the pigs. At least the pork and bacon could be sold at a profit.

To sell potatoes was to take part in a lottery. James Fenton, an early farmer to the west of Devonport, hoarded new potatoes he had dug at the end of the 1843 season. Rumours insisted that the price of potatoes would be high, and so when a merchant offered him the mouth-watering price of twenty pounds a ton, he said no. To his dismay the price suddenly slumped. Three years later he decided to dispense with the middleman and to escort his latest crop of potatoes from Tasmania to the new port of Melbourne. He sailed with his crop in a little schooner to supervise the sale. The owner of the ship was aboard; and within sight of Melbourne, he decided to speculate. On the spur of the moment he offered Fenton the meagre sum of one pound for every ton of potatoes stacked below. Fenton, remembering his bad luck in recent years, said yes. He was paid on the spot in gold coins. His decision was sensible. An hour or two later, when the ship reached Melbourne, it was discovered that nobody wanted potatoes; and eventually the whole cargo was dumped in the bay.

Five years later, after the gold rushes began, enormous quantities of food had to be imported into Victoria to feed the rich gold diggers. The price of Tasmanian potatoes soared. For decades Circular Head, a small potato and timber port, was also the general name for all Tasmanian potatoes sold in Sydney shops.

How did cooks serve the potatoes that probably appeared at two out of every three Australian meals? The simple things in daily life are often undocumented. It is sometimes assumed that the overwhelming majority of Australians boiled their potatoes and then ate them with the skins attached. It is doubtful whether this was a universal habit. The simple boiling of peeled potatoes, with salt added to the water, was common. Another method was recalled by George Dunderdale who in the 1850s ate with a family who lived largely on mutton and home-grown potatoes. He noted that Mother Shenty 'always boiled the potatoes in their jackets'. The diners, rather than eat the skins, discarded them on the wooden table.

In the ashes of a camp fire it was common to bake whole potatoes wrapped in wet newspaper. Curiously these were known as 'roasted' potatoes in old diaries. This method was favoured by bush cooks who owned only a billy and wished to set it aside for making tea, or by cooks who, confronted by too many visitors, had no pot big enough to cook all the potatoes.

The Marquess of Salisbury, who inspected Victoria's gold-fields nearly half a century before he became prime minister of England, was entertained to a meal in a tent in 1852. The potatoes and mutton were cooked in the embers – or 'half cooked', if the entry in his diary is read correctly. Hot tea was also drunk, with small fragments of stringy-bark floating in the black liquid. He noted that knives and forks were handed to only two of the five diners, and so it can be assumed that cutlery was scarce.

Potatoes were served in many ways. Once cooked, they could be mashed with a fork, and the resulting flour-like mix could be sweetened with sugar and a little milk or butter. Medical opinion argued that this was the safest way of serving potatoes to young children. Yet again, potatoes could be cut into fritters and fried in dripping or lard, though potato chips as we know them were not yet in vogue.

Sometimes fish and potatoes were served together. One favoured recipe called for the mashing together of fish and potato, after which the mash was shaped into small rolls and fried in hot lard. Or potatoes were slowly roasted in a pot, along with meat, and basted from time to time with the sizzling fat. Potatoes formed the heart of a stew of meat and vegetables, and were the main ingredient in a hot broth. Cooked potatoes could also be converted, with the aid of oatmeal or flour, into scones. In the streets, vendors sold hot potatoes, and Melbourne in August 1868 was excited by the arrival of the 'Young England hot potato and saveloy engine'.

Other families relished a potato pie in which small pieces of meat or turnip were mixed with chopped potatoes. If the household was comfortably off, it could afford the luxury of the yolks of four eggs to enrich the pie. Some home cooks liked to serve hot cheese-and-potato cakes. In one recipe this cheesy mix was further enriched with eggs, sugar and butter, and – an exotic extra – a handful of currants.

Even in the boiling of potatoes the recipes varied. One

school of opinion argued that the hot potatoes, before they were placed on the dinner plate, should be dried quickly with a towel so that not a drop of water remained. Some cooks, when setting out to please guests, would place boiled potatoes in hot fat, quickly moving them around the bottom of the pan or saucepan so that they were lightly fried.

There was frequent debate about what kind of potatoes should be planted in the home garden or bought in the shops. In the rich potato-growing districts of south-western Victoria, where the Irish were the main growers, the 'snow flake' was the favoured potato in the 1880s, though later it gave way to the New Zealand pink-eye. In Adelaide, Ernst Heyne, a seedsman who had learned his skills in the botanical gardens of Dresden and Melbourne, recommended that his customers should plant in autumn the pink-eye or early rose, the white rough, purple-eye, Prince Regent, and maybe the fluke and ashleaf kidney. For the seed potatoes sown a few months later, he was already selecting potatoes bred in Australia, including the Sydney red and that well-known Tasmanian potato, the Brown's River. As many families grew their own potatoes in the backyard, they were quick to learn which varieties suited their own soil and the different planting seasons.

A Green Salad – Not on the Menu

The Victorian government, a busy collector of statistics, regularly recorded the average prices of twenty or more vegetables even in the 1860s. They set out the price of bunches of green onions, dry onions, green peas (which competed with imported tins of green peas), marrows and pumpkins, parsnips, turnips, carrots, radishes and horseradish roots. They recorded asparagus, broccoli and rhubarb, cauliflowers – their extraordinary size excited new migrants – and cabbages, celery and kidney beans, but not french beans. Lettuces were not on the list. The green summer salad was still in its infancy.

Herbs were surprisingly plentiful. Sage, parsley, mint and marjoram were often for sale in Melbourne's big market. Watercress, a product of flooded paddocks, and not so easily bought today, could be bought by the dozen bunches. On the other hand the varieties of basil, now so popular, were a relative rarity in Australia as late as 1885 and not found even in the catalogues issued by the more venturesome plant nurseries. Curiously, garlic, which is now said to have arrived with the inflow of Italian and Greek immigrants, was on sale long before these people arrived.

There is evidence to suggest that herbs were used more widely in Tasmania than elsewhere, perhaps because its climate nurtured the herbs favoured in English cooking. It was a Tasmanian, Edward Abbott, who in 1864 produced Australia's first serious cookery book: the charmingly titled *Cookery for the Many, as well as for the 'Upper Ten Thousand'*. He conveyed the impression that garlic was grown in his own Hobart garden, that three kinds of parsley were available, and that basil was in 'everyday use' . If his remarks were true, then perhaps Tasmania was an exception to the cooking practices on the mainland.

Thirty years later some Australian doctors emphasised that cool salads were healthier than hot meat on a sweltering day. Dr Philip E. Muskett lamented that hardly any variety of lettuce – except the cabbage lettuce – was available in Sydney and that few herbs were for sale. He even looked in vain for the watercress which was common in Melbourne a generation earlier and was hawked around the streets of London and New York in season. He said he had little time for the English method of cutting a lettuce into shreds, dousing it with water, and then adding a few slices of hard-boiled egg and a greasy salad dressing. The lettuce leaves, in his opinion, had first to be separated, washed lightly, and then wiped clean with a fresh towel. Cos lettuce, lamb's lettuce and fetticus were his favourites; as for the dressings, he called for endives, chives, tarragon, salad burnet and the aromatic chervil, and a pinch of dry mustard mixed with egg yolk and a sprinkling of Crosse & Blackwell's white vinegar. He argued that Australians would be healthy only if they ate far more salad, drank more wine, preferred a small cup of coffee to a pot of tea, and walked ten or more kilometres a day. His dietary advice was long ignored.

The salad was not common, nor the tomato. The throwing of a rotten tomato at unpopular politicians was unlikely because a fresh tomato – let alone a rotten one – was not often seen in a private garden. Tasmania grew tomatoes in some quantity in the 1860s, but possibly they were a species that liked the cold climate and the mild summer. As tomatoes had to be protected from the bouts of intense cold when they were seedlings, fern sprays were placed over the young plants when

The city markets and their piles of Queensland bananas and pineapples and their array of vegetables and flowers astounded newcomers from Britain. This was the main Sydney market.

a frosty night was likely. A glasshouse, or a hothouse of any kind, was still uncommon for tomatoes or any other sun-loving plant.

Tomatoes were viewed as a fruit as well as a vegetable, and those who preferred them as a fruit selected the yellow varieties and the smaller ones: a favourite by the 1880s was Carter's greengage. Many people who ate the tomato as a vegetable tended to prefer the conqueror, little gem and acme varieties. Even then there were consumers whose sense of aesthetics dominated their sense of taste. They preferred a pretty tomato to a tasty tomato.

In 1900, strangely missing in the fruit shops were two tropical plants. The avocado, now produced in its millions in Queensland and Western Australia, was absent. A tree of central and South America, it had not yet been taken up by horticulturists in the United States, whence it came to Australia. The other absentee was the macadamia, itself a native of rainy areas of coastal Queensland. This evergreen tree, with its crop of fatty and delicious nuts, had been named after a Melbourne chemist, John Macadam, who is now remembered primarily as one of the two umpires presiding over the first recorded match of Australian Rules football, played in the parklands outside the Melbourne Cricket Ground in 1858. Half a century later, few Australians had ever tasted the macadamia nut. Not until the nut tree was improved and cultivated in Hawaii did it return in triumph to its native Queensland.

Fruits: Their Dangers and Delights

Many migrants fresh from Europe exulted that they were in a land of exotic fruits. They experienced the excitement of planting, the nervousness in watching shoots and buds develop, and the sheer pleasure when the first flowers and fruits appeared. Annabella Boswell, living on a farm near Port Macquarie when it was one of the most northerly towns in Australia, kept a diary which, in Scotland years later, she transformed into the most charming of books. Her diary for 1848 recorded her pleasure in the sweet potatoes, Cape gooseberries and other plants growing with a profusion that surprised her:

10 January:

> We went out to gather some fruit and found the trees covered with parrots . . . they will not consent to be driven away.

14 January:

> Got up very early, gathered up all the fallen apples, and picked all the ripe raspberries . . .

7 February:

> I picked some fresh apples for a squab pie, and prepared some grapes for jam, which occupied me till lunch was ready.

20 February:

> A lovely day with a north wind . . . Gathered some figs, which are just now both good and plentiful.

Pineapples ripened in her garden but nobody in the household liked them, so strange was their taste. Perhaps they should be made into a jelly? That was almost the highest compliment that could be paid to a rare fruit. So two heavy pineapples were peeled in the hope that they could produce a tasty jelly.

31 March:

> I made the jelly as we do apples, but it never jellied properly, and is more like honey both in colour and substance.

Meanwhile more and more orchards were planted, the preference being for those fruits familiar in the British Isles. Tasmania and Victoria grew prolific crops of the raspberry, strawberry, redcurrant, blackcurrant and gooseberry, which, oddly, were sold by the quart. Mulberry, cherry and quince trees were planted with enthusiasm, and their fruit could easily be found in the markets in summer. Today it is very difficult in a fruit market to find even one punnet of juicy, finger-staining mulberries. Other English favourites such as apples, pears, plums and almonds were grown in abundance. The cheapest fruit in many years was the apple, especially pippins and golden russets.

Oranges, grown in orchards on the north shore of Sydney Harbour and along the Parramatta River, were served mainly as a dessert or used in cooking. The drinking of fresh orange juice at breakfast was rare. Slowly, new varieties of citrus fruit arrived, including the navel orange. Almost seedless, it had been discovered in Bahía in Brazil as late as the 1860s and transplanted to the west coast of the United States where it became the Washington navel, under which name it reached the irrigated settlements on the banks of the Murray River.

Citrus fruit was dear enough, out of season, to reward Australian merchants who imported oranges and lemons from Messina in Sicily and boxes of oranges – and stone fruit too – in fast mail steamers from California. The Melbourne agent for the Mildura fruit growers was himself an importer of Sicilian citrus fruit. Today the importing of fresh fruits into Australia is seen as the outcome of cheap transport and globalisation; but the practice is more than one century old.

For decades, oranges were seen as expensive. Even in the harvest season most Australian children did not eat more than one orange in the course of a month. Orange juice was for the prosperous families. Eventually footballers helped to popularise oranges and lemons. As late as the 1940s, when major football games were played, several small circles of discarded orange peel could be seen on the Melbourne Cricket Ground at the end of three-quarter time.

Fresh fruit was not yet synonymous with good health in the eyes of doctors. Around the kitchen table, where the wisdom and folklore of one generation was passed on to the next, there was clicking of tongues and shaking of heads when the eating of fresh fruit was discussed. Apples were seen as healthier when baked than when eaten straight from the tree. The French idea of eating fruit sparingly, with the frugal support of a slice of bread, won supporters in Australia.

Summer fruits were said to cause fatal diseases in children. Taken late in the evening rather than in the morning, fresh fruit was viewed as risky: 'The old saying that apples are gold in the morning, silver at noon, and lead at night, is pretty near the truth.' So announced the editor of the popular English book of general knowledge, *Enquire Within Upon Everything*, which sold 167 000 copies in the space of five years. A well of information on every topic under the sun, it expressed the prevailing medical views held in the early decades of Queen Victoria's reign and especially the suspicion felt towards fresh fruit.

Seed fruits were preferred, on medical grounds, to stone fruits. Apples, grapes and other fruits containing seeds were generally seen as healthy, but peaches and apricots were viewed as a risk to health. Francis Bushby, a young wheelwright who emigrated from England to Brisbane, fell sick in 1866 from a 'bilious fever', which he seems to have attributed partly to the eating of stone fruits. He recovered after abstaining from such fruit. Whether most Australians shared his views is far from clear, but the idea persisted that fresh fruit was a hazard. The fear was still held by some outback Queenslanders a century later.

Much fruit was eaten as the final course in the midday or evening meal, but this custom emerged slowly. Eventually, in perhaps the majority of family households and boarding houses, the meal called 'dinner', irrespective of whether it was eaten in the middle or at the end of the day, often contained a concluding course of prepared fruit. In 1891, that arbiter of sensible eating, Mrs Wicken of Sydney, set out for ordinary families what she called 'economical dinners'. For Sunday she prescribed apple tart and custard, for Monday a currant pudding made with suet, and for Tuesday she prescribed stewed fruit. For the next three days were set down a jam tart, tapioca pudding, then bread-and-butter pudding, followed by a college pudding to complete the week. For a more prosperous family she set out costlier menus.

On most days of the week, except perhaps at the height of summer, the final or 'sweets' course was usually served hot. Admittedly most houses did not yet own an ice chest, and so the serving of apple tart and lemon custard and other cold puddings in the summer was difficult. Even then, the rule about fruit was emphatic. Fruit was healthier when cooked.

Tens of thousands of Australian families grew fruit in their own backyard and tried to preserve the surplus. Apples – and of course almonds – were most easily preserved. How to carry out this task was explained by country journals including *The Border Post Almanac*, published in Albury in 1878: 'Wipe every apple dry with a cloth; and see that no blemished ones are left among them. Have ready a very dry tight barrel, and cover the bottom with dry pebbles. These will attract the damp of the apples. Then put in the fruit, head up the barrel, and plaster the seams with mortar.' The barrel was then stored in a cool place, perhaps a cellar. For the preserving of lemons the recipe was to place them well apart in a barrel of dry sand, with the stem of each lemon facing downwards. Oranges were also preserved in sand.

Preserved fruits shipped in drums and boxes from the other side of the world were on display in shops even in the 1850s. In grocery shops it was easy to buy imported almonds, including the Jordan almond, Patras currants, and dried figs. Many shops sold bottles of French plums, packets of Barcelona nuts, and dried American apples. For cooks wishing to bake a large apple pie, the dried American apples were a bargain compared to the fresh and expensive local apples. Australian growers were slow to produce dried fruits. By the end of the century several Hobart factories produced 'evaporated apples' and a dry soup mix consisting of evaporated vegetables and herbs, while the new irrigation settlements on the banks of the Murray River produced increasing amounts of raisins and currants.

Parramatta and the north shores of Sydney Harbour were dotted with orange orchards, long before the orchards of the inland irrigation areas were planted.

To grow fruit and vegetables for a living was the equivalent of buying a ticket in a lottery. Most orchards experienced occasional dry years, after which might come a glorious spring and summer in which fruit was produced in such a glut that prices fell disappointingly. Near Adelaide in bumper years the ripe apples littered the ground, and it was not worth collecting them. Instead the pigs were let into the orchard, where they fattened on the ripe fruit. In southern Tasmania, at times so many raspberries arrived at the fruit shops and jam factories that later loads were dumped in the river. On the south-eastern fringe of Melbourne during the Christmas season of 1862 the market gardens were so withered by drought that cabbages sold at the huge price of one shilling each, but they quickly fell to one penny after March rains fell. A few years later cabbages were so scarce in the small river port of Brisbane – they were normally shipped from Sydney – that the price of one cabbage was worth two hours' pay. Later, the multiplying of locomotives and steamships tended to level out prices, for the surplus produce of one region could be moved quickly to another.

Orchardists cursed the pests, both native and imported. Several pests were the result of the nostalgia felt by many Australians. Common British garden birds were imported in cages, and released in the countryside. They would surely devour the caterpillars that spread like a plague. In the spring of 1867 a horsedrawn passenger coach arrived at Ararat in Victoria with a cage carrying fourteen English sparrows, and there was jubilation after the cage was placed on the upper verandah of the Bull and Mouth Hotel and the birds released. At first, residents gathered in excited knots to look at any sparrow hopping about the gardens. 'We trust that parents will warn their children against throwing stones at the sparrows', warned the local *Advertiser*. Before long the sparrows and starlings far outnumbered the boys as orchard thieves. In South

Yarra the Presbyterian clergyman counted, in his couple of high-yielding cherry trees, about 250 of the immigrant sparrows. He himself was lucky to save one basket of ripe cherries. A dozen plum trees were raided even more effectively by the creature he referred to as Master Sparrow.

The price of fruit varied widely from town to town. Adelaide was the city of purple grapes. British travellers in the early 1870s marvelled when they saw plump, shining, mouth-melting bunches, selling at a few pence a pound. In Edinburgh and Manchester a bunch of grapes was a luxury, and the flesh of the first grape was sucked almost like ice cream, so as to prolong the delicious taste. Accordingly, in Adelaide a party of Scottish vocalists thought that their hotel room was like a Roman banquet when they saw a large bowl overflowing with fresh grapes.

In Banana Land

Tropical fruits, at first, were expensive. A banana in Brisbane usually cost more than a large fresh apple in Melbourne. And then banana plantations appeared on the banks of coastal rivers in north Queensland. The Chinese around Innisfail, having cleared away the jungle, soon produced bunches by the million and carried them to the river bank. With long oars they punted the fruit in homemade sampans down to deep water where coastal steamers loaded it, often as deck cargo. Eventually arriving in Sydney and Melbourne, many of the once green bunches were now ripe and bruised. The crates in which the bananas were packed in the 1880s were made of fine tropical woods. In Sydney a new banana case from the Johnstone River was worth keeping even if the contents were rotten.

Bananas, even before they were commonplace in southern fruit shops, were seen by southerners as symbolising Queensland. The term Banana Land, as a nickname for Queensland, was first used in print about 1880. Bananas – not as large as today's – became plentiful in a normal season. Recipes for bananas multiplied in the cookbooks. One Sydney recipe of 1893 called for the stewing of twelve green bananas in a pot of boiling water. Over the soft bananas – spiced with a squeeze of lemon juice – was poured a brown sauce consisting of soup stock and such vegetables as onion, turnip, celery, carrot and brown peppercorns.

Early in the twentieth century, in abundant seasons, fruit and vegetables became cheaper. Many fruits were kept in cool stores and so the selling season was elongated. Faster ships, sailing more frequently, moved fresh produce from colony to colony when a glut occurred. Thus Tasmania in some seasons of the 1890s sold more apples in Sydney than in its booming London market. Melbourne cherries, sold in boxes weighing 25 pounds, were sent by rail to Sydney, and Tasmanian pears were sold in Brisbane, while Adelaide table grapes were sold in New Zealand. In southern cities the hawkers selling fruit from a barrow on the pavement sometimes offered three Queensland pineapples for sixpence, which was less than one tenth of their price a generation earlier.

Increasingly the latest breeds of fruit were given imaginative names, as if they were racehorses or roses. Women in the more fashionable greengrocers' glanced at their shopping lists and – if they were enthusiasts – enquired after the Red Warrington gooseberry, the Trollope's Victoria strawberry, the Falstaff raspberry, the Crittenden damson plum, the Lisbon lemon, and Hunt's large tawny nectarine. Favoured varieties of melon included 'ice cream' and the frighteningly named rattlesnake. Apples were available in wider variety than today, and the names of many of the popular apples of 1900 are now unknown. So the merry-go-round of fashion and experience runs its perpetual course.

Vegetables, too, acquired lofty-sounding or cute names. Among the lettuces, green drumhead, Paris green and Carter's giant white all had their followers. In the contest for the best cucumber, 'tender and true' was an early leader, while Daniel's Duke of Edinburgh was a contender. Among the cauliflowers, a favoured variety was Early London, as was little pixie among the cabbages, and rosebery among the brussels sprouts. Already the brown globe was a popular onion, but many gardeners who preferred a British rather than a Spanish onion planted James's keeping. A hundred other newborn names were on the lips of the nurserymen and seedsmen who flourished in the big towns. Few of these once glamorous names survive.

While the cities offered a wide choice of greens and fruits in season, the outback rarely saw even one cabbage or other green vegetable in the course of a year. Most of the outer sheep and cattle stations had no vegetable garden because the water to irrigate it was inadequate or movable only with the aid of a pump or a human chain of buckets. After artesian bores were sunk for water, the occasional garden was planted near the homestead and tended energetically by Chinese labourers. The stockmen and drovers living further out still had an inadequate diet. One solution was almost obvious: to eat the little-known greens which Aborigines traditionally ate. Few tried that experiment. Michael Terry, who was in the last generation of explorers, testified to the merits of a spinach-like leaf he found in central Australia. Boil the leaves of the portulaca in the billy for an hour with a dash of salt, eat it regularly and, he wrote, 'the misery of barcoo rot is vanished'.

The name Barcoo rot had been used as early as 1870 to describe the scurvy that stemmed from a scarcity of fresh vegetables and fruits. Named after the Barcoo River in outback Queensland, its suppurating sores and circular ulcers were vividly described by bush doctors. As the name Barcoo had a touch of the devil, it was allotted to another illness. The Barcoo sickness, sometimes called the Belyando spews, gave rise to bouts of vomiting.

Many bushmen who fought at Gallipoli in 1915 recognised the old malady. It returned with a vengeance in the summer months; and hundreds – perhaps thousands – of Australian soldiers in the trenches suffered from festering sores, especially on their hands. The gums and teeth of many soldiers were also affected. Naturally they called it the Barcoo rot, though the Barcoo was far away. Clearly their diet was lacking in fresh fruit and vegetables, though they did receive an allowance of lime juice. In Palestine the Australian horsemen suffered again from septic sores. In July 1917 at least one quarter of the men of the Anzac Mounted Division suffered. And then the fighting front moved towards the orange groves of Jaffa, and the orange juice, freely consumed, erased the illness.

Long into the twentieth century some bushmen made a virtue out of the absence of fresh foods. They insisted that lettuce and fruit were harmful either to their digestion or to their general health. The prospector who in 1923 discovered the Mount Isa mining field always maintained, echoing the trusted medical opinion widespread in his youth, that fresh fruit was often a source of harm. His one exception, his one indulgence, was a loaf of raisin bread which he bought on the rare occasions when he passed by a country bakehouse.

The character of vitamin C was a late discovery. For long it had been known or suspected that scurvy was a result of a diet deficient in fresh vegetables and fruit; but it was not until 1912 that the British scientist, Francis Hopkins, and the Polish scientist, Casimir Funk, formed this idea into a well-argued theory, and not until 1928 that vitamin C, or ascorbic acid, was isolated. But already the medicinal magic of orange juice was being proclaimed, especially in orange-growing California.

A long book could be written about the growing and eating of vegetables and fruits in Australia. It would be a story of ups and downs in orchards and market gardens, of scarcities and gluts, of new and fading fashions in medical knowledge, and an impressive willingness to import the seeds and seedlings of pears, plums, potatoes and everything edible, in endless variety, so that the fittest species could multiply.

10

THE SPARKLE OF BOSTON ICE

In the kitchen and at the dining table it was far easier to heat food and drinks in winter than to chill them in summer. And yet chilled food and drink were craved the most.

During the gold rushes of the 1850s, on hot days, wealthy Australians longed for ice in their drinks. At times they could actually buy it. It was not made artificially, but cut from winter ponds near Boston in the United States and carried to the southern hemisphere in sailing ships. As early as February 1853, American ice was on sale in Melbourne, the expensive Criterion Hotel being the main server of it. The price of two shillings for a pound of ice was exorbitant for almost everyone, but it was cheap to a digger carrying gold dust and gold sovereigns.

The trade in ice in Massachusetts was sophisticated. The thick ice covering the ponds was cut neatly with the aid of an ice plough, and in the more severe winters two harvests of ice could be taken off. The heavy horses that pulled the ice plough also hauled the ice to the storage house on the shores of the lake.

There the ice was conserved until warmer weather spurred local demand or an order arrived from a distant city. The blocks of ice – many of them weighing more than 45 kilograms – were carried by railway to Boston and other ports where deep-sea sailing ships were at anchor. In the hold of a wooden ship the blocks of ice were stacked side by side, and one on top of the other, so that in the end the ship's hold was one huge block of ice. The cargo stretched all the way from the wooden bottom of the ship to within an arm's length of the deck beams.

The narrow space between the ice and the deck was filled with a layer of insulation. In ships about to sail from Boston merely to New York, the top of the ice was covered with a layer of meadow hay or thin, curly wood shavings collected from a sawmill or planing mill. Sometimes barrels of fresh apples from New England were placed in the hay or shavings and sold along with the ice. But those cargoes of ice bound for tropical ports were insulated on both sides of the hold with layers of hay and sawdust or wood shavings.

Perhaps 10 per cent of the ice melted in the course of a short voyage – between, say, Maine and Washington – and maybe 20 per cent was lost in the longer voyage to New Orleans. In 1833 a shipment to Calcutta suffered the slow loss of one third of its ice. On a prolonged voyage to east Asia half of the ice might be lost while it passed through tropical waters, firstly the tropical zone in the Atlantic and then, after the ship had rounded South Africa, the tropical zone in the Indian Ocean. In 1846 a sailing ship carrying 600 tons of American ice spent so many months in traversing tropical seas that she arrived in Hong Kong with only 80 tons intact. On a long voyage, the pumps had to be kept at work in order to discharge the melted ice.

On Asian routes the losses were probably larger than on the route to Australia, during which the tropics were traversed only once. An ice ship leaving Boston for Melbourne passed through warm seas when crossing the equator but soon after the ship entered the far south of the Atlantic Ocean where she met the cold waters and westerlies of the roaring forties and fifties. There the melting of the ice was slow. Oddly, an ice ship on that route must have very occasionally passed close to icebergs. Some captains must have wondered whether it might not be easier to hack the ice from an iceberg in the Southern Indian Ocean rather than a pond near Boston; but first they had to find the iceberg and then they had to risk the ship and the lives of its crew by approaching close to that iceberg, much of whose ice was concealed below the sea. An iceberg could never be a source of ice for Australian ports.

The ice that melted during a typical voyage to Melbourne was rarely more than one third of the cargo. Additional ice, however, would be lost after it was unloaded in Melbourne and transported to the ice-storage house or to city hotels. More ice – distributed by fast horse teams and the new railways to Ballarat, Bendigo and other towns – was melted by the heat of day or broken into pieces by jolting vehicles. The melting on up-country journeys was higher in January and February. A block of ice that reached a goldfield 150 kilometres from Melbourne was by then perhaps only half of its original size. In the eyes of rich and thirsty gold diggers, that made it all the more precious.

*Ice and fresh fish were among the cargoes of the express trains that linked
the ports and the interior. This train is steaming through the Adelaide Hills,
just after the Adelaide–Melbourne line had been opened.*

Most of the ships that arrived in Melbourne with ice carried virtually no other cargo. In October 1858, for example, the sailing ship *Alma*, more than 100 days out from Boston, sailed into the bay near Melbourne with 531 tons of ice. While October was not the best month for the sale of such a cargo, the ice was promptly sold to hotels and restaurants.

In Ballarat a few of the wealthy buyers not only wanted ice but ice harvested from a particular Boston pond. Wenham Lake was a favourite brand of North American ice. In Melbourne in the early 1860s it could sometimes be bought for a mere two pence a pound, which was about one tenth as much as the early cargoes of Boston ice had commanded in Australian ports.

How strange that ice from Wenham Lake could be dispensed by a fashionable hotel in Ballarat as well as by royal palaces in London! The first cargo of ice from Wenham Lake had reached London in the summer of 1844. The ice gave sparkle to that summer's entertainments and festivities. On the dining tables of grand hotels, below the gas-lit chandeliers, blocks of carved ice acted as centrepieces and reflected the flicker, sheen and shimmer of light from the chandeliers. In certain London embassies blocks of fresh ice placed in the stately corridors acted as a cool fan for the air passing by. William Thackeray, a novelist who was alert to changing fashions, noticed that American ice sat ornamentally on almost every table in the genteel circles of London: 'Everybody has the same everything in London. You see the same coats, the same dinners, the same boiled fowls and mutton, the same cutlets, fish, and cucumbers, the same lumps of Wenham Lake ice.' After about

1850 the crystal-clear ice from Wenham Lake was increasingly driven from London dinner tables by ice shipped from Norway. The fading of the English markets encouraged the owners of Wenham Lake to seek other outlets for their ice. Australia, which was painted gold to the fingertips, was such an outlet.

Melbourne, as Australia's richest and biggest city in 1860, was the main goal for the ice ships but a portion of the ice was shipped on to Sydney. There the Union Club placed a permanent order for 500 pounds of ice, whenever it could be obtained, but the club was unable to store the ice for longer than a few days. In January 1862 it complained that it had been without ice for a week and a half.

The artificial making of ice was one of Australia's more remarkable innovations. James Harrison, a Scottish-born newspaperman, edited the Geelong daily paper; and in his spare time he experimented with the making of ice. In 1851, on the banks of the Barwon River, he succeeded in manufacturing ice by mechanical means. His ether-compression process was full of promise, and he went to England to patent and promote it. Before the end of the decade he was making artificial ice on a commercial basis, and in Bendigo a brewery installed one of his refrigerating machines. At first, however, he was unable to cope with the competition from Boston ice. Sceptical buyers vowed that the Geelong ice was not as cold as the Boston ice. Many people furrowed their brow and wondered whether they should risk buying the Geelong ice. But the making of artificial ice became more efficient, and eventually it defeated the Boston ice.

In 1873 Harrison seemed on the verge of solving the more difficult task of how to ship fresh Australian meat to the huge market in Europe. He froze meat on shore, and packed it into an insulated chamber in the ship *Norfolk*. The ship, however, had no refrigerating machine. Aboard, the temperature slowly rose, and the decaying meat had to be thrown into the sea. Meanwhile in other lands, more and more experiments were made with refrigeration, and Harrison lived to witness the next breakthrough. A consignment of Australian beef, mutton and butter reached England in the steamship *Strathleven* in 1880. During the voyage the meat had been kept at a temperature of about 15 degrees Fahrenheit by a refrigerating machine designed in Glasgow.

The chilling of milk, butter, fish and meat so that they could stay fresh during long voyages became commonplace. By the late 1880s the more expensive hotels and clubs had refrigerated rooms or ice chests. At the same time the main passenger ships plying between Australia and England also had small refrigerating machines and cool rooms for the preserving of food and the making of ice, but the typical sailing ships, coastal passenger ships and older ocean steamships offered no such luxuries. In 1888 the China Navigation Company's 2300-ton steel steamship, *Taiyuan*, advertising its passages from Sydney to Thursday Island, Port Darwin and Hong Kong, announced that on board was a Haslam patent refrigerator. The owners asserted that this was the only ship that, sailing between Australia and China, supplied ice to passengers throughout the long voyage.

Back on shore, an incoming cargo of ice transformed social life in the wealthier circles – in those months when ice was available. Often on hot evenings a bead of ice was dropped into a glass of claret. At banquets a chunk of ice prevented the butter from melting. Fruit seemed fresher when chilled by ice. That novel delicacy, ice cream, could be concocted for a few guests when the chef heard that the ice ship from Boston had just dropped anchor in the harbour.

Jelly and blancmange were special gainers from the import of ice. It seems unbelievable that one should feel a need to explain what blancmange is, but such has been its decline. Usually made from cornflour and boiled milk and poured into a mould, it was ethereal and opaque. When made by the best cooks it appeared to have descended ready-made from the white clouds.

Jelly was made usually with very hot water, jelly crystals or gelatine, and sometimes fruit or fruit juices. After an hour or two the typical jelly became firm, though rarely so firm as not to wobble when it was served onto the pudding plates. A dish full of jelly – red or yellow, green or orange – was pretty in the candlelight. At night, in a banquet room, the light played brilliantly across its smoothness. When still a warm liquid, it could be poured into metal moulds and, when firm, could be tipped from the mould to stand in dome-like glory. There was one catch. In very hot weather the jelly would not set. Or, if it did set, it remained flabby.

As country balls were held in the warmer weather, the creation and conveying of jelly was risky. Newly made in

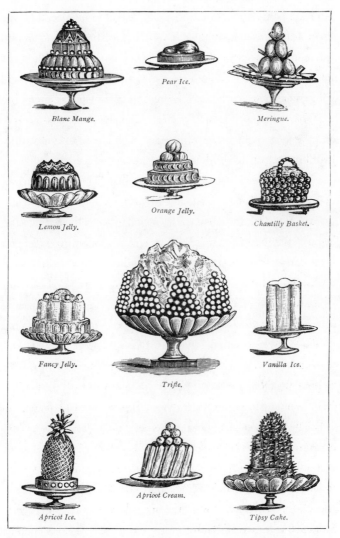

Blanc Mange.

Pear Ice.

Meringue.

Lemon Jelly.

Orange Jelly.

Chantilly Basket.

Fancy Jelly.

Trifle.

Vanilla Ice.

Apricot Ice.

Apricot Cream.

Tipsy Cake.

With the coming of fresh ice, the making of jelly, blancmange, trifle and other watery desserts was transformed. Mrs Beeton's Every Day Cookery and Housekeeping Book, *widely read in Australia, displayed these tempting dishes.*

a private home and still in its mould, it had to be placed on the floor of the horsedrawn buggy, a wet cloth being wrapped around the mould to keep the jelly from sagging in the heat. When the hall was reached, the moulds of jelly, a long line of them, were gently placed on the floor, it being the coolest place. Once the dancing commenced, the floorboards might shake just a little, and the jelly might vibrate. Indeed it might cease to stand stiffly to attention. As Mary Gilmore recalled, ingenious recipes helped some jellies to withstand the evening heat: 'They stood when everyone else's ran. It was talked about for the rest of the year.'

Eventually, blocks of ice appeared in a few districts. At the sight of the ice, women as well as children must have clapped their hands. The making of jelly and other watery desserts was revolutionised.

Ice was craved by ill people whose temperature was soaring. Richard Hart, who was a founder of that influential nationalist organisation, the Australian Natives Association, was a young teacher and musician in the Victorian town of Stawell. In October 1884 he became fatally ill with peritonitis. His fever and thirst were intense. The doctor called for ice. Hart's sister recalled the family's dilemma: 'as ice was not procurable in Stawell we telegraphed to Ballarat for a supply, and were informed a quantity would reach Stawell by eight o'clock p.m'. From five o'clock onwards her dying brother, at brief intervals, asked her what was the time, for he eagerly awaited the arrival of the evening train and the consignment of ice. His sister could not stand 'the silent pleading of his eyes' and temporarily had to leave the room. When the ice reached the sick room, the sense of relief, though short-lived, must have been overwhelming. It is a sign of the slow spread of ice-making that Stawell – then one of Australia's thirty largest towns – should possess no iceworks.

A decade later, an ice chest suitable for a suburban kitchen could easily be obtained. It was possible to arrange for ice to be delivered by horse and cart twice a week to suburban addresses in the main cities, but most houses in Sydney and Melbourne possessed no ice chest. An ice chest cost only about two pounds – or just one week's wages for a semi-skilled tradesman. The weekly ice bill, of course, added to the cost. A piano or a sewing machine cost much more than an ice chest; but far more people heard the sound of the piano through the front window than heard the knock of the iceman at the back door.

Coolgardie and Other Safes

As meat did not last long in summer and could be polluted by blowflies even before it reached the shop of the butcher, a simple way of avoiding the heat and flies was essential. A meat safe was an extremely simple answer. It was a ventilated cupboard, standing in a cool place, and often made of perforated zinc, a very heavy version of what is now called flywire. Some of the larger hotels probably used a meat safe even before 1850. In the outback the more sophisticated housekeepers later used them, but they remained expensive until late in the century. In Melbourne in 1885 *The Australian Housewives' Manual*, written especially for people on a low but not a *very* low income, advised readers to build a cool safe for keeping meat, butter, bacon, milk, eggs, cheese and even the bread. Families who could not yet afford an ice chest saw advantages in this cheap, cool safe.

The Coolgardie safe was probably the outback version of the meat safe. A wooden upright frame, like a refrigerator in shape, it stood on four wooden legs with ample space between each leg. Its sides were made of hessian, a cheap, lightweight alternative to flywire. On the top of the safe was a flattish tin of water, positioned so that water slowly percolated down the hessian walls to a drip tray on the floor. If a breeze was blowing, the damp hessian walls produced – even in a heatwave – a mild cooling of the meat and other items stored inside the safe. Usually the safe was placed on a shaded verandah, or beneath a peppercorn or other shade tree. It was a wonderful asset in those outback towns where the typical house, being made of corrugated iron, was extremely hot in the daytime. As the Coolgardie safe stood in the backyard, it could easily be robbed. Its very existence was a sign of the honesty prevailing in outback towns and even in the suburbs.

Where this safe was invented is not known. It was not necessarily an Australian invention. Even its connection with the gold town of Coolgardie is uncertain, though probably it first became popular on the West Australian goldfields, whence the idea was taken to other cities by the stream of people emigrating from the fields. Eric Partridge, an authority on the Australian language, thinks that the name 'Coolgardie safe' came into popular currency about 1920. My inclination is to think that the safe itself, under another name or no name, was in existence at least twenty years earlier, in small numbers. Sidney Baker, another authority on Australian words, suggests that the name gained favour accidentally, because the word 'cool' forms the beginning of the name. This suggestion, which at first seems naive, could well be correct. The name, with its connotation of coolness, *sounds* just right. In its heyday it was simply called 'the Coolgardie'.

Tens of thousands of houses owned no Coolgardie. Accordingly, on a hot morning the butter tended to melt with alarming rapidity. In an effort to keep the butter cool, the house-wife wrapped it in a wet cloth, put it on a plate, and rested the plate on the cool brickwork of the unused fireplace in the dining room. In most simple houses, the dining room was not used except for special occasions. As for meat, it was placed in the meat safe, which often stood in the shade outdoors in summer-time. That meat safe offered no coolness. Its sole merit was that its galvanised-iron wire kept out the blowflies.

Eventually the Coolgardie safe was everywhere. Nothing was more typically Australian. It could be that three of every four households in Australia possessed such a safe in the year 1930. It was so simple that any bush carpenter could make it in half a day. It was cheap to operate, its only running cost being fresh water. It was to be superseded in the towns largely by the ice chest.

Soon after the end of the First World War, maybe one fifth of the city houses in Australia possessed an ice chest. The ice, supplied to houses only in summer, came by horse and cart from the local iceworks and was carried into the kitchen by a man who perched the block of ice on a hessian bag on his shoulder. Many of the icemen sold firewood to the same house in winter. On farms and in small towns the ice chest was unknown. A housewife in the wheat town of Jeparit once wrote: 'I never saw an ice chest till 1930.' By then, in the new city houses, the ice chest was already being challenged by the domestic refrigerator.

The old Coolgardie safe, looked back upon with fondness, is hailed as being almost heroic in its capacity to fight the butter-melting heat. But it supplied coolness, not coldness. It was a poor cousin to the ice chest, which in turn was a poor cousin to the refrigerator.

Schnapper, Snapper and Murray Cod

The land of meat was not the land of fish. Immigrants arriving from western Europe and hoping to find the familiar, and cheap, cod, mackerel and other fishes of their homeland looked in vain. It was not even easy to find a fish shop in a typical town and suburb. The Australian seas were poorly endowed with fish compared to the cold waters of the North Sea. And yet fish was a useful and sometimes a triumphant part of the Australian diet.

In Victoria in the 1860s, the most popular fish was the schnapper, or snapper. Caught in Port Phillip Bay it was sold fresh in the markets in large quantities. It was also caught by Chinese fishermen who cured it with smoke and then sent it to the goldfields, where it was sold in Chinese general stores. Knowledge of the breeding, growing and feeding habits of the snapper, like most local fish, was accumulated slowly. Thus in Sydney this same fish was known by four names. Red bream, caught by young boys in the estuaries in the summer holidays, was actually a baby snapper; the squire was a half-grown snapper, less than three years old; while the fish usually known as snapper – the prince of fish – was older and might weigh up to a dozen kilograms. Finally there was also an old, solitary fish known as the rock snapper.

The main sporting fish to be found around Sydney, the rock snapper was the target for hundreds of amateur fishing expeditions each month. Anglers set out from Sydney Harbour in steam launches to catch it, using starfish, squid and mackerel as bait on their lines. The sunken reefs where many of the fish fed were known locally as the snapper grounds. To catch a large snapper was a joy. As one patient angler reported, a snapper tugging and jerking at the end of the line was an exciting sensation, giving a feeling in the hands that no true fisherman could mistake: when the snapper tries to escape, with all his might and cunning, 'he goes off with a rapidity that makes the cord whistle again, either through your fingers or over the boat's gunwale'.

The larger cities provided a wholesale fish market where retailers gathered early in the morning. Sydney in 1872 built in the bayside suburb of Woolloomooloo a grand market resembling, from the outside, more a high-roofed railway station than a fish bazaar. Its clock tower looked down on the casually clothed fish suppliers and hawkers who, around five in the morning, arrived with horse and cart or pushed a small handcart. Beneath the lamps could be seen, laid out side by side on the wet floor, thousands of gleaming fishes; and white lines, drawn in chalk, marked off each fisherman's catch from the other.

The fish trade was already falling into the hands of colourful traders of many nationalities. The auctioneer gave to nearly every buyer what he thought was an appropriate nickname. Graball had big hands, Dundreary presumably was named for his whiskers and Ivo Bligh must have been named after the famous English cricketer. And there was a fish-buyer named Ice Cream, who perhaps also hawked that delicacy in summer. When the auctioneer sold fish to a man known as Nebuchadnezzar, the watching journalist saw 'an individual with a decided facial prominence gravely step forward and begin to shovel his fish into his basket with hands that certainly never could have been like those of his kingly namesake'.

The ray of light from the South Head lighthouse was a dazzling sight to the Sydney fishermen returning with their catch early in the morning.

Fish auctioneers followed tradition, selling the small fish such as sand whiting in lots of two dozen, sea mullet by the dozen, snapper by the half-dozen, and big jewfish, weighing as much as 15 kilograms, one at a time. The owners of fish shops and the door-to-door hawkers carried their new-bought fish to the stone troughs at the end of the long hallway and gutted them, finally washing them in salt water from nearby Sydney Harbour. Within an hour or two the fish were being sold from horse and cart in the streets or from the counter of the fishmonger's shop.

Every strip of coastline had its own mixture of edible fishes. Thus in the Launceston market in 1882 the mullet and flounder were the most conspicuous fish, while in hotels in Townsville and the Gulf ports the baked barramundi was a favourite. The public was slow to appreciate some of the edible local fishes. In Tasmania the conger eel, weighing up to 25 kilograms and caught by hook and line, had virtually no sale. Three kinds of leatherjacket were caught, and not one was really saleable. The big and plentiful kingfish was shunned by Hobart's fifty fish hawkers, and when left unsold these wholesome fish were mainly consigned for garden manure. Silver perch and black perch, caught throughout the year, vexed the professional fishermen. Robert Smith, a Hobart fisherman who kept his live perch in salt-water wells, reported in 1882: 'They will not live long in the wells; they prick each other with their fins and become disfigured thereby.'

Fish was much dearer than meat. For many families in city and country a meal of fresh fish was a rarity – unless the father and sons were amateur fishermen. How Catholics managed in Australia is not always clear. Traditionally they abstained from meat and turned to fish on Fridays and on holy days. Many who faithfully chose fish on Friday ate tinned fish, imported from Europe.

By 1900 the fish trade was more sophisticated. Fast steamers, supplies of artificial ice, and refrigerated chambers enabled fish to be carried long distances, and New Zealand even sent chilled fish to Australia. One Melbourne wholesaler set up a fishing village at Lakes Entrance where in pens of wire netting he kept up to 30 000 'baskets' of live fish, ready to kill and chill for the Melbourne market. Not all the customers accepted the novelty of chilled fish. Some shoppers asked themselves: was the fish chilled in order to quell the smell?

The Murray cod, a freshwater fish, was abundant in the Murray and Darling rivers, though now it is scarce. In the fish markets in Adelaide and Melbourne it was marvelled at by newcomers, for some fish in old age weighed as much as 100 kilograms. The cod was appreciated even more when young, for its flesh was then tastier. In the 1840s huge specimens were sometimes carried over the Blue Mountains in horsedrawn coaches and served at Sydney banquets. Some of these fish were older than the diners consuming them. On the Murray River, Aborigines were among the professional net fishermen whose catch was sent almost daily in fast carts and coaches to the Bendigo goldfields, and increasingly to Melbourne in the early 1860s after the inland railway was extended to the river port of Echuca. In the same coaches came also the occasional exotic consignment – thousands of leeches packed in moist blue clay for the long journey to London, where presumably they were bought by doctors in order to suck the blood from ill patients: this was the inverse of blood transfusion.

Murray cod, sometimes called the cod perch, was often the second-most abundant fish in the Melbourne market in the 1860s, coming behind the seawater snapper, but regarded as superior in taste. A few gourmets went further and acclaimed Murray cod as one of the tastiest freshwater fishes on the whole globe. This fish is no longer so esteemed. Its fatty taste has not changed: it is the taste of the eaters that has changed. The wonderful Murray cod is now rarely seen in fish shops, and it is the ecologists more than food connoisseurs who lament its decline.

The cod was so prized in the colonial era that specimens were caught and released in other rivers. It flourished in Lake George near present-day Canberra – until the mineral waters from nearby coppermines entered the lake. Introduced to the Yarra River, the Murray cod neither flourished there nor did it completely vanish. Regrettably it caused other fish to die out.

Another delicacy, the large freshwater crayfish or lobster, was found with ease. In Victoria it was known as the Murray crayfish and in New South Wales as the Murrumbidgee lobster. Beautiful in its colouring and most easily caught in the winter, it reached the Melbourne fish markets, 'alive in great numbers'. In the 1860s, Frederick McCoy, professor of the natural sciences at Melbourne University, praised it as a gourmet's fish, far above the seawater crayfish caught near Port Phillip Heads.

A large lobster 'lifted from the Murrumbidgee was supper enough for father, mother, and two of us children', wrote Mary Gilmore. In rivers in western Victoria, settlers used to go fishing with a landing net and a kerosene tin in the confidence that they would catch a couple of lobsters for the evening meal. The older lobsters were so big that two virtually filled the tin. Smaller ones, slightly more delicate in taste, went three to the tin. These giants of the inland rivers became scarce. Forty years later, people could fish for a whole day and bring home only the small lobsters, many of which were so tiny that twenty might fit in the one kerosene tin.

In the muddy stretches of rivers in the south-east corner of the land, the blackfish was widespread and in faster, clearer water it was often taken by a fishing line at sunset. Nature writers described it lovingly, as if it were a pet cat or dog: 'The blackfish is of stay-at-home habits', wrote the journalist Donald Macdonald in the 1880s. 'You cannot easily tempt him from his favourite river cavern into the broader stretches of water.' Skilled in hiding in crannies, they hid beneath submerged logs and in the shadows. More than twenty years later they were becoming scarce in the Victorian streams that Macdonald had wandered along as a teenager. He wrote: 'alas, the blackfish is dying out'. Some thought that the Murray cod, released in these streams, was the main offender.

In the eyes of many immigrants the native fishes were no substitute for the trout and salmon of home. Attempts were made as early as the 1840s to ship the eggs of trout and salmon from Europe to Tasmania. Two decades later, the imported eggs of brown trout were hatched successfully in the uplands of Tasmania and later they thrived around Ballarat. The rainbow trout was flourishing by the 1890s, eggs having been carried from New Zealand. The idea of breeding trout in a fish farm belonged to a later era.

When the Oyster was King

Love of oysters was a tradition in England, where oysters were cheap enough for working people to buy. In 1851 it was estimated that in the course of a year some 300 000 bushels of fresh oysters – equal to nearly half a billion oysters – were sold at Billingsgate market in London. The appetite for oysters was carried to Australia where very different oysters, smaller but often sweeter, were found.

Along the estuaries and harbours of New South Wales the Aborigines had gathered oysters for thousands of years, and the British immigrants soon appreciated their taste. On all the rocky shores between Sydney Town and the Heads, it seemed that every protruding rock held an oyster or two. Year after year hundreds of picnic parties, arriving in horse-driven vehicles or in rowing boats or steam launches, set to work to eat the oysters, while the professional oyster collectors gathered them in baskets for the fish market. The supply seemed inexhaustible. On crisp sunny days the oyster picnics could be heard and seen along the shores, with men and women plying hammer and chisel to prize shells from the rocks, a knife to open the shells, and pepper and vinegar to pep up the freshly opened

303

oysters. Often likened to the oysters of Carlingford, a seaport in Ireland, the Sydney species was considered to be slightly inferior and smaller. A later generation of Sydney oyster eaters, more nationalist, reversed this verdict.

Oysters were so plentiful that for many decades they were collected and burned in limestone kilns; one Sydney contract called for the providing of 6000 bushels of lime from the shells of live oysters. In 1868 the New South Wales parliament passed a law to prevent the dredging and the burning of live oysters for the making of lime. Two years later a serious attempt at large-scale cultivating of oysters was made by Thomas Holt, who tried the French system of growing oysters in a network of canals.

Oysters were not a food for the wealthy or those arranging a celebration. For decades, oyster eating continued to be more popular among working people. When on a spree, they ate them almost as if they were grains of rice. In Collingwood in the 1870s one workingman, to start his meal, ate 6 dozen oysters, having first spiced them with cayenne pepper. We know of this orgy only because he refused to pay the bill, and so the dispute reached the newspapers.

In many country towns fresh oysters were swallowed with speed when bags arrived by train from the distant coast. In the small Riverina town of Narrandera around 1890, two oyster bars competed for business. In the cities, oyster saloons and bars were numerous, and in 1888 the main streets of Melbourne held at least sixty oyster saloons. If today the city were to have the same proportion of oyster bars to people, it would need about 500 oyster bars.

During the gold rushes in Western Australia in the 1890s, oyster saloons flourished in Kalgoorlie. They sold mainly oysters that had been shipped as deck cargo from New South Wales and Queensland, a voyage often lasting a fortnight, and then sent on in the train from Albany or Fremantle. In coastal ships bound for Western Australia one task of a deckboy was regularly to hose, with sea water, the bags of oysters lying on the deck. Each month about 3 tons of oysters were shipped across the Great Australian Bight.

The medical value of oysters was buttressed not only by folklore but by medical opinion. According to the senior resident doctor at Sydney Hospital, fresh oysters restored the strength of those suffering from anaemia and cleared away the phlegm from sufferers of bronchitis. They were also valuable in coping with nervous diseases and indigestion. As for those suffering from tuberculosis, the oyster 'conserves the vital powers'. One can imagine the medical concern when the supply of rock oysters began to fail.

From time to time there were fears about the reliability of local oysters. In the early 1870s a gentleman's club in Sydney, receiving complaints about the quality of local oysters, arranged for oysters to be imported from New Zealand. A steward in the steamship *Hero* acted as the club's oyster agent, and every time his ship reached Sydney he sent ashore two big bags of fresh oysters to the Union Club's kitchen. More and more oysters had to be shipped in from distant ports, for the local supply fell away. In 1871, New South Wales had harvested 93 000 bushels of oysters but twenty years later the harvest fell to a mere one sixth of that tally. What had caused such a decline was the topic of endless debate among oyster eaters.

Tasmania's native mud oysters passed through the same sequence of boom and slump. Maybe twenty-two million were dredged in a bumper year of the 1870s. Quickly the annual catch declined, and in 1882 only one oyster was dredged for every fifty that had been caught in the prosperous years. By then the scallop, whose flesh was larger than that of the oyster, was being fished in huge numbers. A favoured dish of the poorer part of Tasmanian society, its annual catch rose and fell until eventually it, too, became scarce.

The Australians' hunger for prawns was not as pronounced as it is today. Tiger prawns could be easily bought in Sydney in some years of the 1890s but not in others. As for the Sydney crayfish, it was almost too plentiful to be prized to the full. Douglas Ogilby, one of the few fisheries experts, argued in 1893 that if sensible conservation laws were passed, large lobster canneries could be set up to preserve in tins the 'apparently inexhaustible' supply of lobsters. In nearby Broken Bay, however, fishermen had already harried the crayfish to the brink of extinction.

A common sight was the fish hawker, moving along a city street with a large basket of fresh or almost-fresh fish and calling out his wares. Dr Muskett, the evangelist for healthy food, gave high praise in 1893 to what he called the costermonger, or basket man, who sold most of the fish eaten in Sydney: 'It is true that he is given to making strange outcries, and that he is at times boisterous in speech. Yet, notwithstanding these things, he is a

Cray fishing in the western Victorian harbour of Portland.

valuable member of society, and personally I have a very great respect for him.' The fish hawkers far outnumbered the fish shops. As for fish and chip shops, they hardly existed in 1900.

While the fish shop was rare, the restaurant specialising in fish began to multiply after Greek migrants increased. Greeks in this country had been few. Whether they exceeded 1000 in 1891 is open to doubt. But new arrivals began to open fish shops and oyster saloons as far apart as Fremantle and Cairns. Originating from fishing villages on small islands rather than from Athens, these migrants had a flair for cleaning and selling fish. Some took over oyster leases in the estuaries and supplied their own oyster saloons. In Perth, Greeks started their own oyster beds. In Sydney several Greeks came to be known as oyster kings.

Young Greek relatives, coming out to join these rising businessmen, supplied cheap labour in their shops and fish cafés. One was Georgios Lianos who, on reaching Sydney in 1898, immediately began work for his family's restaurant. He rose at 3 a.m. and walked to the fish market where he cleaned the fish that his relatives had bought. He then returned to wash the tables and floors of the café, to open oysters by the hundreds, and to collect at lunchtime and dinner the dirty plates from the busy dining tables, before retiring to bed at midnight. His long hours of work may well have been exaggerated – three hours' sleep and a midday siesta were hardly enough rest – but hard work was the rule in the Greek oyster saloons, cafés, and fruit and lolly shops. Sheer hard work helped to lower costs and make fish and oysters cheaper. Nonetheless in 1900, a meal of seafood was usually dearer than steak and eggs.

A Craving for More Calories

It is now often argued, by connoisseurs of food and wine, that earlier Australians should have adapted to the warmer climate; that they should have eaten more greens and fruits and cold salads; that they should have rebelled against a diet centred on bread, meat and potatoes. This criticism has validity but it overlooks one crucial fact. Most working Australians in the period from 1850 to 1900 needed more calories than do their descendants.

Most people stood up or moved about while they worked. The proportion of the workforce that could sit down during working hours was tiny. Most workers lifted heavy weights. On the wharves, in the wheat fields and railway yards, the bags, bales and containers were so heavy that today the lifting of such weights, except in a gymnasium, is virtually banned. Most workers walked long distances in the course of the day, either at work or in their journey to and from work. Labour-saving equipment was becoming more common but it still called for muscle power. The jobs that required physical strength could be numbered in the several hundreds, and included the farrier shoeing the horse, the man in the foundry, the pick-and-shovel labourer, the miner drilling a hole in the rock, the axemen and sawyers in the forest, and the men unloading a ship.

In districts where roads were few and the hills were steep, men and even women often had to carry heavy loads. These human packhorses were remembered long after they died. A Frenchman in Gippsland once carried a piano from the railway station to a hotel. Countless farmers could carry a bag of wheat – there were eight bags to the ton. Prospectors pushed their possessions day after day in homemade wheel barrows. All these people were hungry for solid food that filled their stomachs. They were working machines, and food was their fuel.

Most women in the course of a day carried considerable weights. Washing day, if the family was large, called for the carrying of heavy buckets of water, the lifting of masses of hot sodden clothes, and the pegging of those clothes on the long washing line. The making of jam, sauces, soap, candles, pies and biscuits in the kitchen called for heavy and persistent labour. So many kitchens were really backyard factories. In the same kitchen the family's clothes had to be made and repaired, boots repaired when possible, and meals cooked. While servants were on hand in the houses of the wealthier 10 or 15 per cent of the population, elsewhere the housewife was an unpaid servant.

Numerous children were called upon to work regular hours. On a typical dairy farm the older children and sometimes the younger helped to milk the cows from, say, 5 a.m. to 8 a.m., and then again from 5 p.m. In between the milkings they walked to school and back again.

A major milestone was the inauguration of the eight-hour day in Melbourne in 1856, but it applied only to some of the building trades in that city and was slow to spread. Forty years later, about half the paid workforce in the land worked at least sixty hours a week, often in shifts of ten hours a day, six days a week. Sunday, the day of rest, was eagerly awaited. For the typical mother Sunday was less of a day of rest. But if she was religious, and if she believed that little work should be done on the Sunday, she prepared Sunday's food on the previous day.

The culinary critics who rebuke the earlier generations for not selecting a midday menu suited to a warm climate overlook one simple fact. Most Australians rejoiced in meat and potatoes more than lettuces and salads because their hunger was thereby satisfied. They were not yet weight-watchers. Daily work made most of them fit and lean. Indeed, it was the gruelling nature of their work that made them long for a smoke-oh, a pause in which they could enjoy a pipe of tobacco. And tobacco is the theme of the next chapter.

11

TO TIPPLE AND TO SMOKE

Many who try to imagine what Australia was like during the
first gold rushes see black Indian tea-leaves being tossed into
a camp-fire billy, and smell the smoke of cigarettes. But did
most Australians smoke cigarettes then? Did they even drink
Indian tea? Were Australians heavy or light drinkers of alcohol,
and what exactly did they drink? Some of these questions have
surprising answers.

Tobacco came in the First Fleet to New South Wales in
1788. Thereafter it arrived in nearly every ship though not
in eye-catching amounts. Some of this syrup-sweet tobacco was
bought in Brazil, which was sometimes a port of call on the route
to Australia. Tobacco became a bribe that helped to tame the
behaviour of convicts. It was given to Aborigines, who, men and
women alike, rejoiced in it and asked for more. Many free
colonists also liked to smoke.

A Pipe of Tobacco

In the mid-nineteenth century most tobacco was bought in small, dark, heavily flavoured lumps known as plugs. The smokers had to cut the aromatic plug with a knife and then fill their pipe with the tobacco pieces: each piece was rubbed in the palm of the hand and teased out by the fingers before being edged into the bowl of the pipe. Every smoker carried a knife or had to borrow a knife. In the outback many men used the same knife to cut their tobacco as to cut their meat at dinner.

'I hate that beggar', exclaimed a bushman in Joseph Furphy's novel *Such is Life*. The bushman instantly thought of a punishment fit for such a despised opponent: 'I wouldn't lend him my knife to cut up a pipe of tobacco, not if his tongue was sticking out as long as your arm.' To refuse to lend a knife was almost a declaration of war in an equalitarian society.

Perhaps the biggest tobacco merchant was Dixson and Sons of Sydney. A Scottish emigrant of 1839, Hugh Dixson first sold tobacco in George Street, sending home an early order for 400 gross of pipes. He was a faithful Baptist – an indirect sign that the minor religious sects did not oppose smoking. Eventually his firm became a big manufacturer of plug tobacco, which was not normally wrapped or labelled but was simply set down on the counter where customers could sniff it before buying. In about 1880 the Dixsons introduced a gimmick that neatly advertised their product. Into their own plugs of flat tobacco they pressed a tiny round disc of tin, the size of a

314

threepenny piece. The disc named the brand of tobacco, either the bestselling Yankee Doodle or the Conqueror.

The clay pipe, not the wooden pipe, was used by the ordinary smoker. A pipe had a short life. It might last only a fortnight for a heavy smoker. Remote sheep stations kept a stock of these cheap pipes so that their employees would not be deprived of the pleasure of smoking. If there was no pipe, the tobacco was placed in the mouth and slowly chewed.

As most men performed hard physical work during the day, they did not find it easy to smoke a pipe while they worked. The fire in a pipe often went out, and to re-light it took time because the burnt or half-burnt tobacco had to be rearranged or teased out or pressed down, and the match had to be lit and the pipe started again. If the daily work called for all one's energy and breath, a pipe in the mouth was a hindrance.

In nearly all workplaces in 1860, smoking by wage earners was banned because it wasted time. Those who worked on their own or for themselves, whether in gold diggings, on farms or in repair shops, made their own decision. In most shops and offices smoking was banned, at least during working hours, because it gave clients the impression that the workplace was slack and undisciplined. Morever the smoke hanging in the air, and the floating aroma, offended some clients.

At Williamstown in Victoria in 1869 the government's railway workshops were widely said to waste materials and time. An inquiry by a parliamentary committee gathered evidence on whether time was wasted in the smoking of pipes inside the workshops. Apparently workmen did not smoke openly. That would have called down official thunder and lightning. Instead workmen went to the lavatories – 'closets' they were called – and sat down to smoke their pipes. So much smoking went on that those who visited the closets late in the day saw piles of 'wax lucifer matches' scattered on the floor. The workshops' manager, his reputation at stake, was summoned to give his evidence. Yes, he did concede that pipes were smoked in the closets but added with a touch of indignation that 'a man must be a very bad man who would waste his time in the closets'. Indeed, he suggested that a workman who puffed away while seated in the closet was not deliberately wasting his employer's time but trying to get rid of the smell: 'there is always a smell; perhaps that is the reason they smoke'. Almost certainly, smoking was allowed in the railways workshops more often than it would have been tolerated in other workplaces. To smoke at work was a rare privilege.

As the trade unions became powerful, they agitated that a small amount of smoking time be permitted in working hours. But they also felt some sympathy for those employers who argued that a worker who was too often filling his pipe or borrowing a match was not fulfilling his work obligations. Gradually, in various manual jobs, a break for a smoke or a cup of tea was allowed at midmorning and midafternoon: it was called a smoke-oh. If the union was weak, however, smoking at work was usually banned. In 1900 a total ban on smoking was more likely in a woman's place of work than in a man's, partly because so few women smoked.

Australian smokers – whether of cigarettes or pipes – were offered the choice of dozens of varieties of boxed matches in the decade before the First World War. (Mimmo Cozzolino collected these and hundreds of other trademarks for his book, Symbols of Australia.*)*

Most bosses gave preference, when choosing a semi-skilled labourer from a circle of applicants, to those who did not smoke. Between the world wars, when the roll-your-own cigarette was at the height of its popularity, some foremen would look at a prospective workman's fingers; and if they saw tobacco stains they would be inclined not to employ the smoker, other things being equal.

Clues to the gradations of Australian society were found in the way people handled their tobacco. Harry Heathcote of Gangoil, owner of 30000 sheep in south Queensland, is the tall young hero of one of the lesser-known novels by Anthony Trollope. He wears a battered hat of straw, a flannel shirt and moleskin trousers with an all-purpose belt. The leather belt holds up his trousers. It also supplies a safe pouch for his money or tobacco, a safe place for his knife, and a loop on which he can hang his pipe.

Harry, like most rural folk, smoked more in the evening than in the day: 'When the work of the day was over, he would lie at his length upon rugs in the verandah, with a pipe in his mouth', while his wife read aloud to him Shakespeare and other uplifting books. The books were probably not typical of the tastes of most sheep owners of the 1870s, but a wooden pipe, as distinct from a clay pipe, was probably typical. Trollope had come to Australia on two occasions to visit his son, a sheep owner, and so he had an eye for Australian social habits as well as what his big English readership would expect.

William Clarke, a pipe-puffing squatter of enormous wealth, was observed closely by journalists from time to time because he was worth several million pounds and was called the Croesus of the southern hemisphere. Clarke was very observable, with his tall physique, his reddish hair and beard, his large forehead rising rather like a dome, and his pronounced limp and thick stick – it is called a 'club' by his biographer. He had smoked mainly cigars at a time when the importing of cigars was on a vast scale, but later he habitually had a pipe in his mouth, hand or pocket. The pipe was cheap, made of clay and very black. A drawing of him in Melbourne's *Punch* shows that the pipe – almost like a child's bubble pipe – was short in its stem. That the richest of all Australians should smoke such a cheap, small pipe was seen in the 1860s as a sign of frugality as well as eccentricity.

Most pipe tobacco was imported from the United States, though some came from China to cater for the Chinese-born smokers living on the goldfields. Eventually, the Chinese opened tiny tobacco farms in the river valleys near the Great Dividing Range but much of their tobacco leaf, being dark and coarse and second rate, was set aside to make the potion in which sheep were washed.

Colonially grown tobacco was despised. 'I am a native of the soil and I am proud of my birthplace', affirmed Charles Harpur, an early Sydney poet, but he exempted the locally grown tobacco from his pride in native products. One of his barbed insults was that the local politician W. C. Wentworth was not even worth 'a fig of colonial tobacco'. A fig was an English word of contempt – 'I do not give a fig' – and also an American word for a small piece of tobacco. It was said that the penetrating aroma of colonial tobacco even competed, in odour, with the coal smoke from a puffing locomotive.

Please Put on Your Smoking Cap!

A large book called *Australian Etiquette*, published in 1885, advised people to cultivate a 'sweet and pure breath' and to avoid onions. As for tobacco, no gentleman 'should smoke in a room which ladies are in the habit of frequenting'. Even to allow his clothes to smell of tobacco smoke was to insult the women in his company. In essence, when ladies gave permission to the men to smoke, it was really permission to smoke their pipe at a safe distance. Which worthwhile family, warned the author, would wish to live in rooms whose air smelled like that of an inn?

The private rules forbidding the smoking of tobacco inside the home were strictly obeyed in many households. In the houses of the rich a smoking room might be set aside. Perhaps smoking was also permitted in the billiards room. Smoking at the dinner table was allowed in some houses and strictly prohibited in others. A visitor did not even bother to seek permission to smoke at the end of a meal if he suspected that the answer would be no. In the typical house, the habit of smoking, like drinking, was either permitted or downright discouraged. Thus in many of Bendigo's cottages, married miners wishing to smoke in the evening would go outside and sit on the verandah or tank stand. They often wore, while they puffed at their pipe, a special smoking cap, with its coloured tassels hanging down. Consquently, when they came inside, their hair did not reek of tobacco fumes.

Aborigines tended to love tobacco and in 1877 the older women at Lake Tyers in Victoria received, along with their rations of food, a regular allowance of two figs of tobacco a week. Most women, however, disapproved of smoking. A stigma was attached to a woman who smoked or handled tobacco. The Dixsons for a time refused to employ women in their vast tobacco factory in the heart of Sydney. It was true that the famous dancer Lola Montez, on her sensational visit to Ballarat in the 1850s, smoked cigars, but that was seen as a sign of her depravity. Those who denounced Lola could not possibly dream that a century later, around countless dinner tables from Perth to Cairns, women would be the first to take from their handbag a cigarette, and light it – or call on a willing gentleman to light it – even before the first course of the meal was served.

The gentlemen's clubs were a mirror of the altering attitudes towards tobacco. Inside the Australian Club in Sydney no member was allowed to smoke but eventually a special smoking room was set aside. In 1855 members were allowed also to smoke in the billiard room, though only after 8 p.m. One decade later they could smoke their pipes in the billiard and smoking rooms at any time they wished. Eventually the aroma of tobacco, especially cigars, permeated all the corridors and rooms.

Puritans deplored the increasing popularity of cigars, with their strong-scented tobacco, and yet one remarkable cultural effect flowed from the smoking of cigars. Many of the choicest cigars were sold in wooden boxes, and scores of the wooden lids were commandeered by the rising young artists of the Heidelberg School. In August 1889, an art gallery in the heart of Melbourne publicly displayed more than 130 of their new paintings, and most had been painted on the back of the cigar-box lids. Perhaps the most influential display in the history of Australian art, and profound in its influence on our perceptions of landscape, it was called 'the nine by five impression exhibition' – nine inches by five being the dimensions of the cigar box.

Tom Roberts, Frederick McCubbin, Arthur Streeton and Charles Conder were among those who painted the lids of discarded boxes. These paintings, originally purchased for one or two guineas, are now prized in auction rooms.

Where did the young painters find so many wooden cigar boxes? After all, only the most expensive of cigars were packed in fine ornamental boxes. Louis Abrahams, a keen amateur artist, employed some forty people to manufacture cigars in a little factory in Melbourne, his Sonadona cigars being known as among the classiest in Australia. A friend of the painters, he found most of the cigar boxes they required. Some of the lids were of cedar, and formed a fine surface on which to paint with oils. Early in the new century Abrahams was to commit suicide in the cellar of his factory, but the lids of his cigar boxes live on; each year in the larger public galleries hundreds of thousands of visitors see on these lids the paintings of Tom Roberts and his friends.

Tobacco, whether consumed in cigars, pipes or cigarettes, was increasingly smoked. In about 1890 perhaps eight of every ten Australian men were smokers. The annual consumption of tobacco was now about 1.5 kilograms for each man, woman and child – double that of the United Kingdom but much less than that consumed in the USA, Turkey and Holland. In Australia some of the money that formerly went into beer and spirits now went into tobacco, which was seen as being far less disruptive than drink in a married household. The married household was undermining a society long dominated by single men. Women were becoming more powerful, outwardly.

One simple change increased the amount of tobacco smoked each day. The tobacco could now be easily lit. From about 1850 the matches called wax vestas were on sale. In turn came the safety match. Finally came flint cigarette lighters in the early 1900s: with one flick of the finger, or maybe two, a flame was created. Smoking would have been on a humbler scale but for these innovations. Back in 1800 it had been easy for people to smoke only when they were near a fire, from which they could take a light directly.

Light up a Vanity Fair!

At one time nearly every adult could remember the day or night when they first saw someone smoking a cigarette. The pipe, favoured for centuries, had a new challenger. The cigarette, at first, was an incredible sight. So flimsy, so slender and so short, it sent the smoke curling upwards in a strange way. The aroma, too, was not quite the same.

Cigarettes had gained a little popularity in Spain, Portugal and Italy, though it was the French who called them 'cigarettes'. Turkish-made cigarettes first attracted British soldiers during the Crimean War of the 1850s, when Britain fought on Turkey's side. Britain began to manufacture them, using Turkish tobacco, but the initial market for them was small. They were more expensive than pipe tobacco. They were also seen as effeminate by some critics.

Cigarettes were slow to attract the typical Australian smoker, and they do not appear separately in Sydney's import statistics until about 1884. Six years later, of the tobacco smoked in New South Wales, only 3 per cent was in the form of cigarettes. Many of those were American-made cigarettes such as Richmond Gem, Virginia Bright, Vanity Fair and that popular New York cigarette, Gypsie Queen. But Gypsie Queens were rarely seen on a woman's lip. It was not necessarily that women were unliberated: rather, their liberation took the powerful form of banning male tobacco smoke from their home.

Dixsons imported to Sydney a version of the first American machine for manufacturing cigarettes. With the help of a lot of hand labour, it could make 12 000 cigarettes an hour. Cigarettes, increasingly, were thought in some city quarters to

In the first three decades of the twentieth century, various brands of Australian cigarettes adopted nationalist and patriotic trademarks. The wattle was a more fervent symbol then than now.

confer a certain dash and style. In the main cities, larrikins – the young men who stood around street corners in a gang and dressed in the same style – began to smoke cigarettes at the weekends when they were on show.

In Melbourne as late as 1888 the woman who smoked a cigarette was a rarity. Henry Handel Richardson (Ethel Richardson in real life), who was to become celebrated as a novelist, set out from Melbourne with her mother and sister in the steamship *Ormuz*, bound for Europe. One handsome English passenger soon caught the attention of all. A singer of Gilbert and Sullivan, she arranged herself like a statue on the deck or in a public room, 'lying about in becoming attitudes, and taking no share in the ship's amusements'. In her pretty hand was usually a cigarette, which she smoked in a languid way. Many female passengers were so astonished at this sight that in embarrassment they turned the other way. For many this was their very first sight of a woman smoking.

Men were still the main customers at tobacconists' shops, and they began to think well of the new cigarette, while also condemning it as too expensive and the tobacco as too mild. The all-round solution was to choose one's own tobacco and roll one's own cigarettes. The big tobacco firms began to produce a cut tobacco that suited this demand. These thin strips of tobacco, neatly packaged in cardboard packets or small tins, removed the smoker's need to carry a knife. Morever more malleable, fine-cut tobacco could be teased by the hand into thin threads, and then rolled into the shape of a cigarette. Indeed, the smoker using this tobacco could either put it in his pipe or make it into a cigarette, using a small piece of news-paper or wrapping paper. The burning of a little ink along with the tobacco did not seem to alter the flavour. C. E. W. Bean, later a war correspondent, noticed in western New South Wales a man using a strip torn from a copy of the *Sydney Morning Herald* to roll his cigarette.

There was a disadvantage in buying a tin of the thin slices of cut tobacco, especially in summer. They dried more quickly than the larger lumps of plug tobacco. A new invention – the hermetically sealed tin – pleased the smoker. From about 1902 it enabled a smoker in such arid towns as Oodnadatta and Longreach to keep his tobacco moist.

The craving for cigarettes – whether made in a factory or by the smoker's own nimble hand – was to sweep swiftly through Australia. Ned Kelly, hanged in 1880, presumably had never smoked a cigarette, for it was a novelty and also despised as sissy. But little more than a generation later, maybe half of the soldiers who sailed away to Gallipoli smoked nothing else.

Women experienced their own social revolution with tobacco, though it lagged far behind the men's. Most of the girl-friends and wives who farewelled those soldiers bound for Gallipoli did not touch cigarettes – or were careful to not let their parents know if, by chance, they did occasionally light up. After the next world war, 30 per cent of Australian women were to be smokers. The factory-made cigarette would be their preference, especially the cork-tipped cigarette.

Men still preferred their roll-your-owns. At the peak of popularity of this simple activity and artform, the tally of rolled cigarettes totalled many billions each year. It is said that Norway and Australia were for a long time the strongholds of the roll-your-own cigarette. Sadly, that simple, hand-shaped commodity has almost vanished from public life.

With the growing fashion for rolling your own, a market arose for special cigarette papers. They were eventually supplied in Australia by such firms as Boomerang and Tally Ho, which made tiny strips of thin, high-quality rice paper and sold them in packets of fifty or so. Each white oblong strip of paper offered, on one side, a sticky edge to be licked once the tobacco had been rolled into a tube-like shape. With one lick the cigarette was tightly enclosed by the paper. A few loose shreds or tobacco at each end were plucked off, and the cigarette – not quite as neat as a factory cigarette – was ready to be lit. There was something gregarious and generous about this custom. 'Could you lend me the makings?' or 'Could you pass me the makings?' asked tens of thousands of Australians of their friends or colleagues each day. The makings consisted of a tin or pouch of Havelock, Golden Ruby or Grey's tobacco, and also the little packet of cigarette papers.

More sports players took up smoking, and most preferred the cigarette to the pipe. Some sportsmen, without much backing from physicians, thought that heavy smoking was an enemy of fitness. When H. C. A. Harrison, one of the creators of Australian Rules football, wrote his life story he finished with the proud observation that most athletes of his own remote sporting era had never smoked. Smoking, he pondered in the 1920s, must be pleasurable, but was it sensible? His parting advice to young athletes was, 'Avoid cigarette smoking!'

Many boys began to smoke as soon as they entered the workforce. One of the first public glimpses of Ned Kelly is in a police cell at Benalla. He is smoking a pipe: his age is fifteen. Smoking by the very young was frowned upon in certain circles but those circles had a limited influence. Probably the first attempt to ban juvenile smoking was made in the South Australian parliament by a Methodist politician in 1882. The motion received only one vote of support. But in the next generation, public opinion turned against the young who smoked. By the First World War every state parliament – Western Australia was the last – had passed laws that tried to restrict smoking by the young. At the same time, when young men turned eighteen years of age, and were fighting on the Western Front in France, their smoking was indirectly encouraged. The main gifts sent from Australia to the boys in uniform were tobacco and cigarettes.

At one time a few Australians favoured snuff as their

In the 1930s one million or more Australian men always carried in their pocket these small packets of papers from which they rolled their own cigarettes.

tobacco. Snuff was powdered tobacco inhaled through the nose – the words snuff and sniff were cousins. Those who liked to sniff only the freshest of snuff carried their own grater with which they ground down the tobacco. The snuff itself was carried in a small box – made of wood and brass if the owner was poor, and made of gold, silver or enamel if the owner was richer.

In England early in the nineteenth century the taking of snuff was ceasing to be so fashionable. In Tasmania, at the time when it ceased to receive convicts, about 1 per cent of all tobacco was still consumed in the form of snuff. Indeed snuff was far, far more popular in old-fashioned Tasmania than in up-and-coming Victoria. A pinch of snuff continued to convey class and breeding. 'My grandmother', recalled Mary Gilmore, 'when she wanted to show her ladyhood to the less important who came to see her, took snuff as a part of her status'. Some men took snuff only on a Sunday and then in the most frugal of doses. In the morning they took their first tiny pinch, at noon they took the next, and in the evening the last.

The sailing ship *Loch Ard*, one of the later ships to be wrecked in the dangerous western approaches to Bass Strait, carried in her diverse cargo various parcels of English clay pipes, a lot of tobacco, many cigars, and nearly one tenth of a ton of snuff. Almost a quarter of a century later the first prime minister, Edmund Barton, received from the royal family the gift of an ornate snuffbox to mark the birth of the Commonwealth. By then snuff-taking was such an exotic diversion that Barton, if he had filled the ornamental box with fresh snuff, would have found few parliamentarians willing to sniff it.

Others preferred to indulge in chewing tobacco. That habit was never as popular in Australia as in the United States; but at one time those who worked at jobs where it was either impractical or hazardous to light a match satisfied their craving for tobacco by chewing it. Many sailors and coalminers chewed tobacco, spitting the last residues onto the ground. In some public buildings, in the long corridors, a spittoon was in place to receive tobacco spat out with force. In the 1870s one visitor to Sydney noticed sunburnt old sailors, wearing round hats and trousers that were broad at the ankles, walking along with a rolling gait as if lower Pitt Street was part of the sea. These were the tobacco chewers.

Killers of Pain and Boredom

Opium was smoked or swallowed in various ways. In its purer condition it was reddish brown; some of it was fawn in colour; and when low grade it was blackish. Chinese smoked it but in India and Europe it was chewed more often. To the mouth it tasted bitter and to the lips it gave a burning sensation; but the bitterness and the burning were minor defects when measured against the short-term pleasure. Opium in the nineteenth century was not simply a dangerous drug of addiction but a general painkiller welcomed from time to time in millions of Christian households. It was also widely used by doctors in the form of morphine.

It is impossible to write of opium without touching on the pain that summoned it to the sickbed and stretcher. Opium, hemp and other drugs had a vital place in that era when pain was more a part of daily life, and when mixtures that healed pain were few, expensive and often ineffective. The scalding by boiling water accidentally tipped from the stove, the pain from accidents in mines and on streets, falls from a horse, childbirth, and the onset of typhoid and cancer – the sources of pain were innumerable.

With the sparseness of dentists and the abundance of sugar in the diet, toothache was a frequent cause of pain. The intense pain was prolonged when the family was poor and living far from a dentist. In the 1870s the Hickeys were small farmers who every three weeks would travel in the dray to Mudgee, the nearest town. Reaching home after one such trip a daughter with an aching tooth began to cry, whereupon Dad soothed her by saying, 'Don't cry, and we'll take you into Mudgee next trip and get it out.' Three weeks was a long wait.

In 1850 aspirin and a variety of other pain-easing tablets were unknown. The first anaesthetics were just appearing, having reached Australia with astonishing speed. Less than a year after the first painless surgery was conducted – in 1846 in Boston – Dr William Pugh in Launceston decided to make one of his patients inhale ether so that he could treat the large tumour on the left side of her lower jaw and extract the offend-ing molar. She inhaled ether for five minutes, her arms fell limp, and she felt some pain in her mouth as the operation proceeded. Later she confided that the pain was 'far short of what she had fortified herself to bear'. After a short rest she walked home.

Less than two months after this dramatic event, a Victorian settler in his early fifties was shooting native ducks on the far side of the Great Dividing Range, about 150 kilometres from Melbourne. Suddenly his left arm and hand were severely wounded, indeed almost shattered, 'from the bursting of his fowling piece'. His arm was bleeding so rapidly that he fainted several times from loss of blood. A neighbour bound his arm to stem the bleeding, and placed him in a spring cart in the hope that he could be treated by the local doctors. But they were away. After six days, jolting on rough roads in wet weather, the man reached Melbourne. The pain must have been intense and at various times on the journey he fainted.

Dr David Thomas was summoned. He found that the man's face 'was expressive of great anxiety, his face and lips pale, his pulse 140'. Preferring not to operate that day, the doctor requested that the patient be given a small dish of warm mutton broth with a little dry toast. Significantly he prescribed tincture of opium to ease the pain. Next day he persuaded the man to inhale ether – the first general anaesthetic to be used in Victoria. Swiftly, in about forty seconds, the doctor sawed off the arm below the elbow. The patient, not even realising that his arm had been severed, casually observed that he could feel no pain. A Melbourne newspaper, reporting the event, hailed the arrival of what it called 'painless surgery'.

Soon, chloroform replaced ether as the main anaesthetic, and was sometimes used during a difficult childbirth. This astonishing medical innovation, besides easing the pain, enabled an amputation to proceed at a safer speed. It was dangerous, however, and many patients died from the chloroform rather than the surgeon's knife or the complications of childbirth.

Even after the invention of the general anaesthetic, opium was welcomed by the growing numbers who, whatever their race, were in search of quick relief from acute pain. Imported from Turkey, opium was widely used in the British Isles as a reliever of pain and even boredom. In some of the textile districts, many mothers who worked all day in the mills had to entrust their children to a single nurse who, for a few pence, looked after a small gathering of the tiny in the neighbourhood. To keep the children quiet, a little opium was administered to them. At home some babies sucked away at a dummy soaked in a mild opium mixture. In the Lancashire mill town of Preston in 1843 it was estimated that some 1600 families consumed Godfrey's Cordial or similar opium-based medicines. The prevailing opinion, whether correct or incorrect, was that too many young children died from this practice.

One popular Australian opiate was a mixture of aniseed, peppermint and opium tincture or laudanum. Likewise many chemists sold to their female customers a flask of Steedman's Teething Powders, which used opium to ease the pain felt by teething babies. Mary Gilmore recalled that in the lonely country, opium was given to women after they had given birth to a child. It sent them to sleep. The midwife also helped herself to a little as the reward for doing her duty. Gilmore recalled that even in the 1870s the everyday folk took opium 'as a sedative, pretty much as we take aspirin nowadays'. So in Australia, opium had twin uses. It was used mainly by white settlers as a relief from pain and mainly by the Chinese settlers as a way of escape.

The Chinese entering the Victorian goldfields were followed by chests of Asiatic opium. The habit of many Chinese diggers was to go to an opium shop, inhale for a minute the smoke coming through a long pipe from the burning opium, and then drowse away. Victoria, even in 1867 when its large Chinese population was declining, was estimated to have eighty opium shops or dens, each with a large clientele. Opium was an expensive habit, absorbing a quarter or more of the wages earned by many Chinese diggers. Not all Chinese smokers, however, liked opium in their pipes. Some preferred American tobacco, or a hot kind of Chinese tobacco that was smoked in water pipes: both of these tobaccos could be bought in the Chinese general stores that dispensed the opium.

Medical opinion initially did not think that the smoking of opium, in moderation, was damaging. But many Chinese were not moderate smokers. Some became addicts, partly because they were suffering from physical pain, especially the rheumatism arising from long hours of immersion in cold water on the alluvial diggings. Such addicts were likely to earn little money because their regular opium smoking as well as their injuries sapped their physical strength.

The importing of opium at Australian ports was legal. It was virtually impossible to ban imports when the same material in its raw state was not only smoked in a Chinese den but also carried in the wallets and bags of hard-working women and men who envisaged that, in the case of an accident or illness, far from medical help, they might need a grain of opium.

When 40 000 or more Chinese were working on the Victorian goldfields, the import duty on opium was one of the main sources of revenue at the customs house. As the Chinese population declined, the imports of opium fell away. Medically, opium was also losing its high place in the hierarchy of painkillers. Chloroform as a general anaesthetic and such palliatives as the new cocaine and the older ether spray were now relieving pain in Australian hospitals. The simple sedatives sold in chemists' shops were also gaining strength, and many of them ceased to contain opium.

In the western world a campaign against opium addiction was now waged side by side with the campaign against alcohol. South Australia, radical in its social reforms, enacted a law in 1895 against the sale of opium, and a decade later the federal government banned its import except for medicinal uses. China tried to reduce the area of its own territory where the opium poppy was grown. British India curtailed the export of opium, much of which had gone to China. By 1915 some politicians felt relieved that they had not rigidly opposed the growing of opium in India. Suddenly, millions of doses of morphine extracted from the opium of India were needed to ease the pain of soldiers wounded during the First World War.

The Old Bush Inn

Alcohol was at first the opiate of most Australians. The size of a town was increasingly measured, in a rough and ready way, by the number of its pubs or inns. In Hobart in 1854, one in every twenty-three dwellings was an inn. In 1873 Ballarat had nearly 500 inns, or one for every sixty people, including children. Two decades later the little port of Normanton, close to the Gulf of Carpentaria, was fairly typical of an outback town: it contained 800 people and eight inns.

For many decades the inn possibly had more influence on social, sporting and political life in Australia than in the British Isles. The typical Australian male had more money and more leisure than his British cousin. Morever home life was weaker here. In the 1830s, New South Wales held three males to every one female, and so the public house was a male meeting place and news exchange as well as what is now called a watering hole.

Australia, seventy years after the arrival of the British, was spotted with inns. They crouched at the crossroads of the farming areas; they stood under the hot sun on lonely stretches of inland road; and in the cities they were about as plentiful as corner stores are today. The typical inn was small, and its narrow bar room did not hold many customers. Many such inns were run as a part-time activity by farmers or housewives. Initially their guests – if they wanted to sleep – slept mainly on the floor.

The outback inns were not only drinking dens. Here the hat was passed round for worthy causes; here people celebrated and mourned; and here the latest information was found. Sometimes that information was given verbally; but in certain classier inns there could also be found the latest Australian newspapers and the English weeklies and monthlies that had just arrived by sea. The early hotels were forerunners of the web and Internet.

*A shearer, pipe in his hand and his swag dumped on
the pub floor, is spending his earnings. Spirits,
not beer, were the favoured drink in remote
pubs in the pastoral regions.*

Thus the first publican in Melbourne was John Pascoe Fawkner, and at his inn or hotel he published the town's first newspaper, written by hand. He also ran a small library for his guests. All his books he signed in black ink with a very large signature. To make doubly sure that his ownership of the book was not in doubt he inked his name, in large letters, not only in the front of the book but right across several of the middle pages. Occasionally items from his library turn up today in second-hand bookshops.

In the discovery of major mining fields in Australia, the wayside inn was important. In areas lacking newspapers the hotelkeeper and his customers formed – between them – an oral library of local knowledge. It often included mineral knowledge.

Edward Hargraves had dug for gold in California and then returned to New South Wales in the hope that he could find gold there. Crossing the Blue Mountains on horseback in 1851 he called at a small inn run by the widow Lister: women were often innkeepers. Hargraves noticed that the mantelpiece of the inn held specimens of copper, pyrites and quartz, for a small coppermine had been worked in the vicinity and there was keen interest in finding other minerals. Whether it was at this Guyong Inn that Hargraves heard of the isolated pieces of gold found by shepherds nearby is not certain. From the inn he conducted his search for payable gold, recruiting the publican's son and other men. Soon they discovered the gold that led to the first major Australian rush. The vital role of the bush inn, as a mineralogical museum and a source of information, can be seen in other discoveries in early Australia.

For a long period a hotel was known more often as an inn. There must have been, in various regions of Australia, at least one hundred that called themselves The Bush Inn. The bush shanty was a rival institution: it was definitely down-market and usually unlicensed. The police had the right to pull to the ground an unlicensed shanty; many of the buildings were so hastily and flimsily built that their destruction, by time or by the police, was almost effortless. In the gold rushes a bush shanty was nicknamed a 'sly grog shop', which meant that it was a furtive business. By the end of the nineteenth century the words inn and shanty were in decline, and 'hotel' in the city and 'pub' in the bush were the common names.

It was not easy to run an inn, miles from the nearest town, or to maintain order in a house where many of the clients were disorderly before they swallowed their first drink. Some of the publicans were scoundrels, and some were as welcoming and homely as they could be, in the circumstances. Most of the surviving inns were to improve during the thirty years after 1850.

When Louisa Meredith and her husband entered the inns that spaced themselves along the up-country roads in New South Wales they wished that they were back in an English village, where the landlady of the inn had apple cheeks and a 'cap of driven snow and smart flowered gown', and the landlord in velveteen coat and blue stockings stood to welcome them. Occasionally, Louisa was pleasantly surprised. In what she called Blind Paddy's Inn, she was shown into a bedroom no larger than a ship's cabin, but to her delight clean curtains shaped the window, while in the dining room with its newly lit fire the evening meal was laid on a table covered with a neat, white, coarse cloth. A bottle of English ale was served with the chops and eggs and – luxury of luxuries – 'a dish of hot mealy potatoes' cooked in skins which were just beginning to crack.

In any new district, accommodation was scarce. G. O. Preshaw, a very young clerk, was posted to a new bank in the Snowy Moutains. At the lonely port of Eden he bought a horse and set out on the long journey. He found few inns along the way. One night he called at a sheep station, owned by a former publican, and was invited to spend the night in an old four-poster bed, its mattress filled with feathers. To his dismay he learned that he had to share the bed with 'a dirty looking fellow'. Fortunately the 'bed was large, and I gave him a wide berth'. The following night he spent at the Rose, Shamrock and Thistle at Bombala, and on the next night, when rain seemed likely, he halted at a two-room hut along the track. In that congested hut the husband, wife and six children treated him with kindness, and he slept on a sofa while the boys lay on the floor. On his final afternoon he forded the fast-running Snowy River and arrived at a dirty shanty called The Diggers' Rest, where he had to share a large bed with a policeman sleeping on either side of him. He hoped his destination, the high town of Kiandra, would be less comfortless but there, on his first bitterly cold night he was given a shakedown on the wooden floor of the bar parlour. In the bush the sharing of beds was common, so long as the hotel rooms remained scarce.

At first sight many of the shanties and bush inns were uninviting: deep dust and fresh manure in the yard where the coach horses were changed, a bar room hot in summer and most of the shabbily dressed drinkers standing up, with perhaps a bullock driver and shearer sitting on three-legged stools. Outside, sitting on a form, with their backs to the verandah wall, three or four people might wait for something to happen. When a meal was served – on a rough table perhaps wiped clean by a woman using the end of her apron – chops were the likely food, and the black tea poured from the spout of the tall teapot tasted bitter.

Those who tried to go to sleep in the bedrooms felt the straw in the pillow tickling their face and ears, and saw through the thin calico walls the silhouette of those in the next room. On the west coast of Tasmania, Gam Webster, a publican at the little port of Trial Harbour, did not think highly of city guests who, before going to bed, placed their shoes outside their door for cleaning and polishing. Once he took the shoes and nailed them to the floor. This was in the 1880s, when luxury and finesse were not to be expected in remote places. And yet most bush inns and hotels were far superior to those thirty or forty years earlier. It was easy for the guest to complain; it was hard to run a bush inn.

In a tiny township everyone who drank used the same inn. In the big towns, hotels tended to be more specialist, catering for people who wanted to feel at home in their own watering place. In one hotel the Irish might drink, in another the Germans, in another the brickworkers, and in another the wharf labourers. The names of the hotels often mirrored either the customers who drank there or those whom the owner hoped to attract. Thus a business directory issued in Melbourne in 1868 lists three different Butchers' Arms hotels, eight Freemasons' hotels, and two Cricketers' Arms hotels.

On the long routes to the interior, in places where no railway penetrated, the inn was the lifeline for travellers and horses. If the mail coach arrived in the middle of the night, the passengers had to be fed, and the coach's tired horses had to be replaced by fresh horses. Alert innkeepers did everything to encourage this passing traffic. When Samuel Lambert renovated his Commercial Hotel in Tamworth in the late 1870s, he advertised that 'an efficient ostler was always in attendance' to look after travellers' horses and place them in the hotel's stables for the night. For passengers on the Cobb and Co coach, a 'night waiter' was ready to serve hot or cold refreshments.

Hundreds of hotels announced in the local newspapers that they had 'excellent stabling', even if they did not have excellent stables. Tattersall's Hotel, in the remote copper town of Cobar, boasted that its stables were under the care of 'a sober and careful groom'. Next door, ever so convenient, was a blacksmith who could shoe horses at his 'Veterinary and Shoeing Forge'. The ostlers, grooms, stablemen and night waiters formed a whole set of occupations that were destroyed when the railway replaced the horsedrawn coaches and the private vehicles that used the main country roads.

Hotels were so vital to Australian life and leisure that it is hard to think of a national activity that was not shaped by them. At first sight, sport seems to be an exception. Spectators, even some of the players, went to the nearby hotel before the sporting match began. Lo and behold, they returned to celebrate or commiserate when the match was over. The links between hotels and Australian sport were often crucial. The game of Australian Rules football was shaped in Bryant's Parade Hotel, opposite the East Melbourne parklands where the early games were played. Bryant, a professional cricketer who had played for Surrey, kept a football at his hotel and allowed customers to borrow it. It was in his hotel in May 1859 that the original ten rules of the game were drawn up. The footballer who did most to shape those rules was Thomas Wills, who became a fatal victim of alcoholism.

When billiards became popular later in the nineteenth century – more popular than today – hotels were one of its homes. It was in a Sydney hotel in 1881 that the first professional billiards championship of Australia was contested. The finest billiard player the world has seen was Walter Lindrum, a child of the hotels. Born near Kalgoorlie – his father ran a billiard saloon in the Palace Hotel – Walter learned to play as a tiny child on the hotel's billiard tables. The table was too high for him, and he developed a round-arm style. When his father ran a country hotel at Donnybrook in Western Australia, little Walter was in the basement playing with the mangle. Alas, several of his fingers were crushed, and the top half of an index finger was amputated. In the end he gained by using the stump as a natural bridge.

In a newly settled district, divine service was sometimes held in the inn: Sunday, in theory at least, was a day of quiet in an inn. In Chillagoe in far north Queensland it was a tradition that a publican would not charge a visiting clergyman for his board and lodging, so long as he stayed for only the one night. A hotel was also useful for political meetings. Many of those politicians who in the 1890s ardently preached the cause of federation spoke from hotel balconies. Hotels were used, too, for meetings of lodges, friendly societies and trade unions. The first meeting of what became the Australian Workers Union, for decades the largest of all unions, was held in a Ballarat hotel.

Wine, Brandy and Rum

In the outback, spirits were the popular alcoholic drink. The tyranny of distance favoured spirits rather than beer, because the high freight from city breweries to the remote inns and shanties far inland made beer a very expensive form of alcohol. Alongside some of the outback pubs, piles of empty spirits bottles, broken or unbroken, crept upwards until they formed a small hillock that sometimes gleamed in the sunlight as a beacon or a warning for approaching travellers. In the mid-1880s the average Queenslander drank two and a half times as many nips of spirits as the average Tasmanian.

And what exactly did the travellers drink in the early inns? Mostly rum! The rum from India – and not from Jamaica – was the early favourite. Later the Dutch gin known as geneva gained in popularity. But by the time of the gold rushes brandy was the favourite spirit in most places.

Brandy was drunk in oceanic quantities. Ship after ship arrived at the major ports with kegs of French brandy. The finest came from the port of Bordeaux, and the bulk product – often called dark brandy – could come from anywhere. Brandy was sometimes drunk with water and often with ice, when at last ice became available. This drink, even before 1860, was known as a 'smash'. South Australian brandy was slow to snatch a fair share of the market but by the 1870s it was selling well.

Spirits were served hot in some bush inns. In Kiandra, which was probably the highest and coldest goldfield, a glass of hot spirits was preferred. The young bank clerk sent to that bleak new diggings in the Snowy Mountains recalled how his friends, after the day's work, would play cards and smoke. The landlord would set off their evening ritual by ringing a bell and announcing in his lordly voice when Isaac the waiter appeared: 'Gentlemen, I am just going to have some whisky hot, and shall be glad if you will join me.' Thereafter the losers of the successive games of cards played for the next round of drinks. So the landlord made his money.

Nearly all the spirits consumed in that hotel parlour in winter were hot. The heyday of hot spirits was probably in the early gold-rush years. In Ballarat's inns the heating of spirits was so common that hot brandy was mentioned in popular songs.

It is sometimes said that while the crowds that gathered in goldfield inns liked to drink brandy, the richer businessmen and squatters preferred Scotch whisky. At first sight this hypothesis makes sense, partly because whisky ultimately became the favoured spirit in urban Australia. Morever the Scots acquired so much of the finest sheep country, especially in Victoria and the Riverina, that they would be expected, when wealthy, to have imported their native drink. Whisky's popularity, however, came later.

For a long time imported bottles of drink, whether beer or wine, were considered far superior to any local drink. French champagne and French brandy were high on the list, and imported port and sherry had their followings. French claret was preferred to almost any red wine grown in Australia. But in white wine the New South Wales vineyards around Camden and the Hunter Valley had their disciples.

South Australia began to make its mark with wine. Queen Victoria, whether she knew it or not, was presented with a case of South Australian hock produced at Echunga in 1845. Many of the well-known names in Australian wine – Seppelt, Hardy, Reynell, Penfold, Gramp – were early grape-growers in the hills and valleys close to Adelaide. Thomas Hardy planted his first vineyard, along with olive and fruit trees, in the valley of the Torrens, between Adelaide and its port, in 1853. His first wine was drunk four years later. Another Englishman, Dr Christopher Penfold, had planted his vines in the village of Magill, close to Adelaide, and became the master of fortified red wine. At Magill a century later the first vintage of the most famous of Australian red wines, Grange Hermitage, was produced.

The Barossa Valley, a showground of German culture, is now popularly viewed as the pioneer district of wine making in Australia. Curiously the name Barossa is not German – the valley took its name, meaning a hill of red mud, from the site of a British military victory in Spain in 1811. Prussian, Bavarian and British vignerons opened this South Australian valley to

Vineyards and wineries near Wodonga and Albury.

wine but at first it was more a valley of wheat. Here arose the winery of Johann Gramp. Originally a baker, he knew about fermentation. His vineyard was on Jacob's Creek; but almost a century and a half passed before that creek became the brand-name of the bestselling red wine in Britain and Scandinavia.

In early Victoria the vineyards, often planted with cuttings from the Hunter, were few, but by the 1880s they were the most productive in the land. And then phylloxera, a small insect from California, attacked the vines. Whole vineyards had to be rooted out. The insect, however, was probably no more damaging than Victoria's unsound economic policies and the low-quality grapes the vineyards had grown. Eventually South Australia became the leading winemaker. On the eve of the First World War it produced just over half of the wine in the land, and much of that wine was drunk in the British Isles.

Australian wine offered little foretaste of the popularity it now commands as a social or contemplative drink. Thus in the 1880s a bestselling brand had been Atkin's Own Quinine Wine. Atkin was a North Melbourne chemist who used sugar to enrich the dubious taste of his popular medicinal wine. Increasingly the vats of riesling and verdelho and other wines from regions such as Rutherglen and Yackandandah were railed to the city to dilute his quinine.

Most Australians did not drink wine but there were territories where it was popular among a large minority. Roma in western Queensland was probably a far larger wine consumer than Brisbane: even in the 1860s Roma had a winery, and it still flourishes. Newcastle and the lower Hunter Valley had a fondness for wine well ahead of Sydney's. Likewise in north-eastern Victoria many rural labourers drank wine rather than beer. The consumption of wine in German-settled rural areas near Adelaide in 1900 was far more above the national average, but in the cities whole suburban streets held not one bottle of wine – unless it was locked away in a cupboard, out of sight of visitors. In Australia as a whole the drinking of wine, while not on the present scale, was more common than in nearly every other English-speaking land.

Beer – Who Shouts Next?

Beer was a minor drink before the first gold rushes. In Tasmania in the mid-1850s, for example, four times as much money was spent on spirits as on beer, porter and ale together. In the country as a whole, beer was drunk mainly in the coastal towns and rarely in the countryside. Much of that beer was imported from Britain.

A decade later, Australian breweries began to boom. Before long, at least thirty different towns in New South Wales operated breweries. In 1870 Victoria had 116 breweries, and Bendigo alone operated more breweries than Sydney operates today. For a time Victoria brewed well over half of all the beer made in the continent, but then New South Wales began to catch up.

The colonial brewers were inexperienced in coping with a hot summer. In Sydney initially, the malting process did not work effectively in the warmer months of the year. Moreover the water did not contain enough lime to satisfy the brewers.

Drinkers with spare money in their pocket much preferred the dear imported beer to the cheap colonial beer. The taste of the imported beer, rather than the erratic colonial beers, was familiar to them. English beer also tended to contain less alcohol than colonial beers, some of which ran to 7 per cent. Eventually the local brewers found ways to produce a more palatable, more predictable beer: the addition of cane sugar to the malt was one of their innovations. They also catered successfully to the demand for lager beers, which were superseding ale in popularity by the 1920s.

As a large proportion of Australians, especially before 1860, had no family to support, they spent freely on alcohol. In the outback the drinking of alcohol often took the form of sustained bouts, followed by penitent sobriety. The sober period commenced when the money ended.

A hallmark of social life was 'shouting'. This was the custom whereby men would drink in groups, and one man would pay for the drinks of every member in the group, and then the next person would take his turn to pay. If four people were drinking together, then they felt honour-bound to drink until the full round of four drinks were completed, or even a double round of eight drinks. It was a practice furthering the interests of the publican, because more alcohol was consumed. The gold rushes encouraged the practice. When a syndicate struck rich gold they would buy drinks for all their neighbours. When a digger found gold he would sometimes go to a shanty and buy drinks for all present, and continue to buy them until the shanty closed or a loyal friend wisely told him to curb his generosity.

Shouting became so general a practice that those who defied it were singled out for banter, sometimes genial, sometimes acerbic. By the 1890s a man who refused to shout, and instead drank on his own, was called a Jimmy Woodser. Whether Jimmy Woods ever existed, whether there was once a solitary drinker of that name, was widely debated. In the pastoral districts to the west of Ballarat they had their own name for someone who refused to join in the syndicate of shouters. He was said to 'go Ballarat'. It was possibly a reference to the fact that Ballarat was in part an evangelical city and a married folks' city.

Married men who drank a little, and were tempted to drink more, might be warned by their wives not to take part in the custom of shouting. Heavy drinking did, in effect, snatch food or shoes from the shouter's own children. Many reformers thought excessive drinking would be curbed if the habit of shouting was abolished. During the First World War, the parliament in Western Australia debated whether to outlaw the habit. The 'shout' eventually diminished in Australian cities, though less quickly in the bush.

Hobart, where the Quakers had formed an energetic temperance society, was the first town to rebel against alcoholic excess. In 1854 it possessed one public house for every 127 men, women and children; and a reformed drunkard could barely design an evening walk that did not include a dozen tempting ale houses along his route. In a colony where convicts or former convicts were so abundant, the causes of crime were widely discussed. And there was widespread agreement, especially among women, that alcohol was the main cause of crime. The Catholic church, which in many decades was tolerant towards alcohol, was at the forefront of the temperance movement in Tasmania. Bishop Willson, calm in nearly all his statements, dramatically announced in 1859 that the sin of drunkenness spawned almost every crime, fostered poverty and ruin, and led to 'premature old age'.

A Crusade Against Strong Drink

Family life became stronger as the proportion of women increased. Many women deplored the fact that hotels were open for sixteen or eighteen hours a day, and therefore a continuing temptation to men. The hostility to alcohol increased in the 1880s when the Blue Ribbon Movement and the Women's Christian Temperance Union both set foot here. In their crusade against alcohol they enlisted mostly the Methodists, Baptists, Congregationalists and other dissenting sects. Soon the wine swallowed by many congregations during Holy Communion was no longer fermented but simple grape juice. The main Methodist sect, the Wesleyans, who had served alcohol at Sunday School picnics as recently as 1850, turned against alcohol. Originally the word 'temperance' had signified those who were temperate with their alcohol, but now the word signified the total abstaining from alcohol.

Medical opinion for a long time had prescribed alcohol as a stimulant, a bodybuilder, a cure and an anaesthetic. Alcohol was used freely to treat fevers, pneumonia, septic disease and to hasten the patient's recovery from a serious operation. In the Children's Hospital in Melbourne in the 1870s, more money was spent on alcohol than on all other medicines combined, according to Peter Yule, the hospital's historian. In 1883 public concern was expressed when at another Melbourne hospital a girl of fourteen was dosed heavily with brandy. At last many physicians turned a somersault, and hospitals ceased to be havens for those who liked their medicine. Sometimes the new approach had dramatic effects. One hospital decided to use less brandy for medicinal purposes, and a patient whose paralysed legs had defied all diagnosis and all treatment suddenly rose from his bed, walked from the hospital, and was not seen there again.

In Victoria in 1885 more than 45 000 women signed a temperance petition which formed a roll of paper half a kilometre long. Their petition denounced the liquor traffic 'as the most prolific source of broken hearts, ruined homes and blighted lives'. In the space of two decades Victoria almost halved the number of its inns and hotels. In several new Australian towns a complete prohibition was placed on hotels, and the irrigation towns of Mildura and Renmark possessed no public houses. Significantly South Australia, the most evangelical colony, became in 1894 one of the first places in the world to give women the vote. The hope was that their vote would help to tame the liquor traffic, and it did.

The crusade against alcohol was perhaps the most powerful episode of women's liberation in the country's first century. Here was indisputable evidence that Australia was no longer simply a man's land. The men, however, were still the historians, and many dismissed the crusade against alcohol as being of little importance during the quarter of a century from 1889 to 1914 – a time when its actual influence was probably as profound as the old-age pension or the creation of the minimum or basic wage.

There may have been short periods in the nineteenth century when Australians drank more alcohol than the people of almost any other western nation, but by the beginning of the twentieth century they were more sober. As a drinker of beer the average Australian could not be compared with the average Belgian, Briton, German or Dane. In those cold lands the beer swallowed by the average person in the average year was

Camels became the main carriers of goods in more than half the continent. Their Afghan drivers did not drink alcohol, and so were entrusted with cases of whisky and rum in the safe knowledge that they would not steal the liquor during the hot journey to towns in Western Australia.

twice as voluminous as that swallowed by the average Australian. In those years, too, the quantity of spirits consumed by the average Australian man, woman and child was less than that consumed in at least eight European nations, and in Canada and New Zealand as well. The opportunities for drinking in Australia were to be curbed further by new laws, and by 1919 the hotels in four of the six states were no longer permitted to sell alcohol after 6 p.m. – unless it was part of a formal meal.

Western Australia was now the outpost of that old hard-drinking, cheque-busting, thirsty and spendthrift way of life. On the other hand, in South Australia and Victoria reigned those people called the 'wowsers'. This strange word was fashioned by the Sydney *Truth*, from 1899 onwards, into one of the most popular arrow-words in the Australian vocabulary. The wowsers symbolised the deep social divisions raised by alcohol and other leisure pursuits. To many Australians the wowsers were killjoys and spoilsports but in the eyes of others they were evangelical reformers fighting on a wide front.

12

IN THAT BLACK BILLY CAN

The popular drink in Australia was tea. Here lived the most obsessive tea drinkers in the world.

In 1850 much of the tea was drunk from a quart pot, which was the forerunner of the billy. The quart pot carried exactly one quarter of a gallon. An old-time drinking vessel, it was originally made of pewter and later of tin. Shakespeare, in his play *Henry VI*, made Jack Cade say how, when marching along, he used the bottom of a metal helmet 'instead of a quart pot to drink in'. In Australia travellers increasingly carried a quart pot, filled it with water, and carefully placed the upright pot on burning embers. When the water boiled, they tossed in tea-leaves.

Australians switched from the quart pot to the billy can, which was made of cheap iron rather than dear tin. The word 'billy' was a shortened name for the billy pot, a cooking utensil. By the 1840s, on Norfolk Island, a few convicts were making by hand their own billies, which, unlike the quart pots, usually had a lid. The billy also possessed an overhead handle made of thin curved wire, thus enabling it to be suspended on a rod or a hook in a fireplace. The history of the billy, like that of many everyday things, is vague, but probably it was mainly an Australian invention, a response to the availability of increasingly cheap iron and wire. The iron roof for Australian houses and the wire fence, which replaced the shepherd on the sheep runs, were also products of cheap iron.

The new billy can was lighter than the old quart pot. Many men on the road actually carried two billies, the small billy fitting inside the larger. Like the quart pot, the billy could be tied to the swag, from which it dangled. But when water was expected to be scarce along a stretch of road, the billy was filled with water at a convenient creek and carried by hand.

The tea billy became a symbol of refreshment, of hospitality and a symbol of a people often on the move. Today the new and the clean are usually admired but at one time the black billy can was admired because it was old and dirty. It performed its task more efficiently when it was uncleaned, its blackened surface enabling the water to boil more quickly. Eventually a mystique surrounded the billy. No tea was said be so refreshing as that which was made in a blackened billy.

The making of billy tea became an artform. Bushmen were proud of a black billy that was almost worn thin by the hundreds of times it had been encircled by flame. E. C. Buley, the author of a lucid book on Australia, observed in 1905 that bushmen fought one another for the title of the best maker of billy tea. He was inclined to think that the excellence of billy tea was due to the 'infusion of the tea leaves at the very moment when the water is beginning to boil'. Soon after the tea-leaves were thrown into the boiling water, the moist brown sugar was added. It became the custom to give the pot a stir with a twig of eucalyptus. On the west coast of Tasmania a twig of manuka was considered by some bushmen to be the most aromatic stirrer.

The Pot of Tea – a 'Deadly Fluid'

Vast quantities of tea were consumed in hot weather by many people in city and country. It was sometimes said that a typical selector or farmer in the 1870s drank four cups of tea with each meal. A thirsty bushman might drink more than 60 litres in a week. In the kitchen, in the vicinity of a hot stove, housewives drank cup after cup of tea.

In summer the stream of perspiration encouraged people to take in more liquid. Tea had the double advantage that it camouflaged water taken from a brown dam or creek. English visitors noticed that many Australians had a passion for drinking cold tea as well as hot.

Tea, as drunk on the sheep stations and the gold diggings, was made in unexpected ways. One common recipe surprised newcomers to the land. People who lived in a hut, month after month, rarely emptied the billy or teapot but simply added more hot water or, when appropriate, more tea-leaves. To throw out the tepid tea and the squelch of used tea-leaves remaining in the billy was considered almost an act of sabotage.

At the end of the evening the bottom of the billy might hold a small amount of black tea and a layer of old leaves, and they remained there. In the morning the billy would be filled again with water and brought to the boil. It was already a hot brew of very weak tea before the new leaves were dropped in. In that way bush tea acquired its distinctive flavour, which not everybody liked on first tasting it. In the opinion of the German-born explorer, Ludwig Leichhardt, bush tea had two special qualities – the exciting and the astringent: the astringency came from the stewing process. In 1842 he told of his recent experiences in the bush: 'My dear boy, you have no idea how sweet a cup of tea with brown sugar and a piece of damper tastes after such a day's journey in the bush. I prefer the tea in the bush to the most excellent wine'.

How is the incessant thirst for tea to be explained? It was partly a habit brought from Britain: of the European peoples, the British and the Russians were the main drinkers of tea. The heat of the day in Australia stimulated thirst, and tea was the favourite way of quenching that thirst. As the local water was usually impure and muddy, tea took away the dubious taste. In addition, tea was a lightweight commodity, and freight was only a small proportion of its total cost. Even after the sea voyage from Chinese ports to Australia, and the expensive dray journey into the interior, it did not become too costly. A packet of tea was not startlingly dearer on the Australian plains than in the port of Sydney or the port of Canton; in contrast a packet of rice and a bottle of beer were far dearer when they were carried into inland Australia. The

Boiling the billy on the banks of the Goulburn River, Victoria.
The plentiful supplies of firewood in so many districts also
encouraged the river steamers to burn wood.

popularity of tea was aided by the fact that it was actually less expensive in Australia than in England, where in the middle years of the nineteenth century the government virtually doubled the price of tea by virtue of the special import duty it collected at the customs houses.

There was another reason why tea was preferred. In the bush it was easy to gather firewood for the boiling of water. If firewood had been scarce, then tea would not have been the favoured drink. In the bush and on the remote gold diggings, tea was especially prized. Shepherds were paid in provisions as well as money, and their weekly ration of food always included tea as well as flour, meat and sugar. Nearly everybody added sugar to their tea, and so tea was a provider of energy as well as refreshment. The idea of drinking tea without sugar belongs to a much later era when people, no longer exercising themselves so vigorously in the course of daily work, had to forgo sugar in order to lose weight.

If the family was very poor or very large the hot water was poured again and again into the teapot or billy so that the last sniff of flavour would be extracted.

The poet Mary Gilmore described how extreme poverty affected the drinking of tea and the lighting of candles. One family with twelve children lived on a farm so poor that even candles were a luxury. Accordingly there was no reading aloud at night, even though the mother loved to read the Bible. But she learned many chapters by heart, stealing a glance at the Bible while weaving the children's hats from grass, and so was able to pass on the chapters to her children in the candleless evenings.

For such a struggling family tea-leaves were precious, and were used mostly on Sundays. When at last a cow was acquired, most of her milk was saved for the making of butter and rarely used in the teacup. The luxury of tea with milk was reserved for those days when visitors chanced to call.

The Decline of China Tea

When television finally reached Australia, and the producers of plays and documentaries needed visual objects to illuminate the past, the chest of tea was essential, for it was well known that tea was a popular drink in days gone by. Thus a television serial based on the life of the bushranger Ben Hall showed, in one scene, a tea container printed with the words INDIAN TEA. As the year of the bushranger's death was 1865, it is unlikely that he ever tasted or even set eyes on Indian tea.

At that time his fellow Australians drank almost nothing but China tea, especially the black tea from the port of Foochow. Tens of thousands of Chinese tea growers, pickers, sorters and blenders, makers of wooden tea-chests, porters or carters who transported the tea, as well as merchants, wharf labourers and watermen made their living from the Australian tea market.

Today, China tea is assumed to be that hot green drink served in Chinese restaurants. Certainly in the 1840s, in some regions of New South Wales, green tea was the favourite of bushmen but in some pastoral regions black China tea was drunk. The tea drunk during the gold rushes was mostly the stronger black Chinese tea. Both the green and the black China tea came from the same bush. The black tea was simply the result of a different treatment process, which produced a kind of fermentation or oxidation. In China it was the heat of the sun which baked the fresh tea-leaves, but in a later era, in east Asia, a steam engine heated the air passing over the leaves.

The falling popularity of Chinese tea was unexpected. The new preference for teas from India and Ceylon was one of the fastest switches of taste in the history of eating and drinking. By 1870 the rival Indian and Ceylon teas had captured one tenth of the tea market in the United Kingdom, and a quarter of a century later their share was nine tenths. Australia was slower in turning away from China tea. The statistics collected at the customs houses of New South Wales for 1886 reveal that the value of castor oil from India – much used as a purgative in simple household as well as chemists' remedies – far exceeded the value of the tea imported from India. A decade later the money spent on Indian tea was soaring. My estimate is that in 1896, when Henry Lawson published his soon-to-be-famous book, *While the Billy Boils*, only about half of the tea poured from billies and teapots was Chinese leaf. A decade later, little of the tea was Chinese. Ceylon even more than India now presided over Australian teapots, sending its tea in air-tight, lightweight boxes, which, when unpacked, were large enough for a small child to use as a cubby or hideaway.

The new tea, stronger in flavour, suited Australian palates. Coming from large plantations, it was cheaper in price. Its increasing popularity possibly also reflected a change in fashion among European peoples. The French historian, Fernand Braudel, once suggested that changes in fashion were more to be expected in a society where generations are in conflict. A change in fashion, he added, is 'a way in which each generation can repudiate its immediate predecessor'. Perhaps the dramatic swing away from China tea was partly such a rejection.

Traditionally tea in Australia was drunk black and piping hot. By around 1900 – the year is not completely certain – the white-aproned waitresses in city tearooms were often asking of their customers: 'Tea? Black or white?' The practice of adding milk, more a habit in the city than in the bush, possibly coincided with the rise in popularity of black Indian tea.

The adding of milk was made easier by the increasing supply of fresh milk in cities and towns. In the hot pastoral districts, where fresh milk was rare and in any case did not long

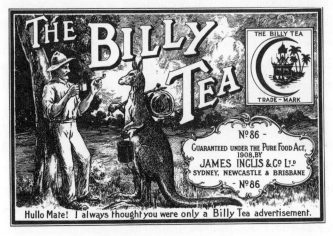

'Billy Tea' was a popular brand, sold in general stores in the early 1900s. The owners enlisted the song 'Waltzing Matilda' to help advertise their product in the newspapers.

remain fresh, the preference for white tea was met in another way. There, the tin of condensed milk, so permeated with sugar that it was sickly, became the substitute for fresh milk. A small hole was punched in the top of the tin, enabling the thick syrup to flow slowly into the teacup. At the kitchen table, when parents were not looking, children would put the tin of condensed milk to their mouths and suck the fluid. Long after the Second World War, the tins of condensed milk were stacked high on the shelves of all country stores. The tins were eventually defeated by long-life milk and the refrigerator.

In 1890 it is likely that more chests of tea were drunk in Australia than in all of Continental Europe, stretching from the western border of Tsarist Russia to the shores of the North Sea. Such was the thirst for tea that in 1906 the tiny population of Australia drank more than twenty times as much tea as all the people of France, and far more than all the people of India combined. At one time in Australia the average person – babies, grannies and all – drank tea at the rate of more than 4 kilograms a year. Today the average Australian drinks less than half that amount.

The craving for tea worried the medical profession. Dr Philip E. Muskett, surgeon superintendent in Sydney, deplored the habit among Australian women of drinking tea between ten in the morning and three in the afternoon. He regretted that they drank tea in immoderate amounts with their bread and butter: 'What wonder, then, that they grow pale and bloodless.' Tea in the middle of the day, he announced in 1893, is a 'deadly destructive fluid'. A cup of tea in the evening, especially after the evening meal, was also to be deplored, for it usually disturbed the night's rest. Such was his indignant complaint.

A Coffee Cocktail

Coffee was drunk less than tea. The only stronghold of coffee was in the few districts peopled by Germans, especially in South Australia and the Victorian Wimmera, the southern tablelands of New South Wales and southern Queensland. Indeed South Australia, with its large German inheritance, was the highest consumer of coffee for many decades, and the coffee it consumed came mainly from Java and Ceylon. In 1890 the average South Australian drank roughly two-thirds of a kilogram of coffee a year. It might not suggest a voracious appetite for coffee but the average for all Australia did not reach that total until the early 1960s, when the Italian espresso café and the tin of Nescafé were satisfying a growing taste for coffee.

Numerous Australians were so fixed on tea that they drank no more than a few cups of coffee in the course of a long life. Much of the coffee drunk was close to unpalatable, being the result of a tablespoon of coffee essence being sloshed into a cup of hot water. As the makers of Symington's Coffee Essence proudly announced, a cup of their coffee could be made at a moment's notice. Sweet and mild, it was more like a warm cup of brown cordial.

While tea was homely, coffee was the drink for excursions and days of daredevilry. It was often seen as the drink for adventurers. Many people drank coffee only on a day of travel.

Americans, voracious drinkers of coffee, initially must have felt elated when in this land they saw the sign COFFEE instead of the eternal TEA. Mark Twain, arriving in the mid-1890s at the height of his writing fame and travelling in trains from Melbourne to Sydney, ordered coffee with his breakfast at the Albury railway station. The food he liked but not the coffee. As his train travelled towards Wagga Wagga he noticed at little wayside stations the advertisements for a certain brand of sheep dip. He hardly knew what sheep dip was but it gave him the opportunity to poke fun at the railway coffee. He wrote that coffee and sheep dip must form a perfect cocktail: 'By itself, railroad coffee is too passive; but sheep dip makes it wake up and get down to business.'

The advocates of temperance and teetotalism gave a boost to the drinking of coffee. In England they founded novel hostelries in the hope of attracting the kind of person who normally preferred an alcohol house, and by 1879 London alone possessed a hundred such houses. They were christened coffee houses – coffee was exotic – though they seem to have served more cups of tea than coffee. As these coffee houses could not readily compete with the traditional gregarious pub, they began to sell cheap meals of sausages and potatoes or a Melton Mowbray pie along with a cup of coffee or cocoa. When a few years later the coffee house was welcomed into Australia by the temperance crusaders, it was reshaped. It was called a coffee palace, which sounded grander. It also supplied accommodation on a large scale but no alcohol. Some of Melbourne's palatial hotels of the 1880s – for instance the Federal and the Windsor – were coffee palaces, built by businessmen whose advocacy of temperance did not always extend to their own financial practices.

In many private houses coffee was kept not as a drink but as a disinfectant. Freshly roasted coffee was said to drive away the smell left in a room by decaying meat. Alternatively the coffee was pounded into a powder and then burned on a hot iron plate, the burned powder then being transferred to a dish placed in the offending room.

Softer Drinks

The sale of soft drinks each summer rose dramatically between 1860 and 1890. The soaring sales reflected the growing prosperity; they reflected the increasing influence of women and children, who were keen consumers; and they also reflected such innovations as steam-bottling machinery and cheaper, returnable glass bottles, which lowered the price of these drinks.

Aerated waters and cordials carried a variety of brand names such as would now astonish us. Around 1890 there were at least 500 different brands of soft drinks. In Bathurst or Port Pirie the local cordial maker, as he was usually called, did not have to compete with some Coca-Cola corporation of that era: there were no international brands and not even one Australia-wide brand of soft drink. Many factories employed only one or two people and a horse and cart.

Larger factories, with perhaps forty employees, produced a diversity of drinks such as the combined factories of a big city no longer bottle. In 1888 in Melbourne one factory made that childhood favourite, raspberry vinegar – concocted, they claimed, from their own vinegar plus raspberries picked on the nearby Yarra river flats. From raw fruits they made a long list of fruit wines – ginger wine, currant wine, elderberry, mulberry, orange and raspberry. They made raisin and quinine wines, lemon syrup, lime juice and sarsaparilla, and more than half a dozen bitters, from orange to hop bitters. In 1888, the centenary year of Australia's colonisation, the firm proudly announced their own registered invention, the new Eucalyptus Wine. A pure, warm preparation for the stomach, it was acclaimed – by its makers – as an excellent tonic and as a sure preventive against fever. The firm has long since gone out of business. If you find in the family cellars a bottle of 1888 Eucalyptus Wine and open it, make sure that no naked flame is burning nearby!

Many cordial makers boasted that they used fresh fruit. Small cordial factories existed alongside orchards and gardens. The time would come when no maker could afford to use fresh fruit and still compete for business. Most of the soft drinks would then be coloured and flavoured by artificial additives.

As the city water was not always trusted, some factories carried their own 'unique and pure' water long distances. Rowlands of Ballarat, which in the 1880s was perhaps the largest soft drinks firm in the land, tapped a mineral spring at Mount Warrenheip for its famous Ballarat soda water, its magnesia water, lithia water, apollinaris water, seltzer water, tonic water, and even for the ginger ale which the firm pioneered in Victoria in 1876. When Rowlands set up a new factory at the west end of Collins Street in Melbourne, much of their water was railed from this private spring.

Mineral water had its admirers, few but discerning. Most lived in those regions where it flowed or bubbled out of the earth. Queensland had its Helidon spa, near a small railway station west of Brisbane, while New South Wales had a spring that was marketed by Tooth's Brewery. When Rowlands of Ballarat set up in Sydney they carted their mineral water from a spring near Katoomba in the Blue Mountains.

The gold town of Daylesford in the hills of central Victoria boasted of the most frequented mineral springs in 1900, Hepburn Springs being the best known. Daylesford received three trains daily from Melbourne and five from Ballarat, and on public holidays people poured in to sample the free mineral waters of the district. A sixpenny horsedrawn cab took them to picturesque Hepburn, which possessed a macaroni factory – Italians were prominent in the town – and four hotels, one of which is still called the Mineral Springs Hotel. It lay in wait for those who took an instant dislike to the mineral water. When the motor car became popular the imbibers of the strong-tasting water could drive to the spring with empty lemonade bottles and fill them. Their enthusiasm was rarely weakened, even after they saw that the inside of the bottles turned brown. The water from most of the mineral springs had a tang in its taste. Above all it was free, and still is.

Spa water seemed likely to become a big business, partly because a back-to-nature movement was in the air not long before the First World War. The railway refreshment cars stocked spa water; and its virtues were publicised in 1909 when a stuntman, undertaking a public fast at the Melbourne

Waxworks, announced that he had lived for fifty-three days on nothing but Rowlands spa water. An ex-governor was also persuaded of its virtues, though he was not willing to undertake a similar period of fasting. Thus the Earl of Jersey wrote to Rowlands, from Osterley Park in England, to praise its mineral water branded as 'Koomah' and bottled in Cooma. 'I am sure that no mineral water comes up to it', he announced. Despite such a hearty affirmation, the real vogue for mineral water did not arise until sixty or more years later.

As half the population by 1910 preferred soft drinks to beer and spirits, they were courted by an increasing variety of soft drinks, including sharp-tasting herbal drinks. Ginger beer, made from the ginger root, also had its devotees. The cola nut, imported from west Africa, saw cola beer being produced in many Australian factories long before Coca-Cola arrived as a competitor. Sarsaparilla, a black fluid based on a plant grown in Mexico and Peru, gained a following among Australian men. Like many soft drinks it was said to have medicinal qualities. Rowlands, on the printed label of the bottle, called it the 'Great Blood Purifier'. Its purifying qualities are now seen as imaginary, but that too will be the fate of some of today's medically lauded concoctions.

Sugar and Jam – and a Word on Tooth Decay

Today, shoppers take a bag of sugar from the shelf and assume it is first class. In the grocer's a century ago, however, they knew that sugar came in various grades, and that the best could be double the price of the worst. In the grocer's shop stood various sugar bins, side by side; and from one the grocer ladled out the superior white sugar while from other bins he took inferior, darker sugars. The brown sugar was very cheap. One sticky kind of brown sugar, often exuding a dash of syrup, was almost black. The lowest grade of sugar had vanished by 1914, and white sugar was added to tea in most households.

Before the sugar farms and mills began to flourish north and south of Brisbane, Australia imported all the sugar it consumed. From the island of Mauritius regularly arrived sailing ships carrying bags of sugar carefully divided into four grades: ration sugar, good counter sugar, fine yellow sugar and fine crystallised sugar. The poorest was the ration sugar, being the kind of sweetener which a pastoralist gave to his shepherds as part of their weekly food ration. Ration sugar remained popular on the goldfields. In Henry Lawson's stories the struggling families tend to tip ration sugar into their cup of hot tea, while on their slices of bread they spread treacle. At the sugar mills in northern New South Wales the treacle was a waste product, and people could arrive with a billy can or cask and fill it with free treacle.

Loaf or lump sugar, more expensive even than fine white sugar, was used only in wealthier households and fine restaurants. At one time the favourite loaf sugar came from England and Holland. For practical reasons loaf sugar was preferred by some of the pioneering shopkeepers in the forests of south Gippsland. They knew that if loaf sugar fell off loaded pack-horses in the course of being carried on muddy tracks to their

SUGAR MILL at BROADWATER
RICHMOND RIVER.

BRINGING DOWN THE CANE

A VACUUM PAN

The cane farms and sugar mills on the coastal rivers of northern New South Wales were increasing suppliers of sugar to the jam and biscuit factories of Australia.

own town, most of it could be recovered and then washed clean. In contrast the grain sugar, if spilled, oozed its way into the mud and was largely lost.

One day, a sharp protruding branch of an uprooted tree tore open a passing pack and sent hundreds of loaves of white sugar tumbling into the mud. 'I was able to collect most of it with very little waste', wrote the horseman, 'and the bag reached its destination minus very little more than I had been able to eat during salvage operations'.

Tea without sugar was considered to be worse than a pie without meat. Most Australians were proud that they consumed such large quantities of sugar – an extravagance which was beyond the income of the average family in Europe. In the town of Camden in 1845 one tenant farmer, when questioned, calculated the tea and sugar consumed by his household of about seven adults and three children. Casually he answered, 'We buy tea by the half chest; use about three pound a week; buy 100 weight of sugar at a time; cannot say how much we use; when the bag is empty we get more, that is all I know about it.' A nearby farmer, Pat Curry, boasted that at his smaller dining table and kitchen they consumed almost 2 kilograms of sugar a day: 'no stint', he added. You can almost hear him saying, 'What a land to live in!'

Much sugar went into the making of jams. The quantity of jam made in private homes exceeded that made in factories. Homemade jam was said to have a precious taste of its own. It was cheaper, too – so long as numerous children were conscripted to help. Children had to pick fruit from the trees in the backyard, and others had to peel it with sharp knives. The core of the apple had to be removed, the root of the hard stem had to be cut from the gooseberry and mulberry, and stones had to be plucked from apricots and peaches. The harder fruits had to be sliced before they were placed in the sugary syrup in the big metal pan on top of the stove. And someone had to break the apricot stones with a gentle blow of the hammer, thus enabling the inner kernels to be removed and cooked. The gleaming white kernels, tiny islands among all that apricot, were the delicacy in the pot of apricot jam. At times all the family was summoned to do these repetitive tasks.

And where did mum find the jars in which her new-made jams were preserved? Jars were expensive, and improvisation was called for. Throughout the year, wine bottles and other glass containers were stored away and then, in the jam-making season, were washed and prepared for reshaping. The delicate task was to break the neck from the bottle – sharply. For this task an iron ring was heated on the coals of the stove until it was red hot. Taken up by a long handle, the heated ring was clasped around the neck of the bottle, which was quickly turned once. The iron ring was removed, and the bottle was plunged into a bucket of very cold water. Normally the neck – with a cracking sound – separated cleanly from the bottle, leaving a long, open-necked jar.

The neck then had to be rubbed with a file so that the jagged edges were smoothed. Into these jars or bottles went the hot jam. Once the jam had cooled, a circle of rice paper was pasted as a seal over the top of the bottle. If a firmer seal was preferred, paraffin wax was poured on top of the jam, forming an air-tight layer.

Now came the time for the labels to be fixed. Labelling was essential because many of the bottled jams looked alike, especially if the glass was dark. While the housewife normally would take a bottle of ink and write out the labels, she might entrust that task to her husband if his handwriting was deemed clearer and more elegant. If the jam was to be sold at a fete, neat calligraphy added to its value. On the white label was written the name of the jam and the name of the month when it left the kitchen.

'Mother was proud of her jam, and rightly so', remember many old people. At bazaars and charity fetes around 1900 were displayed quince and quince-honey jams, and the plum jams made from Kentish cherry and greengage and golden plums, and all those melon jams with ginger and quince or lemon as additives.

Recalling her Gippsland childhood of the 1870s, Mary Fullerton insisted that the work of making jam lacked the romantic feelings attached to that task in the United States and England. Perhaps the sweltering Australian days weakened the pleasure of making jam. 'I have weary recollections', she wrote, 'of stirrings by hot stove-fires on days of fierce heat.' And yet this peeling and boiling, bottling and labelling was essential because 'ours was a family that consumed an amazing amount of jam'.

A few people still make jam at home. Probably they are people whose own parents were raised in the countryside, whether in Australia or Europe. They are people who see the homemade jams as a celebration of the cycle of the seasons, an honouring of old ways as much as a method of saving money. Today, the making of jams and sauces at home is less attractive, partly because most customers can afford to buy factory jam. They can even afford to buy homemade jam, which, packaged in quaint bottles and labelled folksily as Grandma's Own Jam, is even dearer than factory jam.

As sugar was relatively expensive around the time of the early gold rushes, it was used with restraint by the average family, except at feasts and picnics. In 1870 a generous picnic was prepared for the children of the small farmers and orchardists living in the foothills near Melbourne. Crowded together in twelve spring carts, the children travelled for three hours to reach the beach at St Kilda where they proceeded to consume a long list of foods:

> 40 pounds of plum cake
> 30 pounds of seed cake
> 16 pounds of sugar
> 384 tarts and buns

They also consumed twelve loaves of bread, two hams, 12 pounds of beef, 4 pounds of tea and 20 pints of milk. As the first four items on the list were sugary, a lot of sugar was devoured at the picnic.

In the inner city of Melbourne in 1868 a gigantic children's party was staged to celebrate the visit of Prince Alfred, son of Queen Victoria. The caterers provided meat by the ton,

as well as 20 000 buns and 15 000 bags of lollies – or one bag
of lollies for each child expected to attend. At another picnic
in Bendigo, after children welcomed the prince, the food was
apportioned equally in order that the small children would not
be crushed in the scramble. Each child received two buns, two
tarts, an apple and a packet of lollies. A child's bag of lollies was
easily clutched in the hand, and each tooth-breaking sweet
could be sucked for many minutes until finally it shrank away.

The heavy consumption of sugar rotted teeth. Dentists,
however, were few. People either submitted themselves to the
pain or persuaded neighbours or paid doctors and chemists to
pull out the aching tooth. In the early 1880s all the dentists in
Adelaide, then the third-largest city in Australia, could probably
be fitted into a single horsedrawn cab. A quarter-century later
that city employed some seventy registered dentists, and they in
turn were training about twenty apprentices.

The Gorgeous Lollies

The drink of cocoa and the bar of chocolate, like milk and butter,
are almost inseparable. The cocoa bean, originally from Latin
America, is the source of both cocoa and chocolate. The bean
was expensive at the time when the British reached Australia,
and both chocolate and cocoa were luxuries. It is possible that
not one cup of hot cocoa was drunk in Sydney in its first year.

Many of the great chocolate firms of the world were
founded during a tiny span of seven years, beginning just when
Western Australia was colonised. Between 1824 and 1831, the

firm of Menier was founded in France, which was to become the home of luxury chocolates. In the same years, Suchard was founded in Switzerland, and Van Houten in Holland. The English firm of Fry was much older, and as early as 1795 it employed a Boulton and Watt steam engine in its factory in Bristol.

Only the richer people drank cocoa. What is now often seen as a drink for children was at first deemed almost too valuable to be offered to them, except those who were sick and frail and not long for this world. Cocoa was partly seen as that rarity, an enjoyable medicine; and as late as the 1870s Fry's advertised the virtues of their Homeopathic Cocoa with a message from the *Medical Times*: 'Eminently suitable for invalids'.

Meanwhile cocoa was ceasing to be such an expensive drink. Bags of cocoa beans from Portuguese West Africa arrived in European ports in the 1850s, and seventy years later Africa was to supersede the American homeland as the main source. As the price of cocoa became cheaper, it began to compete a little with tea and strongly with coffee. In the United Kingdom in 1870, five times as much coffee was consumed as cocoa but thirty years later the consumption of cocoa was well ahead of coffee. Australia, its average citizen being wealthier, preceded England in its rising appetite for cocoa and chocolate.

Curiously cocoa, as it entered more kitchens, ceased to be hailed so much as a medicine: it was just plain healthy. Moreover it was highly praised by some temperance advocates as a substitute for alcohol. Like spirits it was usually drunk in strong doses. One of Fry's advertisements in Australia in 1890 shows two cups and saucers on a tray. Dark liquid steams almost to the rim of the cups, leaving no room for milk. On the tray there is no room for a milk jug.

The moulded bar of milk chocolate, neatly wrapped, came late in the history of the cocoa bean. The Swiss invented milk chocolate in the 1870s, and dominated this growing trade. Cadbury's Dairy Milk chocolate made its mark just before the First World War. Even then a chocolate bar was expensive, and perhaps half of Australian children under the age of twelve had probably never tasted one – or only one. Boiled lollies, being cheap, were the property of children.

Australians probably coined the word lolly, which was short for the old English word, lollypop. It was long understood that the first mention of 'lolly' in print was in the *Melbourne Illustrated Post*, which in July 1862 drew attention to 'the gorgeous decorations at the lolly stall'. But it is now known that Catherine Spence, the South Australian writer, used the word in a novel published in 1854: 'Fanny ran away to the nearest lolly shop, and all her brothers and sisters followed her.' It is likely that the word was in currency in Adelaide for some years before it was considered appropriate to be in print.

While the richest chocolates and the most luxurious confections were imported from Britain and the Continent, the bulk of simple confectionery was made here by the 1870s. At this time there were no reliable statistics for the manufacture of Australian sweets. My estimate is that more were made in household kitchens than in factories. As the main ingredients for the simplest lollies were sugar and water, as no secret recipes were needed, and as the wood-burning stove supplied the heat for the boiling process, a skilled housewife could easily compete with the sweets factory. Moreover the boiled lollies made at home for picnics, birthdays and Christmas treats looked much the same as those produced in factories, for most factory sweets were not yet wrapped in coloured paper. Even so, the public demand for sweets was so large that the factories continued to expand. By 1890 some Melbourne firms – for instance, the Excelsior Wholesale Confectionary Co – employed as many as 300 people.

Sweets were sold from tall glass jars standing on or near the shop counter. The shopkeeper thrust a hand inside the jar and clutched the lollies and then weighed them or counted them. The sticky sweets were wrapped in newspaper or grease-proof paper and then handed to the purchaser. Most lollies were touched by human fingers – the cheaper varieties had to be counted by the shopkeeper in front of the young customer's eyes. Only the expensive sweets, as late as 1914, were sold in printed packets or in tins, and even they were probably touched by human hands – not always washed hands – at some point in the manufacturing process.

It was believed that glass jars protected lollies from germs and dust. The germs, however, entered the jar at their pleasure. The shopkeeper did not wear gloves and did not use metal tongs, and so the lollies were easily contaminated. But the feeling among medical men was that, if an infectious disease was traced to a shop, goods in jars were safe but goods in the open air were suspect. In 1882 in Swanston Street, Melbourne, a woman caught smallpox while living at the back of a shop which sold fruit and confectionery. Government officials arrived at the infected shop and destroyed the fruit on display but did not touch the lollies in the glass jars. When the shop was reopened the customers who returned had their suspicions about the glass jars and their contents. Even small children wondered whether the lollies were really hygienic. Their doubts, their sense of wonder and even the lilt of their voices were recorded by the shorthand writer at a government inquiry into the episode: 'Look what lollies there are there, will they sell them again?'

Brand-name sweets, like a Mars Bar or a Cherry Ripe, were not yet dominant. Sweets were known not by their maker's name but by age-old categories. Thus at one time toffee and its sister, the butterscotch, were words known to every child who could mouth two or three syllables. The superior kind of butterscotch contained honey and butter as well as sugar. Many children, clutching their halfpenny, pointed a grubby finger at the lolly jars and asked for lozenges and pastilles: these were cheap and could be chewed slowly for some minutes. When barley sugar was demanded, the shopkeeper was happy to supply it in the shape of glassy balls, sticks and bars. And there was the fondant, nougat and bon-bon, liqueur and sugar candy. Some older customers, with a shilling in one hand and a girlfriend in the other, wanted exotic fruits and nuts covered with candy made from sugar and the gum, tragacanth.

Colouring was the elixir of confectionery. Children, especially girls, loved the pretty colours almost as much as the taste.

Most lollies for children were advertised with bare simplicity. The actual price – four for a penny or six for a penny – was the main topic of interest in the inter-war years. 'Braddies' were presumably named after the young cricketer, Don Bradman.

For a long time much of the colouring came from such vegetable products as saffron, brazilwood, cherrywood and fustic. From animals and insects came such colourings as carmine and cochineal. But the chemist and the dyestuffs industry increasingly supplied synthetic colourings, ranging from Prussian blue to magenta; and in some factories by the early 1900s these artificial colours had virtually supplanted the natural ones.

Sugar was basic but many flavourings were used in lolly factories. 'Where is the caraway kept, where are the cloves?'

enquired the new mixer. Also on the shelves were such flavour-ings as lavender, nutmeg, aniseed, peppermint, verbena, oil of almonds and fruit essences innumerable – cowslip and damson, apricot and peach.

Around 1900 it became common for a factory to wrap individually by hand the sweets of medium quality. When the firm of MacRobertson launched its 'milk kisses' in about 1903, it was proud to announce that each chewable lolly was covered by a printed wrapper. 'Know them by their printed wrappers', it advertised. The lolly-wrappers, once the sweet was eaten, were collected by children, for they were pretty and novel. The day would come when they were so common that they were thrown on the ground or in the gutter, left to blow about on windy days.

Macpherson Robertson, the founder of this confectionery firm, became the Cadbury of Australia. He began to make boiled lollies in the bathroom of his parents' house in Melbourne in 1880, carrying his latest batch to shops in the suburbs on a large tray that he perched on his head. His factory in Fitzroy grew and grew, eventually becoming known as the Great White City. He could have employed an estate agent almost full-time to negotiate the later purchases of surrounding houses and other properties which he needed for his storerooms, mixing rooms, assembly line, and the cellars where his Old Gold chocolate could be stored in warm weather. Children loved the surprise packets in which he packed items that had not sold so well. In winter the sniffling public swore by his cough drops. The strong greys that pulled the delivery vehicles became the symbols of his firm. He belonged to the new era of gimmicks and jingles.

On a visit to the United States in 1893 he absorbed new ideas – including fairy floss and the Columbine caramel that would become a household word, as well as chewing gum. In Australia the chewing of gum was only a minority taste when he first made 'chewy' to the American formula. The rise of chewing gum was to be in part a mirror of social tension, and in the United States, the rate of chewing increased rapidly during each of the great wars. The arrival of chewing gum in Australian mouths was one of the early signs of American cultural penetration, and the time came when cleaning women could look beneath the chairs in every Sunday school in Adelaide and every school desk in Perth and find a few discarded wads of chewing gum adhering to the wood. The firm was to sell the chewing-gum section of its business to the American firm of Wrigley in 1918, and in Australia the name of Wrigley was almost to become a synonym for chewing gum. But the name of MacRobertson in this part of the world has outlasted Wrigley, for the founder of the firm gave away money on a large scale, and imaginatively. His is probably the only brand name of any country to have a large zone of the world named in its honour, MacRobertson Land in Antarctica.

The Luxury of Ice Cream

Ice cream was a luxury and unattainable, or unknown, in most parts of Australia. It so happened that in 1906 many school-children went by train from Burnie to Launceston, a slow journey of six hours, to see a trade exhibition, a rare event in

Tasmania. One of the children – later to be the wife of a prime minister – was aged nine, just old enough to marvel at her first sight of a provincial city; and she saw fairy floss being made and tasted the magic sweet. At the next stall the children with a penny to spare were buying small cones filled with a cold, creamy mixture, and Enid and her sister bought one. 'Never in our lives had we tasted anything so delicious', she wrote. 'The filling melted in our mouths – truly melted in our mouths.'

The children thought that their parents and all at home must have an opportunity to taste this gift from heaven. Spending their last sixpence on six cones loaded with the creamy mixture, they carried them away in a paper bag, determined, as a special surprise, to take them in the train all the way to their home. But soon the dollops of ice cream became smaller and smaller, and the children were bewildered that they should melt in their hands. 'And because', recalled Enid, 'we had never tasted ice-cream until that day, we sat on the grass and ate it all and were consoled.'

The first ice cream was made in hotels and private homes long before it became available in shops. In the cities the street hawkers, playing music to attract children, sold ice cream from the back of carts, but only in summer. Usually they scooped the ice cream out of a tin which was kept cold by a surround of dry ice. Far more children crowded around the cart than had the money to buy its produce. Everywhere, ice cream was dear. In remote districts it was virtually unknown. In 1910 in the bustling Tasmanian mining town of Zeehan, a man wrote to Melbourne to buy an ice-cream churn; and his daughter, some sixty years later, thought the ice cream was perhaps the first made in a district whose mountains were capped with snow on some winter weeks. It is possible that less than half of the children then living in Australia had ever tasted ice cream.

In the hot city of Broken Hill an ice-cream seller became a national figure in the early months of the First World War. Perturbed by the news that Turkey and Australia were on opposite sides, he decided to take action on New Year's Day in 1915. He decked his ice-cream cart with the Turkish flag and drove, with a compatriot, to the railway line, where a picnic train was expected. In the train nearly all the 1200 passengers, wearing holiday hats and their best clothes, were sitting in open railway trucks. Suddenly shots were fired at the train. Three passengers and one spectator died, and seven others were wounded. The two Turks fled to nearby rocks to make their final stand, and were quickly 'riddled with bullets'. As the layers of headlines in the *Barrier Miner* excitedly proclaimed:

WAR IN BROKEN HILL
ATTACK ON A PICNIC TRAIN
UNDER THE TURKISH FLAG
MEN AND WOMEN SHOT

To sell ice cream was to ply a marginal trade. The sellers were mainly foreigners who were willing to accept the low income that the seasonal ice-cream trade returned. In many parts of the land, once summer faded away, they put aside their white coat, stored the gaily decorated cart in a shed, and plied some other business – if they could.

Firms that were to become the big names in ice cream were still only minnows. Frederick A. B. Peters emigrated from Michigan to Sydney in 1907 and began to make ice cream in poky premises at the seaside suburb of Manly. He expanded into Queensland. Surely, he argued, if ice cream could be sold on a large scale in Australia, it would be in Queensland! Eventually small factories in Brisbane, Rockhampton and Townsville sold his ice cream under the name of the Peters-Arctic Delicacy Co. Even in 1930 Peters ice cream was still expensive. His strawberry ice cream actually contained small pieces of fresh strawberry, and such embellishments added to the price.

Demand for ice cream fell away when each summer ended and most factories, by Easter, had ceased altogether to make the product. The arrival of American soldiers in 1942 did more than anything to boost the year-long demand for ice cream. They even licked their ice creams in winter. The word 'lick' is significant. The delicacy was so dear that it was usually licked slowly in order that the pleasure would last as long as possible.

Sales of ice cream depended on packaging. The edible cone was really a package. An Italian invention, it reached the United States before the First World War. The dixie – a small cardboard cup of ice cream eaten with a wooden spoon – began to make headway in Australia only between the two world wars. On a Saturday night in the new picture theatres, the dixie was a special treat and a rival for the small box of chocolates.

The Biscuit – Sixty-nine Varieties

In 1850 most biscuits were probably made in the kitchen. By the late 1880s big firms such as Swallow & Ariell of Port Melbourne, in what they called their 'steam biscuit manufactory', baked biscuits in oversized ovens in astronomical numbers. Biscuits, packed in large tins with tight lids, were sold through the grocer's shops. There the shop assistants opened the tins, took the biscuits out by hand and weighed them for each individual customer. Biscuits were not yet sold in packets with bright wrappings.

The taste for factory-made biscuits went hand in hand with the taste for lollies: indeed, in the 1880s some firms made both items, for sugar is an ingredient of each. Simple biscuits were still in demand: the ship's biscuits, nursery biscuits, rice biscuits and soda biscuits, and of course the plain rusks and Sutton rusks. But there was an increasing demand for the fancy biscuit: the currant luncheons, macaroons, lemon ginger-nuts, meringues, raspberry wafers, lime biscuits and chocolate wafers. That thriving Port Melbourne firm, with its five chimneys puffing up smoke, made sixty-nine different kinds of biscuits in Australia's centennial year.

In 1888 the typical housewife probably baked most of the biscuits that her family ate. But when her friends called on visiting day and sipped their tea, they were pleased if 'bought biscuits' were placed on their plates. Such biscuits were given fashionable names by their makers, and at the grocer's shop you could see, identified in fancy lettering on the latest tins, such royal biscuits as Victoria, Prince of Wales, Queen drops, Jubilee (Queen Victoria's jubilee had occurred in 1887), Balmoral – named after the Scottish home of the royal family – and those biscuits called Alberts, named after Queen Victoria's dead husband. Similarly Lord Beaconsfield, as England's prime minister, was immortalised by a biscuit, while that military hero of 1885, General Gordon, was commemorated by a tinned cake, the Gordon cake, after he was killed at Khartoum in the Sudan. Gordon also lent his name to a newborn child of 1894, the future prime minister, Robert Gordon Menzies. His father, a country storekeeper, no doubt sold tins of Gordon cake each Christmas.

Biscuits a century ago were served with a small glass of fortified wine in many households. 'My own people', wrote Mary Gilmore, 'had cracknels with port, arrowroot biscuits with sherry, and a "plain" biscuit with sweet Madeira and Malaga.' The cracknel was a dry biscuit, curved or hollowed, but the word cracknel has vanished, perhaps being replaced by crackers. These special biscuits, the cracknels and arrowroots, were obviously bought from a general store rather than made by Mary's parents in their successive kitchens near Goulburn and Wagga Wagga and beyond.

In the eyes of children with a halfpenny to spend, 'broken biscuits' were a favourite. These were simply biscuits which had been broken somewhere between the biscuit factory and the shelves of the grocer's shop: perhaps the delivery cart passed over a rough road, perhaps someone dropped the tin, or perhaps a biscuit was poorly made. A self-respecting grocer put to one side any broken biscuits and sold them at a fraction of their normal price. It was less the custom to ask for a pound of broken biscuits than to ask for one or two pennys' worth, the grocer himself mentally estimating, from the quality of the broken biscuits, how many he should serve. Many families purchased only broken biscuits.

Dripping and Cocky's Joy

Restaurants were at one end of the ladder of pleasure. At the other end were the private kitchens, thousands of them. They made do in countless ways, depending on the region. Monotony of diet was common.

Some hardworking farming families ate mainly bread and milk. On entering the kitchen at morning and evening they carved for themselves a large wedge of bread and placed it in a bowl. On the side of the stove stood the hot milk and they poured it over the bread and sprinkled a little salt and pepper. A second wedge of bread was later carved from the loaf and again soaked in milk, and so the meal proceeded. 'And that was all they ate', wrote one Tasmanian observer. In an asylum for the mentally ill in Melbourne, meat and vegetables, or a dish equally nutritious, was served for dinner in the middle of the day. But both breakfast and tea consisted of bread and milk, probably with a sprinkling of sugar, and usually a pot of hot tea.

In poor households, bread provided most of the calories, and fatty dripping provided the remainder. At breakfasts the bread was toasted on the coals of the wood stove, spread with dripping and sprinkled with salt. Pepper was dearer and so was used more sparingly by the poor. At lunch the big loaf of bread was again on the table and spread with cheap plum jam or dripping. There was rich dripping and lean dripping – the rich was highly satisfying, especially when melted on hot toast. In the evening, potatoes might be the main food. Pumpkin, also cheap, was widely eaten in season. A popular breakfast was hot pumpkin fritters over which golden syrup was spread. It now seems to be the most frugal of dishes, but children relished it.

As pudding a dish of plain boiled rice was often served with a coating of sugar to provide sweetness. When fruit was plentiful, stewed quinces or plums might be served with the rice. If times were hard, sugar was used sparingly, leaving the stewed fruit with a slightly sour flavour. Sugar substitutes like golden syrup and treacle were prized. Bread and treacle made a popular dinner in a poor household. Golden syrup, which was popular long before 1900, was known as 'cocky's joy', the small farmer being known as a cocky. If the syrup was bought by the large two-pound tin, then it was four times as cheap as jam. It was a disaster, however, when a swarm of black ants found their way into the golden syrup.

Henry Lawson was an alert observer of the miners who, when the gold rushes faded, settled on tiny farms and lived mostly on tea and ration sugar, bread and treacle, bread and dripping. Next door, in a slab hut, a large family often fed on bread, tea and a pumpkin pie. After these farmers cleared the land and paid off some of their debts, they acquired livestock and so produced their own bacon, milk, butter and eggs. But the eggs and butter, being almost too valuable to eat, were usually carried to the nearest town in order to pay for bread, groceries and clothes.

Along the Great Dividing Range of central New South Wales stood the small town of Crookwell and its potato growers, many of whom were of Irish descent. To one farm came a lad who was eager to earn money by digging the new crop. At dinnertime, which we now call lunchtime, he reported that the farmer's wife went outside the kitchen and struck an old ploughshare with a piece of metal – her dinner gong. In case there was any doubt what the meal consisted of, she shouted loudly in the direction of the nearby paddock: 'Taties is biled'. She was simply announcing that the potatoes were boiled: come and devour them! The hungry potato-diggers streamed into the farmhouse and sat at a long table holding a gargantuan dish of boiled potatoes, capped by rising steam. The other item of food on the table was a slab of rock salt.

Was this feast of boiled potatoes typical of farming families? Perhaps it was more typical of Irish families than of others but even that assumption is uncertain. The young man returned to his father's own humble farm and announced that he was not going back to a kitchen where the meal was so simple. This suggests that a meal consisting solely of boiled potatoes and rock salt was hardly typical.

The wife who had cooked all those boiled potatoes came from a family of shepherds. At home, that family also ate meal after meal of the same food. One day a visitor saw, sitting on their table, three meat pies of enormous size. She was told that this one was for lunch and the next one was for the evening meal, with 'the other's goin' shepherdin'. Possibly these pies contained pieces of potato as well as meat beneath the crust.

The poorer rural families, growing most of their food, followed a simple diet. In sheep country one Scottish-born farmer ate cold mutton for breakfast, cold mutton for dinner and cold mutton for tea. On some farms, the daily menu was dominated by eggs. In Western Australia in the early 1900s a lad named Albert Facey went to work for two German farmers. Their hut was made of bags spread over a wooden frame, the floor was trampled earth, the kitchen table was a long board standing on four stout forked sticks stuck in the earth, and the meals consisted of fried or boiled eggs and some damper and black tea. For the tea he was given neither sugar nor milk, which was a severe deprivation, because nearly everybody stirred several spoons of sugar into their tea. Such families, with their monotonous meals, had the consolation that most people in Europe would have envied a menu in which eggs were so plentiful.

When a large family had to economise, it saved money on clothing. The children wore patched clothes and, except in winter, walked in bare feet. But food was the main target for savings. The largest item of the budget, food absorbed maybe half of the family's weekly income.

We see where the savings had to be made by struggling families if we look at the relative cost of each item of food. The cost of certain foodstuffs varied from season to season and from district to district, but the following list, of about 1890, attempts roughly to make a ladder of the cheapest foods available in a typical large town. Pumpkin, potatoes and bread were clearly cheapest – if measured by the pence paid for each kilogram.

Pumpkin	1.5 pence	Pork	8
Potatoes	1.5	Cheese	8
Bread	1.5	Bacon	10
Rice	3	Eggs	12
Sugar	3	Butter	14
Mutton	3	Coffee	18
Beef	4	Tea	24
Milk (quart)	5		

To cut back on beef and pork, butter and cheese, bacon and eggs, as well as coffee and tea was an obvious source of savings. Tobacco, at 18 pence a pound, and beer could also be rationed.

Women and children probably suffered more than men in exceptional adversity. If the husband went to prison, deserted the family, or died in the prime of life, many young families could not cope. Of the destitute women appearing in official records in Western Australia in 1877, more than one in three was married to a man in prison. Such women often wandered the streets of Perth in the daylight hours, their ragged children beside them. Magistrates who investigated the life of women who had appealed for help might find a house with a leaking roof, a bed in which she and three or four children all slept together, and an empty larder.

The sense of helplessness stands out in surviving letters. 'Please help my children', wrote a woman living near the rural

The cottage of a Newcastle coal miner's family. It is washing day,
and the wife washes clothes in the open air while her husband stands
by the large chimney.

village of Toodyay in Western Australia in 1854. She added
urgently that her children were starving, 'which you know Sir
must be heart-breaking to a Mother'. Her neighbours, viewing
the family as feckless, and knowing that the husband was in
prison for theft, lifted no finger to help them. Six years later the
plight of the family was the same.

Throughout this era the social services were sparse.
People had to provide their own, by joining a friendly society, a
trade union that ran a sickness fund, or by taking out a policy
with a life office. All these forms of self-help were imperfect.
They called for a level of financial sacrifice almost beyond the
reach of an unskilled labourer with six or eight children.

Unemployment was a cruel blow, whenever it fell on breadwinners. Fortunately it did not reach 4 per cent in the average year between 1850 and 1890. But the depression and long drought of the 1890s caused massive unemployment in several colonies, hitting Victoria the hardest. There the unemployment in the worst months averaged maybe 15 per cent. It soon fell, partly because so many Victorians, especially young families, paid for their own relief by buying a sea ticket to the Western Australian goldfields; New Zealand; the west coast of Tasmania; Sydney; or wherever the economic prospects seemed shinier.

The land of meat had temporarily become, for many, the land of dripping.

13

RESTAURANTS AND
GENERAL STORES

In the land of the bullock dray and quart pot, restaurants were few. Families ate at home or beside the road.

With luck, however, an appetising restaurant could sometimes be found. Around 1860 the eating room of Kidd's Hotel at the new goldfield at Kiandra, high in the Snowy Mountains, surprised visitors. It was the only real restaurant in the district; Sydney itself owned only a few that were superior. The menu was almost a miracle, for supplies had to be carted from afar, along rough roads and at high expense. The hotel itself was virtually a wooden barn with head-high partitions dividing the main space into a dining hall and bar on one side and cramped bedrooms on the other. Two long parallel tables ran the length of the dining room with seats for up to seventy diners, if they kept their elbows to themselves. Homemade candelabra held a ring of candles that illuminated the patrons, most of whom displayed on their rough clothes the clay and dirt from the mines. Knives, forks and plates were set out on the table, a refinement which elevated Kidd's above other restaurants within a radius of 300 kilometres. To gain a seat, people arrived long before the advertised hour – diggers, officials, shop-keepers, bankers, black men and white, all of them hungry and, often, cold.

At last, from the little kitchen, came waiters bearing Irish stew, 'liver and bacon', roast mutton and the few other advertised dishes. The menu sounded stolid but the food was delicious. After the very hungry finished their food they held their plates high and shouted for more. The chef, Felix, came from Paris. Even if he had originally made his name in a tiny café in an ill-lit Parisian lane, his reputation soared in the Australian high country.

His waiters were noted for strength rather than manners. At the long tables they were skilled in maintaining law and order – except on those occasions when the fighting between diners became completely out of hand. It was the waiters' normal duty to expel all diners as early as possible, for the big room later served as a bar, finally becoming, with the evening far gone, a dormitory for the hotel's overflow.

In the 1870s there must have been no more than 1000 restaurants and cafés in Australia: few if any passing muster by today's standards of cleanliness – not many with a clean tablecloth; few with a wide menu; many of them draughty and cold in the extremes of winter or stifling on hot summer nights; many with an earthen floor; many with a grubby chef who a year or two previously knew little about the art of cooking. And yet a few of these restaurants were triumphs because they quickly established themselves in towns that, emerging in the space of a month, simply vanished when the shallow gold had gone.

Restaurants de Paris and de Darwin

The more enterprising providers, like Charles Jones of gold-rush Melbourne, tried to serve meals in their hotels and restaurants at all hours. For his one-shilling breakfast Jones offered steak, chops, stewed tripe, kidneys, sausages, cutlets, Irish stew and bread and butter. Eggs, bacon and ham were extras. Those customers who arrived at 10.30 a.m. could order soups and bread. Roast and boiled meats were available at dinner. Those who did not wish to be waited upon could go to the east end of the 'culinary department' and try the 'Counter Lunch', in which a glass of the best English ale (or so he said) was accompanied by such delicacies as lobster salad, pork pies and plain pies, fish, tripe, rump steak, chops, steaks, tongues and cold meats. He even advertised his long menu in the country newspapers.

In remote towns, the restaurant was occasionally a surprise. At the tiny port of Darwin in the mid-1870s, visitors disembarking from the small steamship were initially dismayed to see that a large bucket of water cost nine pence, that white children walked around naked in the heat, and that many newcomers slept in hammocks suspended from the branches of trees; but some visitors were pleased to discover a restaurant which somehow managed to find the ingredients for excellent meals. The owner – unable to procure fresh vegetables and meat, or poultry, milk, butter and eggs – had to make do with preserved meat, taken from tins or casks, and even preserved potatoes at times. But he made tasty bread and provided tasty sauces, pickles and jams and caught ling fish, thereby managing to make 'sundry, savoury dishes'.

Hundreds of thousands of people in the course of their whole lives did not once enter a restaurant. Melbourne, the hub of entertainments in 1868, probably possessed no more than fifty restaurants, and some of these were really coffee houses and colonial wine rooms, in which eating was a lesser activity. One, the London pie shop, was not really a restaurant. Another was a business that combined a wine saloon, a billiard saloon and a tobacconist's shop. Nearly all of these establishments were in the city, with the notable exception of two by the sea – at Williamstown and Port Melbourne. Just over half of Melbourne's eating houses were in the busiest shopping street, Bourke Street, and twenty-two of them stood in that stretch running from the GPO up to Parliament House.

As the wealth and population grew, the city eating houses multiplied. Many began their day with breakfast. Their midday meal, called dinner, commenced with hot soup, which might range from mutton broth to ox-tail and vegetable soup. The main course embraced a choice of fried fish, mutton pie, beefsteak pie, corned or roast beef, stuffed mutton, roast lamb, or that sturdy delicacy, roasted ox heart. A few restaurants included poultry but diners could not expect too large a helping, poultry being a luxury which in the typical household was served only once a year. The third course ranged from apple tart and jam tart to plum pudding, blancmange and sago pudding. While a few restaurants offered a free glass of ale, most provided tea or coffee.

There were even 'threepenny' restaurants where the meal had to be eaten quickly so that the seats could be vacated for those waiting outside. Thus Hosie's Hotel & Café, in the heart of Melbourne, set out to cater especially for the visitors who poured into the city in May 1901 for the formal opening of the first Federal Parliament. In the space of six days it served 17 252 meals, at three pence each.

Even more of a bargain was a restaurant opposite the post office that provided, for the down and out each weeknight, a hot meal consisting of the leftovers from the day's previous meals, and chunks of bread to fill any remaining space in the stomach. Many hotels bid for the masses with a simple one-course meal, available freely to those who purchased a beer or ale. At the top end were the shilling restaurants, which included wine in their meal of four courses.

By 1900 the word 'café' was used more than 'restaurant'. It covered bakers and pastry cooks who, on the ground floor of their shop, set up tables and chairs for thirty or sixty diners and employed 'smart waitresses' to serve luncheons and afternoon teas. The word 'café' also described the kind of 'eating supermarkets' that the Greeks especially established in Sydney and Melbourne. These held a dozen different dining rooms in the one three-storey building: rooms for simple meals and snacks, a dining room for ladies and another for gentlemen, a hall where the banquet or smoke night or euchre tournament could be held, and small rooms for supper parties after the theatre.

Saturday night in George Street, Sydney. For the crowds promenading in city streets at night, there were few restaurants. The era of the restaurant arrived in the 1960s and 1970s.

In Melbourne the Town Hall Café, founded by Antony Lucas – first known as Antonios Lekatsas when he arrived from the isle of Ithaca – had seats for 650 people. While Lucas did not compete fully with another Greek, Dinnis Black, who employed a string band to play in his Restaurant de Paris and Oyster Palace, he offered other facilities for his patrons: 'Adjoining the apartment set apart for ladies is a boudoir fitted up with every requisite for their comfort and the completion of their personal adornment before proceeding to the theatre or concert-room'. Such cafés were expensive, and the mass of citizens never stepped inside to see the rows of tables with their immaculate white tablecloths draped almost to the floor, the neatly ironed serviettes arranged in glasses on the tables, the tall thin vases of flowers, and on the walls the ornate mirrors enabling diners to see, without turning around, who was kissing whom at that ultra-convivial table on the far side of the crowded room.

The Fasoli family, which had immigrated from the border between Italy and Switzerland, was widely praised for the restaurant it conducted in Melbourne. The clientele in both Fasoli's and the later Café Bohemia included painters and writers. Louis Esson, the playwright, in a poem of 1906, rejoiced that here could be heard the ripples and gusts of laughter, 'the tongues of all the earth', and the irregular click of the game of dominoes as well as the scraping of knife and fork. 'And there's smoke, and wine, and strumming of the harp and gay guitar', he added.

The years between 1890 and 1910 possibly marked the heyday of dining in cafés. Michael Symons observes in his book

One Continuous Picnic – the premier study of the custom of eating out in Australia – that the 'austerities' of the First World War were to snuff the flare and vitality of what he calls Restaurant Society. The lighting of a new flame was far away. It was not lit until the 1960s and 1970s.

Chinese Cuisine

The major alternative to the British diet and cooking traditions was Chinese. But there was little likelihood of that cuisine wooing British mouths. On the goldfields in the 1850s, when the Chinese were so numerous, rice was their main food. Potatoes and bread they rarely touched.

On the long road to the goldfields the incoming Chinese employed cooks to go ahead and prepare the meal for the large numbers who travelled together. Their diet day after day rarely altered. Rice gruel was their breakfast, along with pickles and salted cabbage. For the brief halt in the middle of the day they usually ate rice cake and drank tea. The evening meal was large but still dominated by rice, perhaps two bowls of hot rice, with pickles again and salted fish. Beans – dried rather than fresh – often were part of that evening dish. Hot water was also in readiness for them to wash themselves.

As fresh vegetables were scarce on the infant goldfields – it was more exciting to dig for gold than to dig the soil – the Chinese ate preserved vegetables. They ate little beef and they did not like mutton. Duck they loved but it was salt-preserved rather than fresh when it reached their pot. Even the fish they ate was rarely fresh, because the bands of Chinese fishermen working on the bay near Melbourne salted or sun-dried their catches of snapper, shrimps and other fish before sending them to the goldfields. Similarly, the vegetables sold in the Chinese general stores were mainly salted turnips, salted cabbages and dry peas. As the Chinese diet was weak in vitamins and protein, they were vulnerable to beri-beri and the Barcoo rot.

The needs of Chinese diggers can be glimpsed in the items held in a shop on the Buckland River goldfield in Victoria on 4 July 1857. We know what was on the shelves and floor of the shop because it was looted by rioters, as a result of which the Chinese owner applied to the government for compensation. His heaviest losses – maybe he exaggerated a little – were tins of opium, bags of rice, chests of tea, boxes of candles, pieces of preserved duck and boxes of Chinese tobacco. Another valuable entry on the list was 4 dozen 'water-tights'. Presumably they were tight-fitting boots that, stretching from the toes to the top of the thigh, were worn by those Chinese miners who stood all day in cold water while they sought shallow gold in the riverbed.

Chinese cafés flourished on the goldfields but most who ate in them were Chinese. In early Ballarat, John Alloo opened a large restaurant and welcomed Europeans, his signs being in English as well as Cantonese. 'SOUPS ALWAYS READY' he advertised in big letters. While waiting for your soup you could buy from John a ticket for a stage-coach journey to distant towns.

Visitors who knew the Chinese restaurants in San Francisco were not impressed with those in Australia. 'The best in the colonies is one near Castlemaine, but even this is small and poor', wrote Charles Dilke, who was travelling around the world before winning a seat in the House of Commons. To ask for shark's fin in Castlemaine was to receive a blank stare.

About 1900 small groups of city bohemians experimented with exotic foods. They provided an opportunity for several restaurants operating in the Chinatowns that flourished in Sydney and Melbourne. In the main rooms pigtailed waiters served the Chinese and the few Europeans – mostly larrikins – who handled the chopsticks. In the inner room were sometimes seen the bohemians, 'in faultless evening dress' and sampling Chinese dishes and sauces. As Chinatown was associated with opium dens, laundries, gambling parlours and narrow lanes, it did not attract the average citizen.

There was also a distinctive German tradition in food, with popular choices including pickled cucumbers, a white cheese flavoured with caraway seeds, 'German' sausages and black puddings. Germans also displayed a liking for wine and coffee. Outnumbering the Italians in 1900, their food tradition was the more influential. Adelaide was its home.

Stores that Sold Everything

The general store was a special institution. In many townships it was the one and only store. Today, in the suburbs it has given way to the supermarket, which is a general store and a half, or the small corner store and the twenty-four-hour shop, which are miniature general stores.

The old-time general store was indelibly linked with the

'township', a word which has also faded away. An Old English word, almost archaic in England in 1800, 'township' was resurrected here and applied to early Sydney and also to land set aside for a town of the future. David Collins, writing in 1802, noted that in one inland area the trees were cut down and the debris burned, 'a small township marked out, and a few huts built'. Eventually 'township', a word that sounded rather grand, became the normal name for a small town. In contrast a bigger town was simply called a town. By 1860, in general conversation, a place definitely merited the name of township if it had a general store. Already in Australia the tendency in civic and political affairs was to overstate.

Hundreds of townships consisted of nothing more than an inn and a general store, either side by side or facing each other across the wide street. If the township was a small stopping place on an up-country railway, the inn was likely to be called The Railway Hotel – the word hotel was in favour by the 1890s – and the shop was likely to carry the sign 'Railway Stores', the plural, not the singular. Henry Lawson, describing such a town in the New South Wales back country, observed that a third building was occasionally in the background. 'There is sometimes a small, oblong, weather-board building – unpainted, and generally leaning in one of the eight possible directions and perhaps with a twist in another – which, from its half-obliterated sign, seems to have started as a rival to the Railway Stores.' This building was empty. Wooden shutters covered its front windows. It was a sign of how perilous was the trade of shop-keeping.

Many of the early country stores stood next to the homestead of the big sheep stations and were owned by the station.
As floods – in the era before bridges – could cut off the station
from the merchant in the coastal cities, and as droughts along
the road could increase isolation, supplies had to be brought in
when the road was open and grass was growing for the bullocks
that hauled the drays. Each station, in early years, tended to
keep three or four months' supply of every important item.
Mrs Campbell Praed recalled such a store in Queensland. Along
one wooden wall the goods are piled up to the rafters, and even
into the dark spaces above: bags of flour, drums of tobacco, a
cavernous chest of tea, new pint pots and quart pots, a pair of
shears for the shearing, and odd bottles of Steven's Red Blister
and other prescribed potions and chemicals. Here are men's
clothing and blue blankets, big bins for the flour, and another
bin in which separate compartments hold the best white sugar,
the middling sugar and the cheap black ration sugar which was
apportioned in weekly lots to the workmen.

A storekeeper looked after this station store, but his customers were few, and rarely did cash change hands. Here the
employees bought tobacco or a new clay pipe, and the cost was
deducted from the wages due to them. In one sense this was the
genesis of the general store at a time when there were only
a dozen country towns and two dozen 'townships' in all the land.

Along the country roads in the 1840s were hovels and
humpies that served as general stores for the passing public.
Lieutenant Colonel Mundy, crossing the Blue Mountains, came
to a bark store in front of which, laid out on a sheet of bark, were

half-a-dozen shrivelled oranges, several bottles of ginger beer, a couple of locally made cabbage tree hats, and 'a tumbler full of bulls' eyes and lollipops'. What made the scene an eye-opener was the sign proudly painted in whitewash above the door, 'General Store and Provision Warehouse'.

Patrick Curtain was the owner of a general store at Ballarat during the Eureka Stockade in 1854. As luck would have it, his simple store of canvas and wood was close to the action. For a day or two he must have sold large quantities of goods because more and more miners came to the fortified stockade with its strong wooden fence. Alas, when the stockade was completed, his shop was inside it. If the government's troops attacked the fortress, his goods and wares would be destroyed.

On the eve of the fighting, the shop must have presented a fine display. There were boxes of sperm candles and boxes of English nails. Sacks, bins or big boxes held flour, crystallised sugar, salt, Epsom salts, tea and coffee, each of which had to be weighed before being sold to customers. Other goods probably were pre-packaged. Certainly Barrett's twist tobacco, the large tins of lollies, the 3 dozen castor oils and the 5 dozen pickles were all packaged, along with the cigars and preserved sardines and oysters. A clothing store and a food store combined, its shelves, cupboards and boxes held seventy-two regatta shirts, a dozen silk cravats, forty-eight blue serge shirts and thirty-six lamb's wool drawers, as well as twenty pilot-cloth monkey jackets and eighteen pairs of doeskin cloth trousers. A few items were stocked in the hope of catching the eye of the goldfields' few female customers – including bonnets and shawls.

When on 3 December 1854 the fighting began, the shop was accidentally or deliberately set on fire. Patrick Curtain applied to the government of Victoria for compensation. In filing the details – true or exaggerated – of his losses, he included one revealing item. Many of his customers had 'booked up' rather than paid what they owed. The account book claimed that a total sum of 315 pounds was owed to him. He said that, alas, he had lost the actual book and therefore could not provide proof of the sums owed to him. Eventually, most goods bought at general stores in the country were probably bought on credit. Stores that did not allow credit called themselves *cash* grocers or *cash* drapers on their signboards outside.

Storekeepers were not necessarily popular. Their goods were dear and often people fresh from a larger town noted the high prices and complained about them. Their prices, however, were higher largely because freight from the coast was high. Moreover many storekeepers, especially in bad times, were generous. Henry Lawson, who was walking at the back of Bourke in the early 1890s, placed on record one of these acts of generosity. As he was in his left-wing phase he did not readily praise commerce, but this praise was unstinted: 'We saw one of the storekeepers give a deadbeat swagman five shillings' worth of rations to take him on into Queensland. The storekeepers often do this, and put it down on the loss side of their books. I hope the recording angel listens, and puts it down on the right side of his book.'

Dances and Laments in the General Store

Francis Daw kept a general store in rural South Australia before he moved west in 1894 to the remote port of Esperance where he opened a store. A storekeeper moving long distances usually did not take sugar, shovels and other produce with him – he carried only skills, experience and maybe a set of weighing scales and other simple items. Six years later Daw sent his son Edgar further west to open a general store in the small mining town of Ravensthorpe. The high cost of transport meant that groceries and other supplies were dearer in the remote districts. Thus at the Daw's general store in Ravensthorpe a pound of dates, a bottle of tomato sauce and a case of kerosene were much dearer than in Perth. Of twenty-five selected items, only a packet of self-raising flour was cheaper than in Perth, and it was much cheaper. Without high prices, many general storekeepers would have become insolvent.

Like a general fighting a war, the storekeeper had to protect his flanks. If a new mine was opened an hour away, he sent out a man to take orders from residents with the promise that he would deliver the goods by horse and cart the next day. If the new mine prospered he opened a branch store there. So in 1907 Edgar Daw sent his brother Harold to nearby Kundip where he opened the new-built general store with a dance, as was the fashion. Fifty people attended and were still dancing at midnight. Within a few years the merriment had gone. Small farmers and miners usually earned small incomes and, in lean years, tended to run up debts.

413

In 1910 another branch store, built of corrugated iron, was opened at the small settlement of Desmond. On the window was painted the sign: BREAD SOLD HERE. The store sold not only bacon and butter but miners' boots, crockery, ink and paper, fancy goods and postage stamps, for it also served as the post office. It even sold steamship tickets for those who wished to return home. The prickly question was, would the departing customers meet their debts to the storekeeper before they used the ticket to return to the eastern states?

Records of the store at Kundip reveal that only three in every 100 customers paid cash. All the other bills were written up in a big book called a debt ledger. This kind of township was kept alive by the storekeeper and his willingness to give credit. When customers ran deeply into debt they called the shopkeeper to one side and humbly – or sometimes defiantly – asked for more credit. How could he lightly refuse credit to a family he had known for years, or who worshipped on Sunday in the same congregation, or whose wife was decent and hard-working though the husband was feckless?

In the end many customers left the district, their debts unpaid. In the Depression of the 1930s, Daw could count seventy-eight such people. Some had abandoned their farms – they had no money. A few actually handed over to him, in payment for years of unpaid groceries, the title deeds to their land; but who wanted to buy the land? It was like a valueless cheque. Fortunately for a rural storekeeper, a city merchant sometimes carried his debt.

At one of the Daws' stores, newly arrived miners regularly

'booked up' nearly all of their purchases. One day, collecting their back pay from the mine, some miners went to the nearest railway station and vanished, their debts unpaid. When the local butcher saw some of his customers about to leave the town he boarded the train just before it departed and called for payment. He was ignored or jeered at. In an outburst he said, 'How can I manage with no income?' To this, one of the passengers cheekily replied, 'The best thing you can do is to come with us.'

On the social ladder of the country town, the bank manager and his wife were seen as sitting near the top. On the economic ladder, however, the keeper of the general store was often more important. He knew what made the town tick. He knew which townsfolk were creditworthy. He knew which family was living beyond its means – well before that private inform-ation reached the bank manager. He was Mr MasterCard. Long before the era of plastic money he – and his family – provided much of the town with its own form of credit card.

Some retailers sold their goods only for cash. As they did not have to borrow money and pay interest in order to carry the unpaid bills of their customers, they could lower the price of their goods. Moran & Cato, cash grocers in Melbourne, opened store after store, and then expanded interstate. The first large chain of stores in the land, it operated more than a hundred branches early in the new century. As Moran & Cato bought in bulk, they could sell tea, coffee, sugar, butter and many other foods at bargain prices. Their ticklish task was the selecting of branch managers and shop assistants who were honest enough to ensure that all the cash, collected in the course of the day's business, ended up in the till.

A competent storekeeper presided over his general store like a judge presiding over his court. He stood slightly aloof, serving the customers' needs while standing behind the strong wooden counter – a counter was a barrier as well as a level surface for weighing and wrapping the goods. He conveyed an air of authority. He also needed a listening ear, though that ear was often provided most sensitively by his wife and daughters. Sometimes they looked after the general store while he was away, delivering goods that had been ordered. Together, husband and wife had to be busy. They also had to dawdle, to twiddle fingers for sixty seconds, so that local news could be passed on to them and to everyone standing in the shop. Storekeepers had to give every sign that they were listening intently. Then, when one second's pause in the conversation gave them the opportunity, they darted away to fulfil orders: to weigh a bag of potatoes, or to take with naked hand the biscuits from a large tin and weigh them. The storekeepers were the handlers, the weighers, the packagers. Much of what they did is now performed by machines in factories.

The old general store was a kind of apprenticeship. A few storekeepers who were successful moved ambitiously to the cities and began those big general stores that later were called an emporium – the forerunner of the supermarket. Thus the now-famous retail firm of Coles Myer began as separate halves in the country. The Coles half was a family of general storekeepers who moved around Victoria and Tasmania, while the Myer half was founded by a Russian immigrant who launched himself as a horsedrawn hawker in the late 1890s and then opened a large shop in Bendigo. In the hierarchy of society and commerce, a hawker stood on the bottom rung. Nonetheless Myer in his lifetime became almost a world figure in city retailing.

In New South Wales the big retailers tended to confine themselves to their home town. David Jones, a Welsh immigrant, started his store in Sydney before the gold rushes, and remained

The travelling hawker, with his covered wagon loaded with clothing and utensils of all kinds, supplied many of the areas where no general store was handy. Sidney Myer, one of the nation's greatest retailers, commenced as a hawker in the Bendigo district.

there. He was a Congregationalist – that was his network. The owner of an emporium or a chain of stores was likely to be a Protestant dissenter or maybe Jewish but rarely a Catholic.

Roll Out the Barrel

The goods that reached the shops in city and country came in a variety of containers and packages, the size of the containers being limited by the ability of men to carry or move them. A host of goods came in wooden barrels or casks. A barrel could easily be rolled along by a wharf labourer and drayman, thus saving the energy needed to carry it. Barrels were used not only for liquids but also a variety of other goods. Those who prised open a barrel might find salt, refined sugar, butter, tobacco, toys, twine, nails, sharpening stones, steel pieces, cement, paint, tar, resin or blasting powder. Today all hooped wooden cylinders are known as barrels, but in those days they were designated – according to their size – as tuns, butts, puncheons, hogsheads, barrels and half-barrels, casks and quarter-casks, kilderkins, firkins and kegs. Merchants knew by heart the weight of a firkin of Irish butter or a hogshead of Dutch gin.

In shops the barrels, once opened and emptied, served as convenient bins. In a general store in the 1860s much of the earthen or wooden floor was probably occupied by standing barrels and casks. Some barrels stood on the footpath where they could display those wares not likely to be pilfered by passers-by. Many barrels were used to collect rainwater which flowed from the roof of the shop.

A boy who was apprenticed as a barrel maker or cooper was learning a craft that was secure – the demand for wooden barrels seemed inexhaustible. Many of Australia's exports, including skins and hides, tallow and whale oil, went away in barrels. But barrels were relatively expensive. They occupied more space in a ship than did oblong boxes, and eventually were to be used less and less – especially after steam cranes and hoists were erected at cargo depots and wharves. 'Roll out the barrel' was an expression appropriate for a popular song only when the barrel was in decline – a century ago a barrel had so many purposes that it did not mainly signify rum or beer.

Sacks and bags were used to carry flour, potatoes, wheat and sometimes sugar from Mauritius and coffee from Ceylon. Fruit was shipped or carted in barrels and packing cases. Cheeses came in cases and boxes, as did drapery, linen, bonnets and hats, hosiery, earthenware and glassware, mats, tobacco pipes and a variety of other goods.

A general store, in handling goods, functioned more like today's fruit shop than supermarket. Nearly every purchase was ladled out and weighed or measured by the shop assistant in the presence of the customer. The flour was scooped from the bag or bin and poured into a bag. Butter was scooped from the tub or firkin and placed, after much fiddling with the brass ounce-weights, on the cumbersome weighing scales – until the customer finally said 'That's just right.' The bacon was cut into slices and weighed and wrapped, and the eggs were counted one by one. Most of these items went into the customer's basket, bag or box with the minimum of wrapping.

In the 1870s arrived the first machines for making paper bags. Such bags were used sparingly, being reserved for the more expensive purchases such as tea or coffee: brown or grey wrapping paper was cheaper. Second-hand newspaper, being even cheaper, was preferred for the wrapping of many items. Even after the Second World War many foods were wrapped with second-hand newspapers, including hot fish and chips.

For most liquids, customers saved money by bringing their own tins and billies: a billy for the honey, a tin for the kerosene. On hot evenings children would be sent to hotels with a jug or billy can in which they would carry home the beer. The idea of wrapping up such commodities as bread, soap or candles was dismissed as extravagant. Few goods were wrapped or packaged in the nineteenth century, and so any wrapping paper or cardboard or twine that came home from the grocer was carefully hoarded because it was valuable.

During the early gold rushes, tins and bottles were used only for expensive goods. English beer and ale, many spirits and cordials, expensive jams, wine and medicines could be bought in jars and bottles. Glass, however, was still expensive and fragile. A few tins of food sat in grocery shops in the mid-1860s – imported oysters, salmon, lobster, sardines, herrings, green peas – but tin and glass, paper and cardboard were used less than wood as containers.

The practice of hoarding old bottles and containers and wrappers – so essential at one time – was to continue long after the need was passing. So by 1960 the pantries and kitchen cupboards of houses had accumulated thousands of kilometres of scavenged string and twine, enough pieces of brown paper to roof a city, and countless bottles and jars. They reflected the old motto, 'waste not, want not'.

The packaging revolution still lay ahead. It belonged to the era of self-service shops, of cheap multi-coloured wrapping material, and machines that could swiftly and accurately apportion, weigh, wrap and label most of the grocer's wares. The advertising and packaging revolutions would be partners.

14

ON PRICING A WAY OF LIFE

It is impossible to discuss this earlier Australia without considering the present opinion, widely held, that life since 1945 has changed so remarkably that no other period can be compared to it. Beyond doubt the basic way of life has been transformed since the end of the Second World War. It can be seen in the rise of wine making, in the proliferation of restaurants serving dishes from maybe half the nations of the world, in the widening range of fresh foods and their availability 'out of season', in the fast-food palaces, and in the more adventurous menus and the new cooking and chilling devices in so many of the households. It can be seen in new means of travel, in the new medicine, in television and email and satellites, in the new flowering of the performing and visual arts, and in the belated appreciation of Aboriginal painting and dance. Most Australians welcome these changes, even if they personally do not take part in all of them.

There is a tendency among those who celebrate this new

Australia to depict the way of life before the Second World War, and even before 1960, as stolid, unimaginative, unchanging and lacking in diversity. But Australia in the last 200 years had been changing in every decade. It is not belittling these latter-day changes to set alongside them, for comparison, the changes that took place in our period extending from the first gold rushes to the First World War.

While a unique transforming of living and leisure habits has recently taken place, another unique change had taken place in the years spanned by this book. A land not fully emerged from the convict era attained – in the span of one lifetime – an enviable way of life. Candlelight gave way to kerosene and, in the cities, to electricity. The tinderbox gave way to the box of matches and the cigarette lighter. The bullock dray was almost superseded by the steam train, and the sailing ship by the steamship, while the car appeared on the streets and the bicycle was everywhere. A postman reached nearly every corner of the country and the telegram reached every town, while the telephone transformed talk in the cities, though it did not yet link the nation. In this quickening of communications, the simple bell, the flag, and the cry of coo-ee were no longer vital. Likewise a land where in 1850 most people did not own a watch was almost enchained half a century later by the ticking of the clock. New ways of weighing and packaging were arriving. A currency ruled by gold and silver was turning to paper, and private currency had been replaced by Commonwealth currency. Not everyone gained by these changes; some even lost.

Eating and drinking habits were bound to alter in an era of such wide-spanning change. Cooking in a few blackened utensils on an open fire, often in the open air, gave way to kitchens with iron stoves and eventually to gas cookers. This alone improved the variety of meals prepared in most households. Whereas in 1850 no sure way existed of cooling food and drink in summer, soon the Boston ice, artificial ice and later the Coolgardie safe and the simple ice chest offered hope, especially to the growing numbers who were moving to regions where the climate was hotter. In cities and townships the access to fresh fruit and vegetables, fresh fish and oysters, was improved by fast transport. Butter and eggs became cheaper, the variety of wheat, breads and biscuits increased, and the eating of lollies became a national pastime. Beer surpassed brandy, gin and rum as the popular alcohol, but more and more people turned away from alcohol – but not tobacco – as the nineteenth century faded away.

Perhaps the far-reaching change affected the most basic of items, water. Once bucketed from a hole in a creek, or delivered by horse and cart to the house at a high price, this precarious supply of cloudy water largely gave way, in the cities and towns, to the turning of a tap and the outpouring of clear water in the kitchen and bathroom. Clothes, hands and perhaps even faces were decidely cleaner in 1900 than fifty years previously.

Australia was, for much of this period, a land of extending horizons. Biddy Burke, who emigrated in 1880 to Brisbane from a thatched farmhouse in Galway as a 21-year-old domestic servant, set out a fairly typical view of the new land in her letters home. Though on hot days the sweat clung to her face, though she marvelled that thunderstorms exploded with less than a minute's warning, and though some of those in her sight were struck down by strange fevers, this was a land of plenty and leisure by the standards of her Ireland. While she could not write a letter with ease, she made her opinion perfectly clear: 'This is the finest Country in the wourld for young people that takes care of themselves.'

What Biddy wrote privately with pen and ink, other commentators wrote in books and newspapers for a wider audience. Marcus Clarke, the English-born novelist, predicted a distinctive future for these people whom he described as hospitable, hardworking and pleasure loving: 'Sail up Sydney harbour, ride over a Queensland plain, watch the gathering of an Adelaide harvest, or mingle with the orderly crowd which throngs to a Melbourne Cup race, and deny, if you can, that there is here the making of a great nation.' Edward Jenks, who lectured for three years in Australia before becoming professor of law in Liverpool, argued in 1895 that Australia displayed material progress on an astonishing scale. It was also blessed by the fact that it was so remote from the British Isles that the 'penniless loafer' was not often an immigrant. It was, he vowed, a land so full of opportunity that 'no one with health and honesty' need be hungry or unemployed. John H. M. Abbott, after enlisting as an Australian horseman in the Boer War, spent time in England where he wrote observant books about his experiences, constantly contrasting the old land with the new. He was almost overwhelmed by the sight of London's 'awful and debasing poverty': the army of the poor, their stooped gait, their sallow faces, and their listlessness. 'A hungry crowd – a really hungry and cold multitude – is strange to an Australian', he wrote.

The standard of living in Australia was among the highest – perhaps the highest – in the world by the 1880s. Various visitors, with an extensive knowledge of how people lived in western Europe and North America, were deeply impressed with the way of life of most Australians: the food in their homes, the style of their houses, the quality of the clothes worn, the conveyances travelled on, the time given to leisure, and the favourable wages and prices. Flora Shaw, a bright young London journalist who in the 1890s was head of what was called the 'colonial department' of *The Times*, issued her own emphatic verdict: 'Never, perhaps, has there been a country in which the condition of the labouring man is more favourable than in Australia.' Twenty years later her assessment was no longer true.

Admittedly, it is easier to measure the material things. It is easier to observe full or empty stomachs, easier to count houses and railway lines, easier to estimate the meat cooked and the tobacco smoked, than to weigh anxiety and to count content-ment in the life of individuals, let alone in several million people. Most Australians, after the slump of the 1890s and the drought which prolonged the anxiety, still had an abundance of the good and useful things of life: food, drink, tobacco, medicine, shelter, clothes, transport, space, light and heat. But those people who sometimes feared for the future were multiplying. In the cities their primary fear was to be unemployed, and on the myriad

427

small farms the fear was to be driven, insolvent, from the land. There slowly arose, too, the fear of a serious war. That war began in 1914.

For most Australians an era of plenty and contentment had come to an end.

The high standard of living of the typical Australian in the early twentieth century owed much to new machines and techniques. This harvest scene near Geelong seems antiquated to us, but in the eyes of European migrants the strong horses and the new reaping machine would have been impressive.

SELECTED SOURCES

I began in the 1970s to collect much of the material that appears in this book. I was provoked by the realisation that while I spent so much time writing and teaching Australian history, I was not well informed about the vital question: how did Australians live from day to day, and how did their way of living change over the decades? My interest in the everyday was aroused partly because of the remarkable increase in the number of folk and regional museums. The people who set up these museums sometimes phoned or wrote for elementary information about candlesticks, tobacco tins, needles and soft drink bottles. Often I could not provide this. At the same time, more movies and documentaries were being made about Australian history, and often they displayed remarkable errors in the little things. I could not blame the producers for the errors. After all, most of us who worked full-time as historians did not write about shoelaces, billy tea and shipboard food. Sure guidance was not readily forthcoming for a film-maker who had to reconstruct a bush kitchen, a hotel or a chapel in 1870 and wished to be historically accurate.

In a spasmodic way I began to collect the evidence in this book long before I decided to write the book. When doing research for other books my eyes would light on something curious about everyday life. Perhaps it was an advertisement for tobacco in the newspaper that I was skimming, or perhaps it was a report of a fire which destroyed a shop and all its listed contents. Sometimes I noted these snippets on a slip of paper; sometimes I stored them in my mind. Occasionally, reading a book written by a traveller, I pencilled a mark on the margin or a short note at the back of the book. Reading explorers' printed journals, I might see a revealing snippet about how they travelled in the moonlight or how they used the coo-ee. Sometimes, after my interest was aroused in a topic, I would chance to meet an old person who was full of knowledge: a country butcher who made his own sausages in 1920 and remembered the strange colourings and preservatives he used, or someone who had kept house in the bush in the 1890s.

Many of the oddments of daily life amazed me. When I was doing research for a book, *The Tyranny of Distance*, I noticed in the shipping notes of the Melbourne *Argus* for 15 October 1858 that on the previous day a sailing ship had arrived from Boston with a cargo of 541 tons of fresh ice as well as lumber and miscellaneous items such as painkillers. I briefly mentioned the ice in that book but I knew nothing of how it had been gathered on shore, how it had been stowed in the ship, and how – in the era before the invention of refrigeration – it managed to cross the tropics, unmelted. Bit by bit that knowledge has come to me, and is set out in Chapter 2. It may be that today I know as much as anybody about that ice trade to Australia. But on that topic, like dozens of other topics covered in this book, a single-minded researcher with plenty of time and determination could eventually discover far more than I know. I hope that this book will temporarily fill various gaps in social history.

I first spoke publicly on everyday life, especially what people ate and drank, at Swan Hill in the mid-1970s when I gave a public lecture in honour of Professor Norman Harper. Thereafter, as I gained more knowledge, I gave after-dinner speeches on such topics as keeping the time, lights and darkness, the coo-ee, or how speeches were made before the era of the outdoor microphone. By publishing none of the speeches I could use them again – a bonus to anybody who speaks in public. If a question-time followed a speech, members of the audience would sometimes put me right or supply fascinating details from their own experience. As I learned more about the common patterns of everyday life I could look at oil paintings and read fiction of the period with new eyes. I came to realise, for example, what an accurate mirror of the trivial things of life Henry Lawson's short stories were.

The following notes are far from comprehensive. For example, on the question – did the typical Australian family eat much fruit in, say, 1880? – I mentally noted many fragments of relevant evidence from newspapers or books or novels, and almost unconsciously came towards a conclusion. When quoting concrete episodes – whether of somebody lighting a candle or eating fruit – I have usually tried to select what seems to have been typical rather than what was exotic. This has meant abandoning some colourful, or pithily worded, reminiscences of events.

In writing the book I received help on a range of historical detail from Peter Yule and John Day of Melbourne. In specific themes I was guided by Tim Sullivan and Jan Croggon of Ballarat's Sovereign Hill, Frank Costa of Geelong, Jim McDonald of Cloncurry, Bill Middleton of Barwon Heads, Tom Evans of Creswick, Mrs E. Madden of Launceston, Professor Ross Fitzgerald and Richard Hagen of Brisbane, Frank Gardiner, S. E. K. Hulme and Ross A. Williams of Melbourne, and my wife Ann and daughter Anna Blainey. I gratefully acknowledge the help received long ago on specific topics from four people who are now dead: K. M. Dallas of Hobart, Stephen Murray-Smith of Melbourne, George Redman of Smeaton, and my own mother. I also express my thanks to my editors, Sandy Webster and Saskia Adams, for their skill and valuable suggestions.

Illustrations

Nearly all illustrations were selected from *Australasia Illustrated* edited by Andrew Garran (Sydney: Picturesque Atlas Publishing Company, 1892). Of other illustrations, those on pages 221 and 291 were selected from *Mrs Beeton's Every Day Cookery and House-keeping Book* by Isabella Mary Beeton (London: Ward, Lock & Co. Ltd, an undated reprint of a nineteenth-century edition). The illustrations on pages 317, 324, 328, 365 and 384 were selected from *Symbols of Australia* by Mimmo Cozzolino (Ringwood: Penguin Books, 1980) and reproduced by kind permission of the author. My thanks are extended to Karen Trump for her skill in solving design problems.

Museums and Galleries

I gained much from inspecting objects in museums and galleries, including the Queen Victoria Museum in Launceston, the Australian War Memorial in Canberra, the railway museum at Port Adelaide, the new national museums in Canberra and Melbourne, the Ballarat Fine Art Gallery, various local museums, including those in Kalgoorlie, Swan Hill and Jindera, and the old blacksmith's shop at Bacchus Marsh.

I thank, too, the Noel Butlin Archives at the Australian National University, the University of Melbourne Archives, and the Sovereign Hill Museums Association, which holds the manuscript papers of Thomas Lang, a Scot whose plant nursery was operating at Ballarat as early as 1856.

Printed Sources

These sources are divided into four sections:

1. Newspapers and Gazettes
2. Catalogues of Trade Fairs
3. Primary and Eyewitness Sources
4. Secondary Sources

The following is not an exhaustive list. Many minor sources I have not included. Well-known novels and poems and some of the other sources that are clearly mentioned in the narrative are not specifically listed below. This selected list does not include most of the voluminous colonial and Commonwealth yearbooks and statistical registers that were consulted from time to time.

1. Newspapers and Gazettes

I acknowledge my debt to many newspapers, all of which were published in some or many years of the period 1840–1918.

New South Wales: *Sydney Morning Herald, Sydney Mail, Bulletin, Daily Telegraph, Silver Age, Town & Country Journal, Wilcannia Times, Barrier Miner, Government Gazette, Newcastle Morning Herald, Mutual Provident Messenger, Medical Gazette, Freeman's Journal, Bathurst Free Press, Border Post* (Albury), *Richmond River Express, Pastoral Times* (Deniliquin).

Queensland: *Courier, North Queensland Register, Queenslander, Government Gazette, Queensland Government Mining Journal.*

South Australia: *South Australian Advertiser, South Australian Register, South Australian Chronicle, Critic, Garden & Field, Burra News.*

Tasmania: *Zeehan & Dundas Herald, Mercury, Examiner, Daily Telegraph* (Launceston), *Advocate, Tasmanian, Government Gazette.*

Victoria: *Argus, Australasian, Age, Herald, Weekly Times, Port Phillip Gazette, Australian Pictorial Weekly, Leader, Ballarat Courier, Geelong Advertiser, Ararat Advertiser, Government Gazette,*

Australasian Insurance & Banking Record, Australian Cyclist. Especially to be noted are *Police News* and *Australasian Sketcher: with Pen and Pencil*. A debt is owed to Michael Cannon for reprinting and indexing several volumes of the latter two journals.

Western Australia: *West Australian, Daily News, Government Gazette, Coolgardie Miner, Kalgoorlie Miner, West Argus* (Kalgoorlie).

Often the value of the files of these newspapers is to demolish subtly – in their advertisements, lists of prices, accounts of lawsuits and shipping notices – erroneous ideas about the past, whether major ideas or trivia. Sometimes it is the silence that tells us what really happened.

2. *Catalogues of Trade Fairs*
The following large catalogues are a mirror of everyday products and how they changed:

Centennial International Exhibition Melbourne 1888–9: The Official Catalogue, Melbourne, 1888.

The Industrial Progress of New South Wales: Report of the Intercolonial Exhibition of 1870, At Sydney, Sydney, 1871.

Intercolonial Exhibition of Australasia, Melbourne, 1866–67: Official Record, Melbourne 1867. For Italian sausages, see p. 15.

Melbourne International Exhibition, 1880–1881: Official Record, Melbourne 1882.

3. *Primary and Eyewitness Sources*

Abbott, J. H. M., *An Outlander in England: Being Some Impressions of an Australian Abroad*, London, 1905. For the intense poverty in England, see pp. 118, 135–7.

Ackermann, Jessie, *Australia, From a Woman's Point of View*, London, 1913.

Adams, David, ed., *The Letters of Rachel Henning*, Penguin edition, 1969. Her letters cover three decades, 1853–82.

Alexander, Colonel Sir James, ed., *The Albatross: Record of Voyage of the "Great Britain" Steamship from Victoria to England in 1862*, Stirling, 1863.

Anderson, Hugh, *Eureka: Victorian Parliamentary Papers and Proceedings 1854–1867*, Melbourne, 1969. For shop losses at Eureka, see 'Claims for Compensation'.

Archer, W. H. and Smyth, R., Brough and others, *Intercolonial Exhibition Essays, 1866–67*, Melbourne, c. 1868. This large collection of essays includes Professor McCoy's opinion of the Murray Cod.

Aspinall, Clara, *Three Years in Melbourne*, London, 1862. For her description of a Melbourne house and kitchen, see pp. 101–5.

Aurousseau, M., *The Letters of FW Ludwig Leichhardt*, Cambridge, 1968. For Australians and tea-drinking in the 1840s, see vol. 2, pp. 549, 600.

Austin, K. A., *The Lights of Cobb & Co.: The Story of the Frontier Coaches, 1854–1924*, Adelaide, 1967. For the huge 'Leviathan' coach used in 1862, see pp. 112–13.

Australasian Dairyman and Farmers' Friend, Sydney, 1897.

SELECTED SOURCES

Australasian Farmer: A Practical Handbook for the Farm and Station, Melbourne, c. 1885. Written by agricultural journalists, its chapters embrace such topics as fruit, poultry, dairying and gardening.

Australasian Intercolonial Conferences and Affairs, 1852–1885, 2 volumes of selected British and colonial parliamentary papers, initially bound and indexed by J. A. Gurner. In private possession.

Australian Etiquette, Or the Rules and Usages of the Best Society . . ., Melbourne, 1885.

Australian Handbook. Published by Gordon & Gotch, this large annual directory, from 1870 onwards, is a valuable guide to the progress of the main towns in Australia, and to notable events, telegraphic rates, shipping timetables, mail, customs duties and many other matters. Its long sections of advertisements, exceeding 200 pages by 1890, are a guide to consumers' changing tastes.

Aveling, Marian, ed., *Westralian Voices: Documents in Western Australian Social History*, Perth, 1979.

Bannow, Waldemar, *The Colony of Victoria: Socially and Materially*, Melbourne, 1896.

Barry, Captain W. J., *Up and Down; Or, Fifty Years' Colonial Experiences*, London 1979. For the hot dogs at Ballarat, see pp. 163–4.

Barton, Robert D., *Reminiscences of an Australian Pioneer*, Sydney, 1917. For the coming of wax matches, see pp. 38–9.

Bean, C. E. W., *On the Wool Track*, Sydney reprint, 1945.

Bird, S. Dougan, *On Australasian Climates and their Influence in the Prevention and Arrest of Pulmonary Consumption*, London, 1863. His book has strong words on the Australian meat diet.

Boldrewood, Rolf, *Robbery Under Arms*, London edition, 1889. For the brilliant gas lights and dense street traffic of Adelaide, see p. 84. For the coach lamps, see p. 229.

—— (anon), *SW Silver & Co's Australian Grazier's Guide*, London, 1881, vol. 2. See chapter 30 for unhygienic milking practices.

Bonwick, James, *The Tasmanian Lily*, London, 1873. An attempt, in the author's words, to portray 'simply, but fairly, the condition of Colonial life'.

Border Post (Albury) Almanac for 1878, Albury and Wodonga, 1979 reprint. For ways of preserving apples and lemons in barrels, see p. 81.

Boyce, William D., *Australia and New Zealand, Illustrated*, Chicago, 1922. For the cry for newspapers, see p. 124.

Bradshaw, George, *Profitable Poulty Breeding for the Local and English Markets*, Sydney, 1899. For the breeding of colonial game, see pp. 18–19.

Britain: *Parliamentary Papers*, 'Correspondence Relating to Emigration to the Australian Colonies', House of Commons, 1857. It is a valuable source on the migrant ships and conditions abroad.

Buckley, Vincent, *Cutting Green Hay*, Ringwood, 1983.

Buley, E. C., *Australian Life in Town and Country*, London, 1905. For the making of billy tea, see p. 56.

Calwell, A. A., *Be Just and Fear Not*, Hawthorn, 1972.

Cambridge, Ada, *Thirty Years in Australia*, London, 1903.

Cannon, Michael, ed., *The Vagabond Papers* (by John S. James), Melbourne, 1969. Among these newspaper essays of the late 1870s is one on the sixpenny restaurants.

Clark, C. M. H., ed., *Select Documents in Australian History 1851–1900*, Sydney, 1955.

—— ed., *Sources of Australian History*, London, 1957.

Clowes, Evelyn M., *On the Wallaby Through Victoria*, London, 1911.

Cornish, Henry, *Under the Southern Cross*, Madras, 1880, 2nd edition.

Deakin, Alfred, *The Federal Story: The Inner History of the Federal Cause*, Melbourne, 1944. For the oratorical skills of the leading politicians of c. 1900, see especially chapter 4.

Dilke, Charles, *Greater Britain: A Record of Travel in English-Speaking Countries*, London, 1868. For the poor Chinese restaurant in Castlemaine, see p. 304.

Dowling, J. P., *Practical Dairying for Australia*, Sydney, 1893.

Duncan, Sinclair T., *Journal of a Voyage to Australia by the Cape of Good Hope, Six Months in Melbourne . . .*, Edinburgh, 1869.

Dunderdale, George, *The Book of the Bush*, London c. 1870, Penguin edition, 1973.

Dyson, Edward, *Rhymes from the Mines and Other Lines*, Sydney 1898. For his poem on the singing camp oven, see p. 51.

Enquire Within Upon Everything, London, 1861. A popular book of kitchen hints and how to do everyday tasks, it reportedly achieved sales of 167 000 in the space of five years.

Evans, William, ed., *Diary of a Welsh Swagman 1869–1894*, Melbourne, 1975. The so-called swagman was named Joseph Jenkins, and his beat was mainly the Victorian farmlands between Ballarat and Maldon. He worked too hard, often for long periods in the one place, to merit the designation of swagman.

Facey, A. B., *A Fortunate Life*, Fremantle, 1981.

Fairfax, William, ed., *Handbook to Australasia*, Melbourne, 1859. For the exact dating of the seasons in Tasmania, see p. 129.

Fenton, James, *Bush Life in Tasmania Fifty Years Ago*, London, 1891. This is a valuable source on early potato growing.

Fitzpatrick, Kathleen, *Australian Explorers: A Selection from their Writings*, London, 1958. For Peter Warburton and the camel bells, see p. 430.

Forrest, John, *Explorations in Australia*, London, 1875. For the use of the coo-ee, see pp. 38, 108.

Franklyn, H. Mortimer, *A Glance at Australia in 1880: Or Food from the South*, Melbourne, 1881.

Freeman, John, *Lights and Shadows of Melbourne Life*, London, 1888.

Froude, James A., *Oceana: Or England and her Colonies*, London, 1886.

Fullerton, Mary E., *Bark House Days*, Melbourne, 1921. For the making of jam, see p. 55. For the precious eggs and bacon cooked for the night visitor, see chapter 9.

Giles, Ernest, *Australia Twice Traversed*, London, 1889. For the camel driver's silver watches, see vol. 2, p. 253.

Gilmore, Mary, *Old Days: Old Ways – A Book of Recollections*, Sydney, 1934. For the handbells, see p. 68. For her charming words on grandfather and the almanac, see pp. 109–12. For a bedtime glimpse of the moon, see p. 96.

Gordon, Harry, *An Eyewitness's History of Australia*, Adelaide, 1976. For the Turkish ice-cream vendor at Broken Hill, see p. 192. For Robert Burke addressing the crowd on his departure from Melbourne in 1860, see p. 66.

Greville, Edward, ed., *The Official Directory and Year-Book of Australia*, Melbourne. Published annually from 1882 under differing titles, this non-official yearbook is a goldmine of fascinating trivia, including medical and travel hints. For weights such as firkin and hogshead, see p. 51 in the 1884 edition. For hints to train travellers, see p. 60. For differences in clock-time in Australian towns, see pp. 67–72.

Greville's Official Post Office Directory and Gazetteer of New South Wales, 1875 to 1877, Sydney. For horse stables in hotels at Tamworth and Cobar, see the advertisements opposite pp. 162, 688.

Griffin, G. W., *New South Wales: Her Commerce and Resources*, Sydney, 1888. For the importing of American cigarettes, see p. 199.

Harrison, H. C. E., *The Story of an Athlete: A Picture of the Past*, Melbourne, 1923. For his advice that athletes should abstain from cigarettes, see p. 135.

Haygarth, Henry W., *Recollections of Bush Life in Australia*, London, 1848.

Herman, Morton, ed., *Annabella Boswell's Journal*, Sydney, 1965.

Heyne, E. B., *The Amateur Gardener . . . Of The Fruit, Flower, and Vegetable Garden*, Adelaide, 1881.

Heywood, B. A., *A Vacation Tour at the Antipodes . . . in 1861–1862*, London, 1863. On the difficulties of exchanging money, see p. 58.

Hickey, Simon, *Travelled Roads*, Mebourne, 1951. For the selector's daughter and her prolonged toothache, see p. 7.

Howitt, William, *Land, Labour, and Gold; Or, Two Years in Victoria with Visits to Sydney and Van Diemen's Land*, London, 1855.

Hume, Bertram, ed., *A Victorian Engagement: Letters and Journals of Walter Hume and Anna Kate Fowler during the 1860s*, St Lucia, 1975. Anna Fowler sailed from the Thames, bound for Queensland, in 1866.

Hutchinson, Frank, ed., *New South Wales: 'The Mother Colony of the Australians'*, Sydney, 1896.

James, G. F., *A Homestead History: Being the Reminiscences and Letters of Alfred Joyce . . . 1843 to 1864*, Melbourne, 1942.

Jenkins, Joseph, *Diary of a Welsh Swagman, 1869–1894*, see Evans.

Jenks, Edward, *The History of the Australasian Colonies*, Cambridge, 1895. For his assessment of Australia's high prosperity, see pp. 314, 316.

Johnston, James F. W., *The Chemistry of Common Life*, Edinburgh, 1855. On the value of charcoal as a deodorant, see vol. 2, p. 308.

Kendell, W. Tyson, 'Notes on the Early History of the Veterinary Profession in Victoria', *Report of the Fourteenth Meeting of the Australasian Association for the Advancement of Science*, Sydney, 1914. For his claim that one quarter of cattle killed in some Melbourne abattoirs had tuberculosis, see p. 706.

Kennedy, David Jr, *Kennedy's Colonial Travel: A Narrative of a Four Years' Tour . . .*, Edinburgh, 1876. A Scottish actor, he was observant of everyday life, especially eating and accommodation.

Knight's Cyclopaedia of the Industry of All Nations, London, 1851. For the annual tally of oysters sold in London, see p. 1294.

Knox, Bruce, ed., *The Queensland Years of Robert Herbert, Premier: Letters and Papers*, St Lucia, 1977.

Lawson, Henry, *Collected Verse*, 3 volumes, and *Collected Prose*, 3 volumes, edited by Colin Roderick and published by Angus & Robertson, Sydney, 1967–72. For his description of the outback New South Wales township and its general store, see his short story, 'In A Dry Season'.

Leichhardt, Ludwig, *Journal of an Overland Expedition in Australia . . . During the Years 1844–45*, London, 1847. For his view of the 'brightest stars', see pp. 280–1.

Lewis, R. B., unpublished, privately held memoirs of an Edwardian childhood in north-eastern Tasmania. These provided some of the material used in the paragraph on jam making.

Lincolnshire Observer: A Weekly Newspaper Published On Board 'The Lincolnshire' During the Passage from London to Melbourne, 1866. Reprinted Melbourne, 1975.

Litchfield, J. S., *Far-North Memories*, Sydney, 1930.

Loftie, W. J., *Orient-Pacific Line Guide: Chapters for Travellers by Sea and by Land*, London, 6th edition, c. 1902.

Lyons, Dame Enid, *So We Take Comfort*, London, 1965. For her first taste of ice cream, see p. 32.

McCulloch, J. B., *A Dictionary, Practical, Theoretical, and Historical, of Commerce and Commercial Navigation . . .*, London, 1854 edition.

Macdonald, Donald, *Gum Boughs and Wattle Bloom Gathered on Australian Hills and Plains*, London, 1887.

—— *The Bush Boy's Book*, Melbourne. c. 1911.

Mackay, Angus, *The Australian Agriculturist and Colonists' Guide*, 2nd edition, Sydney, 1890.

Manwaring, William H., 'Re Daniel Morgan Bushranger', *La Trobe Library Journal*, April 1970.

Martineau, Rev. John, *Letters from Australia*, London, 1869. For his analysis of the too-warm Australian climate, see p. 69.

Meredith, Mrs Charles (Louise), *Notes and Sketches of New South Wales, During a Residence in that Colony from 1839 to 1844*, London, 1861. For her account of the loss of the North Star and Great Bear, see p. 19.

Meyrick, F. J., *Life in the Bush (1840–1847): A Memoir of Henry Howard Meyrick*, London, 1939.

Milner, Rev. John and Brierly, Oswald W., *The Cruise of HMS Galatea*, London, 1869.

Mundy, Godfrey Charles, *Our Antipodes; Or, Residence, and Rambles, in the Australasian Colonies*, 3 volumes, London, 1852. For his descripton of goats wandering Sydney streets, see vol. 1, p. 49.

Muskett, Philip E., *The Art of Living in Australia (Together with Three Hundred Australian Cookery Recipes . . .)*, London,

1893. For the dangers of tea-drinking, see pp. 67–8. For the merits of Sydney's fish hawkers, see p. 142.

Neilson, John S., *The Autobiography of John Shaw Neilson*, Canberra, 1978. For his travels to a city, see p. 79.

New South Wales: *Royal Commission on 'The Fisheries of this Colony'*, 1880.

Ogilby, J. Douglas, *Edible Fishes and Crustaceans of New South Wales*, Sydney, 1893, especially for snapper, crayfish and prawns.

Oliver, Alexander, *A Collection of the Statutes of Practical Utility . . . in Force in New South Wales*, Sydney, 1879, 3 volumes. For the 1835 Bread Act, see vol. 1, pp. 122–7. For digging up Maitland streets, see vol. 2, p. 2056.

Parker, Genseric, *Forest to Farming*, Box Hill, 1996. For the locally baked bread at Gembrook, see p. 25.

Portus, G. V., *Happy Highways*, Melbourne, 1953.

Pownall, Eve, *Mary of Maranoa: Tales of Australian Pioneer Women*, Melbourne, 1964 edition. For the general store at the pastoral station, see p. 177.

Preshaw, G. O., *Banking under Difficulties; or Life on the Gold-fields*, Melbourne, 1888. Preshaw was a bank clerk at the Kiama gold rush, where he used to visit the French restaurant.

Queen of the Colonies; Or Queensland as I Knew It, by 'An Eight Years' Resident', London, 1876.

Randell, J. O., ed., *Adventures of a Pioneer: William Lockhart Morton*, Carlton, 1978. The core of the book is the rural reminiscences published by Morton in 1884–86.

Reid, Sir George, *My Reminiscences*, London, 1917.

Richardson, Henry Handel, *Myself When Young*, Melbourne, 1948. For her astonishment at seeing a woman smoking, see p. 84.

Sands & McDougall's Melbourne and Suburban Directory for 1868, Melbourne. For the system of firebells, see p. 703.

Scott, Ernest, ed., *Lord Robert Cecil's Gold Fields Diary*, Melbourne, 1935.

Shumack, Samuel, *An Autobiography or Tales and Legends of Canberra Pioneers*, Canberra, 1967.

Simmonds, H. W., *The Grocer's Handbook*, London, 1908.

Skemp, John Rowland, *Memories of Myrtle Bank: The Bush-farming Experiences of Rowland and Samuel Skemp in North-eastern Tasmania 1883–1948*, Melbourne, 1952. For the native Christmas tree in the local hall, see p. 159.

Smiles, Samuel, ed., *A Boy's Voyage Round the World; Including a Residence in Victoria, and a Journey by Rail Across North America*, London, 1877 edition.

Sorenson, Edward S., *Life in the Australian Backblocks*, London, 1911. For the mob of cattle smelling water and then stampeding, see p. 163.

Southon Board of Enquiry: *Victorian Parliamentary Papers*, no. 55, 1882. For the confectioner's shop and the smallpox outbreak, see evidence by Joseph Nimbs.

Spence, Helen Thomson, ed., *Catherine Helen Spence*, St Lucia, 1987. This collection includes the novel *Clara Morison* and its early reference to the 'lolly'.

Spence, W. G., *Australia's Awakening: Thirty Years in the Life of an Australian Agitator*, Sydney, 1909. For his description of cooking in the shearers' hut, see p. 65. A matching description is in Henry Lawson's short story, 'A Rough Shed'.

Stanley, Raymond, ed., *Tourist to the Antipodes: William Archer's Australian Journey, 1876–77*, St Lucia, 1977.

Surveyor: The Journal of the Institution of Surveyors, NSW, vol. 5, Sydney, 1892. For discussion of Australian time zones, see p. 338 ff.

Sutherland, George, *The Australasian Live Stock Manual and Breeder's Record*, Melbourne, 1896. For the scalding of pigs and curing of bacon, see pp. 361–2.

Tangye, Richard, *Notes on my Fourth Voyage to the Australian Colonies*, Birmingham, 1886.

Tasmania: *Royal Commission into the Fisheries*, 1882.

Terry, Michael, *Untold Miles: Three Gold-Hunting Expeditions Amongst the Picturesque Borderland Ranges of Central Australia*, London, 1931. For the effect of native greens on the sickness called Barcoo rot, see p. 28.

Trollope, Anthony, *Australia and New Zealand*, London, 1873. A valuable annotated edition, edited by P. D. Edwards and R. B. Joyce, and entitled *Australia*, was published in Brisbane in 1967.

Tupman, W. F., *Grocery*. One of Pitman's 'Traders' Handbooks', London, c. 1911.

Twain, Mark (Samuel L. Clemens), *Mark Twain in Australia and New Zealand*, Ringwood, 1973. For his comment on railways' coffee, see p. 155.

Twopeny, R. E. N., *Town Life in Australia*, London, 1883. For the Sabbath in Adelaide, see pp. 123–4.

Victoria: *Annual Report of Post Office and Telegraph Department*, especially 1860s and 1870s.

Victoria: *Burke and Wills Commission*, 1861–62. For references to travel in the moonlight, see pp. 36–7, 94–8.

—— *Parliamentary Debates*, 1894–5, vol. 76, Legislative Council, 16 January 1895. See pp. 1605 ff, for doubts about the wisdom of setting an eastern standard time.

—— *Royal Commission on the Aborigines*, 1877. For the females fondness for tobacco, see p. 48.

—— *Royal Commission on 'The Operation of the Factories and Shops Law of Victoria*, 1902–03. For the pork butchers and delicatessens, see pp. 111–117.

Vivienne, May, *Travels in Western Australia*, London, 1902.

Ward, Russel, ed., *The New Australia* by Edmond Marin La Meslee. First published in France in 1883, this edition was published in London, 1973.

Westgarth, William and Ellison, 'Three Westgarth Letters', *La Trobe Library Journal*, April 1973. For the Presbyterian lectures on 'moonlight' nights, see p. 107.

Wheelwright, Horace W., ('An Old Bushman'), *Bush Wanderings of a Naturalist*, London, 1861.

Wicken, Mrs, *The Australian Home: A Handbook of Domestic Economy*, Sydney, 1891.

Wildey, William B., *Australasia and the Oceanic Region*, Melbourne, 1876. For the first-class restaurant in Darwin in 1873, see p. 91.

Williams, Rev. Thos, *Assiduity: Being A Memoir of the Late Mr Richard H Hart, of Stawell*, Ballarat, 1886. It was Hart who in his dying days was served ice rushed by rail from the iceworks in Ballarat.

Williamstown Railway Workshops, Enquiry Into, *Victorian Parliamentary Papers*, 1869, for evidence of smoking at work.

4. Secondary Sources

Aron, Joseph and Arndt, Judy, *The Enduring Remnant . . . Melbourne Hebrew Congregation 1841–1991*, Carlton, 1992. For the supply of kosher meat in Melbourne, see chapter 16.

Astronomical Applications: U.S. Naval Observatory, Washington, DC. The web site shows a multitude of tables of the rising and setting of moon and sun in different Australian longitudes, latitudes and years. I have used its specific times as a rough guide, keeping in mind the distinctive and, in retrospect, confusing clocks followed in various parts of Australia in the nineteenth century. The web site is http://aa.usno.navy.mil/data/docs/RS OneYear.html.

Atkinson, Alan, *Camden: Farm and Village Life in Early New South Wales*, Melbourne, 1988. For the heavy consuming of tea and sugar in 1845, see p. 141.

Australian Dictionary of Biography, Melbourne, 1966–2002, 16 volumes. For the rabbit-oh man, see 'Yabba' Gascoigne in vol. 8.

Baker, Sidney J., *The Australian Language*, Milson's Point, 1978.

Bate, Weston, *Lucky City: The First Generation at Ballarat 1851–1901*, Melbourne, 1978. For Alloo's Chinese restaurant, see p. 98.

Belich, James, *Making People: A History of the New Zealanders*

From Polynesian Settlement to the End of the Nineteenth Century, Auckland, 1996.

Bennett, M. M., *Christison of Lammermoor*, London, 1927.

Blainey, Ann, *If God Prospers Me: A Portrait of Frederick John Cato*, Burwood, 1990. The first large chain of grocery stores in Australia was owned by Moran & Cato.

Blainey, Anna, *The 'Fallen are Every Mother's Children': The Woman's Christian Temperance Union's Campaigns for Temperance, Women's Suffrage and Sexual Reform in Australia, 1885–1905*, PhD thesis, La Trobe University, 2000. For the rise of the female platform speaker, see pp. 32–3.

Blainey, Geoffrey, *Gold and Paper: A History of the National Bank of Australasia*, Melbourne, 1958. For the circulation of the banks' own notes, see p. 83.

—— 'The History of Leisure in Australia: the late colonial era', *Victorian Historical Journal*, February 1978.

—— *Jumping over the Wheel*, St Leonards, 1993.

—— *A History of the AMP 1848–1998*, Sydney, 1999. For the high-risk surcharge imposed on the life policies of those who made long voyages from Australia, see pp. 25–7.

—— *The Tyranny of Distance*, Sydney, 2001, revised edition.

Bolger, Peter, *Hobart Town*, Canberra, 1973.

Bolton, G. C., *A Thousand Miles Away: A History of North Queensland to 1920*, Brisbane, 1963.

Bonyhady, Tim, *Burke & Wills: From Melbourne to Myth*, Balmain, 1991.

Boorstin, Daniel J., *The Americans: The Democratic Experience*, New York, 1974. This is a detailed history of everyday life and objects in the USA.

Burgess, H. T., *The Cyclopedia of South Australia*, 2 volumes, Adelaide, 1907–09. For the rise of dentistry in Adelaide, see vol. 2, p. 136.

Burke, Keast, *Gold and Silver: Photographs of Australian Goldfields from the Holtermann Collection*, Ringwood, 1973.

'Burke and Wills Exploring Expedition', Melbourne, *Argus*, 1861.

Butler, A. G., *et al*, *The Australian Army Medical Services in the War of 1914–1918*, vol. 1, Melbourne, 1930; and vol. 3, Canberra, 1943.

Byrne, Neil J., *Robert Dunne: Archbishop of Brisbane*, St Lucia, 1991.

Campbell, Keith O., *Henry Parkes's Utopia*, Sydney, 1994. This is the story of a small farming settlement, Parkesbourn, near Goulburn, NSW.

Cannon, Michael, *Who's Master, Who's Man?*, *Life in the Country; Life in the City*. These three volumes of social history are subtitled 'Life in the Victorian Age', South Melbourne, 1972–1975.

Charlwood, Don, *Wrecks and Reputations: The Loss of* Schomberg *and* Loch Ard, London, 1977.

—— *The Long Farewell*, Warrandyte, 1998.

Clarke, Michael, *'Big Clarke'*, Carlton, 1980.

Coghlan, T. A., *A Statistical Account of the Seven Colonies of Australasia*, Sydney, 1891. The various editions of this work are a treasury of information on meat, liquor, prices, butter and other matters.

—— *Labour and Industry in Australia: From the First Settlement in 1788 to the Establishment of the Commonwealth in 1901*, 4 volumes, South Melbourne, 1969. First published in 1918, this is a deep mine of information on prices, money and some of the byways of daily life. For the use of tokens and shortage of small change, see vol. 2, chapter 10.

Cozzolino, Mimmo, *Symbols of Australia*, Melbourne, 1980. For early Swedish matches sold in Australia, see p. 147.

Cyclopedia of Tasmania, Hobart, c. 1899–1900. For Tasmanian orchards, see vol. 1, pp. 386–419.

Dallas, K. M., *Horse Power*, Devonport, 1968.

Dare, Robert, ed., *Food, Power and Community: Essays in the History of Food and Drink*, Kent Town, 1999. Among the themes tackled by the sixteen authors are food in the Barossa Valley, the swing from ale to lager in Australian pubs, and the high consumption of sugar in Australia.

Davies, J. L. ed., *Atlas of Tasmania*, Hobart 1965. For scallops, see pp. 74–5.

Davison, Graeme, *The Unforgiving Minute: How Australia Learned to Tell The Time*, Melbourne, 1993. This vital work explores what the author calls a 'cultural revolution'.

de Serville, Paul, *Port Phillip Gentlemen: And Good Society in Melbourne before the Gold Rushes*, Melbourne, 1980.

—— *Rolf Boldrewood: A Life*, Carlton South, 2000.

Denholm, David, *The Colonial Australians*, Ringwood, 1979.

Dingle, A. E., '"The Truly Magnificent Thirst": An Historical Survey of Australian Drinking Habits', *Historical Studies*, 1980, no. 75, pp. 227–49.

Dunstan, David, *Better than Pommard!: A History of Wine in Victoria*, Kew, 1994. For the popularity of quinine wine, see pp. 57–8.

Edwards, Ron, *Skills of the Australian Bushman*, Adelaide, 1979. For simple bush ways of cooling food and rooms, see pp. 41–2.

Eunson, Warwick, *The Unfolding Hills: Mirboo Pioneers of the Gippsland Forest 1878–1914*, Mirboo, 1978. For the lighting of slush lamps, see p. 70.

Farrer, K. T. H., *A Settlement Amply Supplied: Food Technology in Nineteenth Century Australia*, Melbourne, 1980. For the rise of meat canneries, see chapter 5.

Ferber, Helen, *Stagecoach to Birdsville*, Kenthurst, NSW, 1995.

Fitzpatrick, David, *Oceans of Consolation: Personal Accounts of Irish Migration to Australia*, Melbourne, 1995. This fascinating book, especially pp. 70–71 and 587, is the source of the Irish emigrant letters discussing the hot climate.

Fitzpatrick, Jim, *The Bicycle and the Bush: Man and Machine in Rural Australia*, Melbourne, 1980.

Ford, Olwen, *The Making of Sunshine 1890–1925*, Sunshine, 2001.

Garden, Donald S., *Albany: A Panorama of the Sound from 1827*, West Melbourne, 1977.

Gilchrist, Hugh, *Australians and Greeks*, Sydney, 1992. For fish and oysters, see chapter 11.

Gittins, Jean, *The Diggers from China: The Story of the Chinese on the Goldfields*, Melbourne, 1981.

Godbold, Norman, *Victoria: Cream of the Country*, Melbourne,

1989, especially pp. 83–4 for milk-foods for babies.

Goddard, Roy, *The Union Club 1857–1957*, Sydney, 1957. For the supply of ice in the 1860s, see p. 32.

Goodwin, Craufurd D.W., *Economic Inquiry in Australia*, Durham, North Carolina, 1966. For the views of J.W. Fortescue on how a hot climate would make Sydney degenerate, see p. 445.

Gregory, Alan, *The Ever Open Door: A History of the Royal Melbourne Hospital 1848–1998*, South Melbourne 1998. For the doses of medicinal alcohol, see p. 71.

Gregory, J.S., *Church and State: Changing Government Policies towards Religon in Australia*, North Melbourne, 1973. For laws on Sabbath observance, see p. 161.

Haines, Gregory, *A History of Pharmacy in Victoria*, Melbourne, 1994.

Hasluck, Alexandra, *Royal Engineer: A Life of Sir Edmund du Cane*, Sydney, 1973.

Hassam, Andrew, *Sailing to Australia: Shipboard Diaries by Nineteenth-Century British Emigrants*, Melbourne, 1995.

Heaton, J.H., *Australian Dictionary of Dates and Men of the Time*, Sydney, 1879.

Hirst, J.B., *Adelaide and the Country 1870–1917: Their Social and Political Relationship*, Melbourne, 1973.

Hume, Stuart Hamilton, *Beyond the Borders: An Anecdotal History of the Hume and Related Pioneering Families . . .*, Canberra, 1991. A member of this family was the perpetual tea drinker who insisted (pp. 63–4) on his wife using the old open fire for cooking and refused to see the new railway.

Hyslop, Anthea, *Sovereign Remedies: A History of Ballarat Base Hospital 1850s to 1980s*, Sydney, 1989.

Inglis K.S., *Hospital and Community: a History of the Royal Melbourne Hospital*, Melbourne, 1958.

—— *The Australian Colonists: An Explanation of Social History 1788–1870*, Melbourne, 1974.

Jamieson, Ronda, 'Country Storekeeping: A Case Study of the Daw Family Businesses in Ravensthorpe and other Country Areas . . .', PhD thesis, Murdoch University, 2000.

Johnson, Joseph, *Laughter and the Love of Friends: A Centenary History of the Melbourne Savage Club . . .*, Melbourne, 1994.

Jones, Dorothy, *Hurricane Lamps and Blue Umbrellas: The Story of Innisfail*, Cairns, 1973. For bananas, see chapter 14.

Kennedy, Malcolm J, *Hauling the Loads: A History of Australia's Working Horses and Bullocks*, Melbourne, 1992.

Kingston, Beverley, *My Wife, My Daughter, and Poor Mary Ann: Women and Work in Australia*, Melbourne, 1975.

Lack, John, 'Working-Class Leisure', *Victorian Historical Journal*, February 1978.

Lanyon, H.M., *Jubilee of the Box Hill Methodist Church 1883–1933*, Box Hill, 1933. For the quantity of food eaten at a beach picnic, see p. 28.

Lemon, Andrew, *The Northcote Side of the River*, North Melbourne, 1983.

Levi, John S. and Bergman, G.F.J., *Australian Genesis: Jewish Convicts and Settlers 1788–1850*, Adelaide, 1974.

Levi, John S., *Rabbi Jacob Danglow: 'The Uncrowned Monarch of Australian Jews'*, Carlton, 1995.

Livingston, K.T., *The Wired Nation Continent: The Communication Revolution and Federating Australia*, Melbourne, 1996.

Love, Harold, *The Golden Age of Australian Opera*. For gaslight in the theatre, see pp. 112–15.

McCorkell, H.A., and Yule, Peter, *A Green and Pleasant Land: A History of Koroit*, Warrnambool, 1999. For many references to potatoes, see the index.

McCulloch, Samuel C., *River King: The McCulloch Carrying Company and Echuca (1865–1898)*, Melbourne, 1986.

McIlwraith, John, and Harris, Anthea, *Striking Gold: 100 Years of the Perth Mint*, Perth, 1999.

McKell, Katherine (K. McK. on title page), *Old Days and Gold Days in Victoria* Melbourne, c. 1902. This short memoir has asides on candles, bread and other everyday objects.

McQueen, Humphrey, *Social Sketches of Australia 1988–1975*, Ringwood, 1978.

Martin, A.W., *Henry Parkes: A Biography*, Melbourne, 1980.

Metz, Nancy A., *The Companion to 'Martin Chuzzlewit'*, Mountfield, East Sussex, 2001. For the English practice, even in the 1860s, of sending the Sunday roast meat to the baker's oven, see p. 154.

Morris, Edward E., *A Dictionary of Austral English*, London, 1989. For fascinating examples of Australians using the coo-ee in London in c. 1850, see p. 96. For Samuel Butler's likening of the Southern Cross to a kite, see p. 427.

Moyal, Ann, *Clear Across Australia: A History of Telecommunications*, Melbourne, 1984.

Mulvaney, D.J., and Calaby, J.H., *'So Much That Is New'; Baldwin Spencer, 1860–1929, A Biography*, Melbourne, 1985.

Murray-Smith, Stephen, 'Beyond the Pale', *Papers and Proceedings*, Tasmanian Historical Research Association, Hobart, December 1973, for the story of the muttonbird industry.

—— ed., *The Dictionary of Australian Quotations*, Port Melbourne, revised edition, 1992.

O'Brien, Anne, *Poverty's prison: The Poor in New South Wales 1880–1918*, Melbourne, 1988. For the children of families near the bottom of the income ladder, see chapters 13–17.

Parsons, T.G., *Brewing Beer in the Colonial Days*, RHSV Journal, June 1984.

Pascoe, Robert, *Buongiorno Australia: Our Italian Heritage*, Richmond, 1987.

Pearl, Cyril, *Morrison of Peking*, Ringwood, 1970. For the walk across Australia, see pp. 26–34.

Pike, Glenville, *Roads of Yesterday*, Mareeba, 1977. For the humiliation of Camooweal's new Ford, see p. 278.

Powell, J.M., *The Public Lands of Australia Felix: Settlement and Land Appraisal in Victoria 1834–91 . . .*, Melbourne, 1970.

Prest, Wilfrid, *The Wakefield Companion to South Australian History*, Kent Town, 2001.

Price, Charles A., *Southern Europeans in Australia*, Melbourne, 1963.

Priestley, Susan, *Echuca: A Centenary History*, Brisbane, 1965. For the trade in Murray cod and leeches, see pp. 46–7.

Proctor, D.V., ed., *Ice Carrying Trade at Sea*, National Maritime Musuem, UK, 1981.

Ramsom, W.S., ed., *The Australian National Dictionary; A Dictionary of Australianisms on Historical Principles*, Melbourne, 1988. It is a valuable guide to Jimmy Woodser, Wowser, Go Ballarat, and many other Australian terms.

Reece, R.H., 'An Immigrant Mechanic in Queensland, 1865–1866', *Archives and Manuscripts*, vol. 3, Brisbane, November 1965.

Ricketts, Andrew, *Walter Lindrum: Billiards Phenomenon*, Canberra, 1982.

Robin, Libby, *The Flight of the Emu: A Hundred Years of Australian Ornithology 1901–2001*, Carlton, 2001. For the first published photo of an Australian bird, see p. 118.

Rodd, L.C., *The Gentle Shipwreck*, Melbourne, 1975.

Roderick, Colin, ed., *Henry Lawson: Autobiographical and Other Writings 1887–1922*, Sydney, 1972.

Roe, Michael, *Quest for Authority in Eastern Australia 1835–1851*, Melbourne, 1965.

Rolls, Eric, *Sojourners: The Epic Story of China's Centuries-old Relationship with Australia*, St Lucia, 1992.

Roughley, T.C., *Oyster Culture on the George's River, NSW*, Sydney, 1922.

Rubinstein, Hilary L., *The Jews in Australia: A Thematic History*, Port Melbourne, 1991. For the ascent of Helena Rubinstein and her bottled face cream from rural Victoria to New York, see vol. 1, pp. 424–5.

Semmler, Clement, *The Banjo of the Bush: The Work, Life and Times of A B Paterson*, London 1967.

Serle, Geoffrey, *From Deserts the Prophets Come: The Creative Spirit in Australia 1788–1872*, Melbourne, 1973.

Shaw, Flora L., *The Story of Australia*, London, c. 1897. For her confident assessment of the Australian standard of living, see p. 146.

Shiel, Des, *Eucalyptus: Essence of Australia*, Carlton, 1985.

Smith, James, ed., *The Cyclopedia of Victoria*, Melbourne 1903–05. For restaurants and fish suppliers in Melbourne, see vol. 3, pp. 158–164.

Smith, Philip Chadwick Foster, *Crystal Blocks of Yankee Coldness: The Development of the Massachusetts Ice Trade . . .*, Wenham Historical Association and Museum, 36-page pamphlet, August 1962.

Smith, William George, ed., *The Oxford Dictionary of English Proverbs*, London, 1974, 3rd edition.

Souter, Gavin, *Lion & Kangaroo: The Initiation of Australia 1901–1919*, Sydney, 1976.

—— *Company of Heralds: A Century and a Half of Australian Publishing by John Fairfax Limited*, Carlton, 1981. For dangers of mosquito nets in 1850s Sydney, see p. 56.

Sutherland, Alexander, *Victoria and Its Metropolis: Past and Present*, 2 volumes. Melbourne, 1888.

Symons, Michael, *One Continuous Picnic: A History of Eating in Australia*, Ringwood, 1984. In the history of restaurants and the fine menu, this is a pioneering work. For the origin of the pavlova, see pp. 147–52.

Taylor, George, *Making it Happen: The Rise of Sir Macpherson Robertson*, Melbourne, 1934.

Technology in Australia 1788–1988: A Condensed History of Australian Technological Innovation and Adaptation during the First Two Hundred years, Australian Academy of Technological Sciences and Engineering, Melbourne, 1988. For the rise of Australian brewing, see pp. 104–6.

Thompson, Lindsay G., *History of the Fisheries of New South Wales*, Sydney, 1893.

Tomlinson, G.W., *Australian Bank Notes 1817–1963*, Melbourne, 1963.

Tranter, Deborah, *Cobb & Co: Coaching in Queensland*, South Brisbane, 1990.

Vamplew, Wray, *Australians: Historical Statistics*, being one of 11 volumes in the series 'Australians: A Historical Library', Broadway, 1987.

Walker, Robin, *Under Fire: A History of Tobacco Smoking in Australia*, Melbourne, 1984. This book pioneered the field.

—— and Roberts, Dave, *From Scarcity to Surfeit: A History of Food and Nutrition in New South Wales*, Kensington, 1988.

Webb, Martyn and Audrey, *Edge of Empire*, Perth, 1983. The history of the remote port of Onslow in the West Pilbara, Western Australia.

Wilson, Gwen, *One Grand Chain: The History of Anaesthesia in Australia . . .*, Melbourne, 1995, vol. 1. For its advent in Australia in the 1840s, see pp. 62, 77.

Yarwood, A. T., *Walers: Australian Horses Abroad*, Melbourne, 1989.

Yule, Peter, *The Royal Children's Hospital: A History of Faith, Science and Love*, Rushcutters Bay, NSW, 1999.

INDEX

INDEX

pubs *see* hotels; inns
puddings *see* 'sweets'
Pugh, Dr William 331
pumpkin 208, 393, 396
Punch 319
punch cards 164
punctuality 175

quail 206, 207
Quakers 351
quarantine 75–6
quart pots 357–8
quarts 152
Queen Victoria 86, 87, 140, 273, 346, 391
Queensland
  banknotes 187
  buildings 27
  coach services 91
  crops 28, 278–9
  southern 24
  tropical north 10, 18, 27–8, 93, 129
  unclaimed letters 88
  weather 24, 26–8
Quetta (ship) 14
quids 185
quill pens 85

rabbits 208–11, *210*
races, horse 89
radio 83, 131, 144–5
railway workshops 315–16
railways *see* trains; stations, railway
Ralph Waller (ship) 70
ration sugar 373, 393, 410
rations
  charity 190
  part of wages 199, 362, 373
  on ships 66, 67
Ravensthorpe 413
reading 46–7, 94, 177, 318, 362
  see also literacy

recipes
  billy tea 359–60
  meals 214–15, 216–17, 265–6, 267, 268, 279
  'sweets' 271, 274, 290–2
The Recollections of Geoffry Hamlyn (Kingsley) 31–2
Red Sea 77, 79, 99
Redfern 59
refrigeration 80, 81, 198, 203, 288–9, 300
regionalism 89–90
Reid, George 143–4
religions 34–5
Renmark 353
repeater watches 161
Restaurant de Paris 405
restaurants 153, 308, 392, 399–406, 407–8
rice 360, 393, 396, 406
Richardson, Henry Handel 325
Richmond River Express (newspaper) 108–9
riots *see* protests
roaring forties 67, 70, 285
roast meats 215, 218, 219, 248
Roberts, Tom 29–30, 322
Robertson, Macpherson 385–6
roll-your-own cigarettes 317, 325–7, *328*
Roma 348
roofs 27, 42, *43*, 358
rotten eggs 244, 245–6
Rowlands of Ballarat 370, 371, 372
Rubinstein, Helena 30
rules *see* social rules
rum 344
running water 36, 40, 41
Ryan, Paddy 200

Sabbath *see* Sundays;
  see also under Jewish religion
safety matches 63–4

ALSO BY GEOFFREY BLAINEY

A VERY SHORT HISTORY
OF THE WORLD

Following the success of his A Short History of the World, eminent historian Geoffrey Blainey has abridged his account of the grand adventure of human history to create an even more accessible version of his absorbing work. In doing so, he has produced a primer to world history that will become a must for every bookshelf.

A Very Short History of the World traces the story of the world's people during the last four million years, beginning before the human race moved out of Africa to explore and settle other continents. It is a story of the inhabited world being pulled apart, and then coming together again in more recent centuries. A consummate storyteller, Professor Blainey makes the past come alive as he touches on the trivial and the grand: on changes in diet and daily work and sport, on transforming attitudes to the night sky, as well as on profound discoveries and mighty empires.

Praise for A Short History of the World:

'One of those rare books that will delight every
kind of reader.'
Peter Craven, THE BULLETIN

'a triumph of literature . . . an enthralling,
insightful page-turner.'
Sarah Hudson, HERALD SUN

SCURVY

STEPHEN R. BOWN

*How a Surgeon, a Mariner and a Gentleman Solved
the Greatest Medical Mystery of the Age of Sail*

In the days of the tall ships, one dreaded foe was responsible for more deaths at sea than piracy, shipwreck and all other illnesses combined. Cruelly culling sailors and stunting maritime enterprise from Vasco da Gama to Sir Francis Drake, this plague of the seas was scurvy. Countless mariners perished from the disease in agony, their early symptoms included bleeding gums, wobbly teeth and the opening of old wounds.

A cure had eluded doctors and philosophers since the time of the ancient Greeks, but in the late eighteenth century the surgeon James Lind, the great sea captain James Cook and the physician Sir Gilbert Blane, undertook to crack the riddle of scurvy. Their timely discovery, just as Napoleon was mobilising for the conquest of Europe, solved the greatest medical mystery of the Age of Sail and irrevocably altered the course of world history.

This is both a history and a detective story; it is about class, wilful ignorance and ludicrous decision-making, and about how a cure for scurvy was found, ignored, lost, and finally implemented to the great benefit of all seafaring nations.

'*Scurvy* is superior popular history.'
THE AGE

'This is one fabulous, accessible look at the history of seafaring...Never was a now seldom-seen vitamin deficiency so interesting.'
Shaunagh O'Connor, HERALD SUN

SHIPWREAKS: AUSTRALIA'S GREATEST MARITIME DISASTERS

EVAN McHUGH

'The wind noise was screaming, howling . . . incredible, plus the rain and the sea spray, it was just like being hit by nails or stabbed in the face.'

From the first wreck in 1622 off Western Australia to the tragedy of the 1998 Sydney to Hobart Yacht Race, Evan McHugh captures all the drama of Australia's maritime history. There are swashbuckling mutineers, violent storms, uncharted reefs, enemy warships, as well as ripping yarns about Dutchmen and lascars, Aborigines and escaped convicts.

In producing this remarkable book, McHugh has made extensive use of first-hand accounts and contemporary records. With characteristic flair, he also delves into the mysteries and controversies that still surround so many of the wrecks.

Shipwrecks is a white-knuckle voyage through chaos and tragedy that proclaims the courage and strength of the human spirit. It is a powerful reminder that even in the twenty-first century the sea remains a great, unconquered frontier.

'The ship seemed not to sink, but the waters seemed to rise around us. The vessel went down suddenly at the last moment, leaving 200 people all huddled together in the water.'